Plunge

One Woman's Pursuit of a Life Less Ordinary

LIESBET COLLAERT

Roaming About Press

The events and conversations in this book have been set down to the best of the
author's ability, based on her memory, notes, blogs, and diaries. Dialogue originally
in Dutch, Spanish, and French has been paraphrased in English to improve
readability. One name has been changed to protect the privacy of that individual.

Parts of this memoir have previously been published on the author's blog and in
sailing magazines.

First published edition: November 2020

Cover design by KAM Design
Section break logo from Freepik.com

Author photos by Duwan Dunn. All other photographs are from the author's
collection.

ISBN: 978-1-7359806-0-7 (paperback)
ISBN: 978-1-7359806-1-4 (epub)
ISBN: 978-1-7359806-2-1 (mobi)

Library of Congress Control Number: 2020920680

Published by Roaming About Press
Newburyport, MA, USA

Dedication

This book is dedicated to my closest friends:
my dear *oma* (†2017) & the fabulous Rosie

Table of Contents

Introduction

Riding the Waves of Adventure

Freedom to do what I want, go where I please, and be myself, no matter what, has always been more important to me than security, comfort, routine, and keeping up appearances. I like to embrace every day as it comes, while exploring the unknown. A new day brings the promise of a new adventure. Most people follow a distinct path, set by social norms, dictated by society. I become antsy staying in a familiar area for months, following certain habits. It's too restrictive. As if I'm running on automatic instead of living on my own terms.

I'm an ordinary woman from Belgium, who fell in love with travel the moment I tasted its extraordinary flavors. Three-week family vacations turned into a controversial month-long hitchhiking trip to Italy with a buddy when I was 17. After college, a backpacking stint to Southeast Asia with friends followed. Two years later, I returned to that part of the world – solo this time – for another year. In 2003, at age 27, I left my home country on a plane to the United States. I haven't looked back since.

Alas, the road of a perpetual nomad has its challenges. Especially for a spur-of-the-moment person like me. Why plan if you can just "see what happens" and seize opportunities as they arise? After all, *plans are written in sand at low tide*. Better to dive in, for good or for bad. I'd rather regret the things I did than the things I missed out on.

However, the unexpected can drive even me crazy. To the extent that I sometimes crave the comforts and conveniences of a real house, a stable income, and close friends. I realize, though, that a conventional life will always be there, whenever I tire of roaming about. Whether I'll be able to fit in remains a question.

We only live once. It's up to us to pursue a life that suits us, tickles our senses, and shapes us into balanced, complete, and satisfied humans. Each fork in the road leads to a new path. Life is about the choices we make and the chances we take.

Welcome to my world. You might be surprised about the normalcy or shocked by the differences – either way, I hope you enjoy this plunge into my less than ordinary thirties.

Prologue

Mid-ocean

For the last ten days, my sweetheart and I have been stuck on our 35-foot sailboat in the middle of the Pacific Ocean. However, there is nothing pacific (or sweet) about this ride, *this life*, anymore.

Mark steps into the cockpit and cracks his head on the sharp edge of the doorway – again. He lets out a yell of agony. Our floating home had briefly gone airborne and landed with a smack and a groan back into the turbulent sea.

"We're putting this boat up for sale the moment we arrive in French Polynesia, so those islands better be the highlight of the South Pacific!" Mark barks at me before scrambling towards the autopilot.

His expression reflects the grim circumstances around us. There is absolutely nothing we can do to change them. Our sailboat is bouncing and jerking and pitching, lunging left, right, up, down, forward, backward, and everything in between.

Holding on, I gasp and shout back, "You're kidding! I'm not ready to sell the boat yet, after all we've been through to get here!"

He glares at me with non-negotiable fury. Blood gushes down his forehead.

I swallow hard as half-digested crackers threaten to escape. It's difficult to care about him when he's this angry.

His head hurts. My stomach churns. He's ready to give up, now, forever – to quit this lifestyle I have come to love.

Our roller coaster ride plummets into the lowest of troughs, and I hover over the foaming crests of the infinite ocean. I'd rather vomit than let his attitude drag me deeper into this depression – and I do. I look up to catch my breath and watch the horizon dance relentlessly. Deep blue, lined with white, morphs into sky blue, curved above, then below me.

I barf again.

You have to be tough to cross oceans on a small boat. These days, it's tough to be tough. That ever-important sense of freedom I strive for tastes salty and feels confined.

In the name of love and adventure, I pull my weight as a sailor. Albeit with a pale face that matches the color of our sails. And that guy I've been with, through sickness and health, frustrations and despair, peace and madness, anger and passion? He increasingly makes me unhappy, crushing my dreams, belittling my choices. Maybe *he* should get off this boat when we finally make landfall.

Hardships are often required to reach goals. *No pain, no gain.* I'm heading to the blissful, mysterious islands of French Polynesia, better known as Tahiti, to stay a while – and not sell the boat. If I have to suffer through weeks of discomfort and watery environs to get there, so be it.

My mate doesn't agree. He hates discomfort. The pay-off, a so-called paradise, a distant utopia, is not worth the cost to him.

"There are enough beautiful countries that are easier to reach. By plane, if necessary," he states.

I can't deny that, but we are here now, in the middle of the ocean. His mindset and grumbles don't surprise me. I should be happy he agreed to do this crossing in the first place.

While well-equipped, our tiny vessel isn't meant to endure conditions like these. Neither are we.

"We can do this. All of us... together..." I say to nobody in particular, despite the fact that our family has shrunk over the years. I don't want to dwell on that; I have more imminent things to worry about.

I hope we don't flip. We're too heavy! Why did I provision like Armageddon was upon us?

My mind keeps racing, unable to forget my stomach.

I don't want to be sick anymore. Should I take more medicine?

I force my thoughts onto a different tack.

I'm glad I don't have children yet. Imagine the chaos! The fear! The mess!!!

I need to think positively.

Should I try to cheer my man up again? Sailing was his dream, after all...

This is probably one of his exaggeration fits and he doesn't mean any of it.

Maybe I should listen to him. Is it time to get off our boat and do something else? No, it'll blow over, like these heavy winds and killer waves.

Bang! The fiberglass creaks and the boat stalls.

Is this the end?

Chapter 1

A True Kiss and a False Start

S an Francisco. A fascinating city I only know from movies and guide-books. So close now! I can almost see the Golden Gate Bridge, smell the salty air of the bay, and feel the breeze in my light brown hair. The promise of a new adventure causes my ear-to-ear grin as I hop into our small camper to grab a CD of *dEUS,* my favorite Belgian band.

After crisscrossing the United States, Western Canada, and Alaska in our truck camper for the last year and a half, my boyfriend Karl, his dog Caesar, and I landed in California. Karl's friend Nik, a DJ, had invited us to share his studio-apartment in Oakland, as a base to explore SF. Nik also rents out two apartments in his house.

CD in hand, I enter the yard again and stop dead in my tracks. Two gorgeous dogs with fluffy tails had run up to me. I smother them with cuddles and praise.

"Hi, I'm Mark. And these two are Kali, the white one, and Darwin, the grey one."

I look up from admiring the wagging furballs.

My eyes meet those of a tall, skinny, short-haired, and attractive man in the doorway of apartment #1.

"Hello. I'm Liesbet," I oblige. *It's interesting how Americans always introduce themselves immediately, as if names are the most important take-away during a conversation.*

"My boyfriend and I just arrived. We're staying with Nik for a week to visit San Francisco. Our home on wheels is parked in front of the house."

"Home on wheels? Why are you living in a camper?"

"It lets us travel around with our own bathroom and kitchen and plenty of storage. A small RV provides much more comfort and security than dingy hostels and a backpack," I tell him with an unfaltering smile and raised voice; telltales of the excitement I always feel when elaborating on my pursuit of freedom.

"I detect an accent. Where are you from?" he asks, after I had described a handful of places I visited while backpacking for almost two years on the other side of the world.

"I'm from Belgium, but I haven't been back in a while."

"I don't know anyone who can just pack up and go. How do you afford that?" He's not the first to ask this question, verbally or with raised eyebrows. Ever since I chose travel over *stuff*, at age 17, people have wondered whether I'm rich. I'm not. And I never will be.

"I live on a tight budget and have always been careful with my income, saving most of it to travel the world."

I think about how to phrase the next part of my answer. Back in Australia, when I met Karl, and he told me he still had school debt ten years after graduating, I'd been shocked. No wonder Americans become work-focused and entrenched in the economic system at 22. They begin their adult lives needing to repay tens of thousands of dollars before actually making money. Stressful!

I can't possibly dump all this on a person I just met, so I simplify it.

"Because I'm from a socially-inclined country, where education is cheap, I'm debt-free. And, because certain incentives are encouraged, the government pays me the equivalent of 300 dollars a month, since my teaching position is now filled by someone who would have required a hefty unemployment check otherwise. That pretty much covers my expenses."

Mark seems entranced, which encourages me to ramble on about my passion. After some time of telling stories and trading questions and answers, he exclaims, "That's incredible! I need to fly to Australia and find myself a Belgian girlfriend!"

I blush. It dawns on me that we'd been chatting for a while.

"Do you know what time it is?" I ask. An hour has passed. I rush to Nik's place next door.

"Where have you been?" Karl asks.

"Talking to a neighbor, the one with the big dogs. He seems like a nice guy." I hand my CD to Nik, who is always eager to discover new music.

Our planned week in the Rockridge area of Oakland turns into four, as all of us become friends and Mark unintentionally draws me closer and closer. We create precious memories together. He buys me a gloriously ripe organic tomato for my 29th birthday, because I like tomatoes and complained about their high price in California. It is the plumpest and tastiest one ever. He and I go on romantic beach walks, take the dogs to nature parks, and spend hours and hours talking in private at night, getting to know each other better.

Karl encourages my contact with Mark. "Soon we'll be out of here and it's just you and me again," he says. "Enjoy the company!"

I embrace Mark's presence until I crave it. During the day, Karl and I discover the Bay Area and take all three dogs for walks in the neighborhood. In the evening, I anxiously await Mark's arrival from work and, after dinner, find an excuse to go over there.

One night, the Hollywood-moment arrives... our first kiss, following days of butterflies-in-the-stomach anticipation. An arm around my shoulders. A fluttering body. Touching of lips. Mutual desire. *He loves me back!*

We never allow anything more to happen. Mark is a realist. He knows I am leaving Nik's place shortly and that I am in a serious relationship.

Our dreadful last evening together eventually arrives. We hug strongly and kiss tenderly.

"I'll come pick you up wherever you are, whenever you're ready to leave Karl." Mark's parting words sound sweet. *Is he serious?*

That night, I lie awake, heart racing. By morning, it's time to pack up the camper and leave our base for the past month.

I exchange glances with Karl. His eyes beam with excitement about continuing our adventures; mine reflect trouble and sadness.

I take the plunge.

"I can't be with you anymore. My attraction to Mark has grown too strong." I sound more determined than I feel.

Shock.

"I was ready to take this relationship a step further," Karl mumbles, his voice breaking.

What is that supposed to mean? Was he planning to propose?

My pounding heart skips a beat. *I don't want to be someone's wife!* I would have had to say *no*. Even worse than breaking up. I avoid his eyes. This decision rips me apart; hurts me as much as it devastates him. I care a lot about Karl, who loves me dearly and with whom I bond well. I had no reason to leave. *Why split up when mutual respect, passion, and interests abound?*

Alas, something else – someone else – happened.

Karl stares at me with intent. "We're driving to Mexico. We both looked forward to this."

Silence.

Did he not notice my enthusiasm to continue our overland journey had diminished these last weeks?

I swallow hard.

Can I really give all this up, our past explorations on the road and whatever adventures await in Mexico? The year and a half of ups and downs before that, where he tried so hard to fit into my Belgian life? How about my American visa that will run out if I don't leave the country soon?

The consequences of my impulsiveness finally trigger some brain activity.

Karl continues, "I love you. Caesar and I will miss you so much."

We both cry. *Three years together is not nothing.* I think about the good times we shared. Karl and his dog – and me, too – had been ecstatic when I showed up at his Maryland apartment, ready to roam North America.

That was the summer of 2003. I had thrown a goodbye party at my parents' house in Belgium and hopped on a plane. Little did I know I was never to return.

I remain quiet. My heart bleeds for him. Karl is a sensitive man who understands me and cares about me. We have the same passion: traveling the world on a budget. Yet, I crave more romance in a relationship with someone else, a new-found love.

Am I seriously giving up my travels for a man?

That would be a first. It's usually the other way around. My gut knows how this predicament will end. My mind has nothing to add.

I face Karl and finally utter, "If I leave with you, I will want to come back here at some point." It is the only conclusion I can muster.

I have fallen in love with another guy, the "guy next door." I can't stay with Mr. Cute, the name fellow backpackers had given Karl before we met. It would be unfair to him.

"If that's what you want," Karl replies with a sigh, "then you should just stay."

In the hours that follow we split the money from our communal account; I gather my belongings; and we discuss a contingency plan for the truck camper. I pet Caesar goodbye and give Karl one last, heartfelt embrace. Then, misty-eyed, I watch them drive away.

I close the door of Mark's apartment behind me. Unlike other times when Karl and I returned his dogs after walking them with Caesar – today, I don't leave.

My pile of clothes and gear clutters the corner of the bedroom. Mark has no idea.

Kali and Darwin join me on the bed. It's a California King. A month ago, I'd never heard of such a thing. Now, I hope it becomes mine. Four in-quisitive eyes stare at me. I reach for my companions. I should be jumping with joy. Instead, I can't stop sniffling. Their fur is drenched in minutes.

This King-size bed should easily fit the four of us.

The Australian Shepherd mixes wag their tails. I continue snuggling with them. Both are rescue dogs; smart, loving, beautiful. It's their fault I'm here. They greeted me that fateful day.

Mark has found his Belgian girl without having to travel to Australia; she appeared right on his doorstep. He probably thought he'd never see her again. *Surprise!*

What will he say when he comes home from work?

What if he doesn't want me here?

As usual, I don't have a back-up plan. The rest of the afternoon, I cry. I feel bad for Karl.

I'm such a selfish bitch.

I contemplate emailing my parents about what happened. Maybe a Skype call?

"Guess what, mom? I broke up with Karl, the man everyone likes so much; that considerate gentleman who has become part of the family." I imagine the frowns. *"Why? Because I chose someone else. Oh, and you'll have to meet him instead of Karl on your upcoming vacation in the US."*

It doesn't seem the right moment to tackle that subject. Besides, computers can't handle salt water.

The front door opens. The dogs jump up and run towards their human. I stay behind in the bedroom.

"Hi, guys," Mark greets Kali and Darwin with a sad voice. "I guess they're gone, huh? They must have forgotten to lock the door before they left." The dogs' collars jiggle. I assume he's petting them.

"You two don't seem too excited to see me. What's up?"

I walk into the hallway. My eyes sting.

Mark looks up.

"What the hell are you doing here?" His words crush me. I shuffle towards him. We hug. I don't want to let go.

"I'm staying with you," I whisper, as if he doesn't have any say in this. Mark's face relaxes into a smile. His grip tightens. I guess that means it's okay.

The following weeks are exciting and emotional. Mark and I discover each other's minds and bodies. Time eases my thoughts, worries, and sadness about Karl. I settle for a sedentary life as house maid, grocery shopper, and dog walker. I have mixed feelings about my new situation. I spend money being stationary without doing anything inspiring. It's against the pact I sealed with myself years ago: I either live somewhere to work and save money for travel or I spend money while traveling. This is neither. I'm in limbo. But at least it's with the man I anticipate a future with.

In Rockridge flair and fashion, everything is in walking distance: a wonderful Mexican burrito joint, the hip café on the corner where we hang out with our dogs, the BART metro station for easy rides into San Francisco, the Safeway grocery store, and any ethnic restaurant that strikes our fancy. Like the Ethiopian place where I eat *injera* with my hands. The tradition reminds me of trips to Morocco.

Mark's shrink has an office close by as well. Once a week, I pick him up at the glass door and we go out for an early dinner. *Do I need to worry about these visits?*

I've never met anyone else who sees a psychiatrist, but on TV many Americans do. I know Mark has depressive tendencies – he told me so – and according to his psychiatrist, "everyone has depression." I find that hard to believe. I'm content about my life choices. I often get what I want and focus on my passions: travel, writing, and recently, dogs. Kali and Darwin have become a major part of my existence.

I let the shrink issue fade.

"Would you like to come with me to San Diego this weekend?" Mark asks one day. "There's a sailboat in a boatyard I want to look at."

My turn to be surprised. He has been scrutinizing ads, but I had no idea how serious he was about actually buying a boat. His dream of sailing the world is within reach, now that he's found a partner who loves trying new things. There's only one caveat. I get motion sickness.

But the heart beats the stomach. I love this guy. Besides, I've never let seasickness stand in my way of experiencing something unique. Anything to start traveling again, even if it means – *gasp* – on the water.

"Sure, that sounds great."

Should I tell him I get seasick?

🌊🌊🌊

I don't think Mark ever asked, "Hey, do you want to go sailing full-time with me and the dogs?" I just assume that's next after he buys *Tovarish* in San Diego. I'm approaching two years away from my home country and, one would think, getting close to wrapping up this nomadic existence. Mark is ready to begin *his* adventure, after ten years of living the "American Dream" being unhappy.

Going back to Belgium and working, or trying out a lifestyle that expands my horizons?

It's an easy decision for me.

We move *Tovarish* to Emeryville Marina and rename her *Four Choices*. The spelling on the hull – *F/Our Choice/s* – highlights the middle part. *Life is about choices.* Mark downsizes by selling most of his belongings on Craigslist and at a yard sale. He gives notice at work and to Nik, the owner of his apartment.

We move aboard for five months and learn the ropes of our Islander Freeport 36, a bulky monohull with a raised saloon and big windows. Three wide steps lead to the living area and a flip-out transom makes it easy for Kali and Darwin to get in and out of the dinghy. It's a dog-friendly ship with lots of storage and headroom; comfortable to live in.

As long as she doesn't move.

Four Choices is 25 years old, so our life in Emeryville is filled with long hours of boat projects, renovations, and maintenance. I'm eager to participate and do my best to understand Mark's engine talk. It doesn't interest me but helping him does. New to diesel engines and some of the systems, he uses books and the internet to figure things out. None of it is fun since every project requires at least one failed attempt. The constant effort, disappointment, and dirt become infuriating. In our darkest hours, I wonder whether we'll ever set sail.

Entwined at night, the dogs curled up with us, I try to soothe Mark's frustrations.

"At least our little family is together, and we love each other. Kali, Darwin, you, and me. Isn't that wonderful?" It is. We're determined to get the work done. Each day that ends with a majestic sun setting behind the Golden Gate Bridge is one day closer to casting off.

With my B1/B2 visa, I'm allowed to stay in the US for up to six months at a time. I've always obtained that maximum amount, finding out the hard way that a month-long visit to Canada does not re-set the clock.

My emotions are put to the test each time I fly into this country. I'm treated with disrespect, disdain, skepticism, fingerprinting, head shots, interrogations, and intimidation. Afterwards, US Immigration stamps my passport, and I'm admitted for six months.

My current time allowance is coming to an end. Mark and I don't know when we're leaving, so I apply for a visa extension. It costs $200 and – unbeknownst to me – is only possible once. An extra six-month period is granted. No rush to sail south!

I learn the basics of sailing from Mark, who's an accomplished sailor and certified instructor. San Francisco Bay is ideal for practicing, with its consistent, blustery conditions every afternoon. I'm a novice and I know it, but I have a patient teacher who appreciates my efforts and determination. Our attempts to train Kali and Darwin to pee on deck with the help of Astroturf remain unsuccessful. Even after we invite other dogs to drop their scent *and* show them how it's done ourselves. Nope. Our pups prefer to go ashore. We can't blame them.

Once the major repairs are taken care of, we embark on weekend trips to see how everyone fares. The protected waters have mercy on us. We finally have fun on our boat.

China Camp, Clipper Cove, and Drakes Bay reveal what the *real* cruising life is about: peaceful anchorages and stretches of pristine beach where the dogs run free. We contemplate our new life. Paradise lies south of the border. We're almost ready to go. On the way home from Drakes Bay, I succumb to seasickness. Kali and Darwin miserably join me inside. Mark is forced to single-hand us back to the marina.

🌊🌊🌊

After nine months of labor and loaded with food, charts, and spare parts, we motor out of the harbor and raise the sails. The wind pushes us through the Golden Gate, into the mighty Pacific. We turn left.

Mexico, here we come!

The first day of our sailing journey, I hang over the railing and puke my guts out. I lie down in our bunk but feel guilty that Mark is on his own, exposed to the elements. I join him in the cockpit. Staring at the horizon eases my stomach contractions. Darwin is uncomfortable but eventually manages to hunker down under the helm seat. Kali remains on four legs, balancing and bracing herself for nine hours. *Poor puppy.* Mark takes care of us all, and of *Four Choices*, which he stubbornly sails south until we reach Half Moon Bay. We pull in for the night.

Tomorrow will be better.

"Okay, sweetie, let's get this show on the road! Are you ready to head back into the ocean?" Mark starts the second leg of our trip with enthusiasm.

"Do I have a choice?" I make it sound like a joke but believe today we'll have a better time *out there.*

"You have four choices!" Mark can't resist, despite disliking the boat name I picked.

We had taken the dogs to the beach earlier and straightened up the interior of our floating home. All items have to be stored, because the rolling motion of our monohull can turn anything loose into lethal projectiles.

Mark presses the start button for the engine. *Nothing!*

"Now what?" he mumbles, before trying again and consequently digging the engine books out of a cabinet. The rest of the day is spent in the engine room. Mark is chief engineer, putting book knowledge into action. I'm his assistant. By the time we diagnose and fix the problem – a corroded ground wire of the starter – it's too late (and we lack the motivation) to reach Monterey. Instead, we dinghy the dogs ashore and talk about our upcoming adventure.

Are we cut out for this?

We try leaving the bay again on day three and regain our positive attitude. The engine starts. *Four Choices* carries her crew towards the ocean. I dread bouncing up and down for an entire day and focus on the horizon.

We follow the California coastline with full sails and enjoy the wind in our hair. Darwin needs time to relax before finding his sweet spot in the cockpit. Kali pants and stands for ages. It hurts to watch this behavior. When I take her inside the tilted boat to comfort her, she climbs the couch, then the wall, thinking it's the floor. I swallow hard and feel mentally sick. Being indoors triggers my physical discomfort as well. Moments later, I hang over the transom again.

Mark has to do everything alone: steer the boat, attend to the sails, make lunch, check the charts, and discourage his loved ones from jumping off the boat right then and there.

Multiple hours into the trip, the mainsail rips. Now we have to motor, which reduces our progress, roars us into submission, and smells nauseating. I feed the fish once more.

"I don't know if I can do this," I mutter.

"Yes, this sucks. Everything is going wrong. The dogs are miserable. And so are you."

We suffer in silence. I don't know how to proceed on this voyage. I don't want to give up, either. As if on cue, at the height of our gloom, a pod of dolphins brightens our wake, followed by an ensemble of sea lions.

"This is amazing! How do they know we're feeling like crap? They want to cheer us up." I wordlessly thank the creatures and smile at Mark. He remains deep in thought.

Our attempt to arrive in Monterey before nightfall fails. Well after the sun sets, we limp into the public marina, where helping hands tie us up. We're exhausted and demotivated.

Unable to do anything about our issues that evening, we walk to the buzzing commercial district to eat out. The restaurant spins. I can barely focus my eyes on the table in front of me. My belly can't handle more than a spoonful of clam chowder. *What a waste.*

I walk home like a drunken sailor. My conversation with Mark halts abruptly when we reach the same sentiment: *Is this what we want? Really? Who chooses to be miserable on the ocean?* But it's Mark's desire to go sailing! We've worked so hard to turn this dream into reality...

The decision is made on day four of our adventure. We quit! We cannot stand seeing our beloved dogs suffer each time *Four Choices* takes to sea. It breaks our hearts. Not to give up this seafaring journey, but to realize our family is unhappy. We have to stop this madness before something serious happens or before we regret sailing forever. *Cruising is not in our cards yet.*

It shouldn't matter that we only made it to Monterey, a whopping two-hour car ride from Emeryville. Nor that we worked on our boat for the duration of an average pregnancy.

Within five weeks, we turn our lives upside down. A sailmaker fixes the mainsail, we resolve outstanding boat issues, and I buy two yellow *For Sale* signs, which I attach on each side of the bow. Our prime location – in plain sight of the pier where tourists and boat aficionados stroll – helps our cause. We sell *Four Choices* for asking price and without a broker, after she's hauled out and surveyed on my 30th birthday. The positive outcome of the sale is a most welcome present and a step up from an organic tomato.

We buy a used, fire-engine-red, F-350 pickup truck and an 11-foot Lance camper to nest in its bed. Our belongings and provisions are transported from the "weight unlimited" sailboat to the "weight constrained" camper. We're disheartened by the amount of *stuff* we still own yet impressed with our ability to cram everything into a tiny space.

One year after my RV travels with Karl and Caesar, I drive south along Highway 1, destination Mexico. With a different man, a bigger truck camper, and two dogs instead of one...

Chapter 2

From Seasick to Lovesick

My heart beats 200 times a minute. I'm in shock. The world around me spins. A haze envelops me, as if I'm wearing fogged-up glasses. It feels like I'm on a different planet, one that looks surreal, where nothing makes sense. Nobody ever dumped me before! When you really love a man and totally commit to the relationship, he breaks up with you, apparently. I'm usually unfazed by life and its twists. Not now. I'm in disbelief; in a weird kind of pain. Most of all, I'm incredibly sad. Abandoned in the middle of nowhere. By the man I chose.

I should have seen it coming.

Our overland adventure had been off to a fabulous start. It was meant to be. *Four Choices* sold fast in Monterey and we found an alternative way to travel south. The four of us left California with a beaming smile, after following scenic Highway 1, taking in the impressive sea vistas and lazing elephant seals. The dogs ran and leaped about on expansive beaches and slept like babies while underway. No more sloped surfaces, discomfort, or seasickness.

My US visa was expiring, so I needed to leave the country for at least six months, enough time to explore Mexico.

Initially, we stopped at bays where Mark had hoped to anchor our own vessel and stared at the bobbing sailboats. Walking hand in hand, Kali and Darwin by our side, we reminisced about our short-lived cruising life. The scenes appeared romantic.

As time progressed, we concentrated on our own journey, which offered enough distraction and excitement. Especially that moment we didn't notice a *tope* and were ejected from our seats. *Topes* are nasty, usually unmarked, speed bumps. Nothing broke, but our little house in the bed of the truck had shifted and our interior needed cleaning up after a handful of objects took flight. Almost like being on a sailboat in the ocean again.

In Oaxaca, Mark's parents paid us a visit, and we first met Sabine and Michael, a fascinating German couple who had brought their small truck camper, *Lucy*, over from Europe to Canada. They wished to continue to South America after their North American journey.

I was impressed and intrigued by these seasoned world travelers and the way they looked at each other with love and respect. Our own hand-holding days were over already, and I wished Mark was more like Michael. His wife meant the world to him.

We agreed to meet up again in Palenque, where pyramids stand grand on well-maintained grounds. Some of the ruins are restored, others purposefully untouched and overgrown by the jungle, like parts of Angkor Wat in Cambodia. We were allowed to climb the steep steps and walk into the ancient structures, unlike Angkor Wat. The stone carvings were impressive and the views over the lush surroundings, dotted with Mayan artifacts, awe-inspiring.

We enjoyed experiencing the pyramids and watching the howler monkeys with like-minded souls. The first time we heard those smallish primates howl, we thought a roaring lion was hiding in the trees!

During my parents' visit to the Yucatan Peninsula, Mark and I were camped at the gorgeous beach of Xpu-Ha, along the dreamy Caribbean Sea.

We reunited with Sabine and Michael after staying in touch via email. I was happy to have a girlfriend around; life on the road gets lonely south of the border.

"You have been married how long?" I exclaimed during one of our conversations.

"Ten years," she answered, her voice casual.

"Ten years! How do you do that?" I'd never lasted more than three years in a relationship. Mark had been my boyfriend for only a year and a half, and I could feel his affection waning. I longed for the connection, caring, and understanding I had taken for granted with Karl. I was still deeply in love with Mark, but the sentiment didn't appear mutual anymore. Did it have to do with being cooped up in a tiny camper for too long?

"We have our ups and downs, like all couples," Sabine responded.

I pointed out how Michael was always courteous and sweet to her.

"Why can't my guy be more romantic?" I whined. I missed that trait in Mark, just as I thought I did with Karl, who had showered me with attention in comparison.

Maybe it is me? Am I that unlikable?

After our family and friends left, Mark and I faced an important question: "What's next?" We had never given our end destination much thought. We'd cross the border and see what happened. Now that Mexico had been conquered, we thought we might as well keep going. A new country called.

Maybe it would bring Mark and I closer again?

My tears run free now.

I was such a fool back then, believing things would improve.

I blow my nose in a cloth handkerchief. Mark hates these and has never understood their attraction to Europeans. As most Americans, he prefers Kleenex. The "disposable culture" my mother calls it.

How could it have turned so quickly from us being madly in love to him wanting to continue his life without me?

"Stop being my mom!" I remember him sneering.

Am I that controlling?

By the time we reached Belize, his behavior had become more distanced. But we were still traveling and enjoying our lifestyle on wheels. I could deal with it.

Or so I thought.

After four months of Spanish signs, faltering communications in Mexico, and Latino music, Belize appeared to be an oasis in Central America. The culture was different: Caribbean and *irie* – which means *all good* in Jamaican. The national language is English, and the people are black. While reggae music joyfully filled our ears, Mark and I had full-fledged discussions with the locals again. Our moods lifted instantaneously.

The first thing we did was give our shiny red truck a mud bath at a river. It looked too fancy after the mechanics servicing it in Chetumal, Mexico had washed it to perfection. We were getting tired of the question: "How much did your camper cost?" We hoped smudging the Ford with dirt would obliterate those inquiries.

It did. Until a tropical downpour arrived.

We hiked among jungle and howler monkeys. One mama showed a keen interest in my thin hair after removing my bandana; I had to claim cloth – and hair – back. We discovered cashew trees and tried cashew wine, cooled off in lakes and waterfalls, slid down slick rocks smoothed by time and moistened by a series of waterfalls, visited a cave and a butterfly farm, and fell in love with the beach town of Placencia – the only place we thought we could settle.

It was sweltering and humid, which made it difficult for our dogs to be comfortable. We preferred camping in places with electricity, so we could run the rooftop air conditioning unit.

Outside of Mexico, official campgrounds were rare. Belize had two. One was located in big, dirty, and crowded Belize City and doubled as a marina; the other was found in San Ignacio on the western road out of the country. There, we were the only campers on the grassy field. Our AC was buzzing, Kali and Darwin cooled off inside, and I was hanging clean laundry on the clothes lines across the yard. The stifling sun would take care of the drying process. Mark had helped me with the hand washing. Few words were exchanged between us.

"What's going on?" I asked, feeling the weight in the air. It wasn't just humidity.

"Nothing."

"You don't seem to enjoy this trip anymore." I poked the fires of doubt building inside me. We had been underway five months. I pegged another T-shirt on the line.

"The trip is fine," he replied.

"What is it then? Are you sick of my company? Don't you love me anymore?"

The silence that followed stopped my heart.

Then, the bomb dropped.

"I don't know whether I still love you."

The blood rushed from my face and my worries were confirmed. Denial had been an easy solution.

Instantly, it made sense why he seemed absent when we sat together on the incredible beach of Tenacatita, why he was all but romantic as we watched the night sky at the ruins of Palenque, and why I felt our connection was faltering.

Ups and downs, Sabine had said. I intended to be my sweetest, most caring self, assist him with whatever I could, and act cheery. I would make him love me once more. I ignored my doubts – again – and wished for the best. I had to be positive, in a contagious way. Plus, Mark needed my "Spani-sized" French help when entering the next country.

In Guatemala, memories were made at lakes and in mountains, savoring the authentic Mayan culture and reveling at inspiring views of volcanoes, waterfalls, and colorful towns. We walked over hot lava rock with a deep red flow underneath on Volcán de Pacaya in Antigua. Our feet steamed, our rubber soles melted, and a stick poked in the bubbling lava initiated an instant flame. I loved every minute of it. I hoped the stimulation of our senses would keep our relationship at peace and at ease.

Isn't that why certain couples have kids? To have an all-consuming distraction? Prioritize away from the immediate problems at hand?

Instead of making a baby, I jumped on a plane to give both of us a break. To detach. When I returned from my three-week visit to Belgium, Mark's happiness to see me matched the dogs' delight. And, he had mastered a Spanish course in Panajachel, on the shores of Lake Atitlán. We were back on track and felt strong to keep going. Big. Sigh. Of. Relief. We had reached the *ups* again.

In Nicaragua, poverty greeted us. From the border with El Salvador, we followed a dirt road in miserable condition. Children dressed in nothing more than ragged underwear performed a highly needed service. Shovel in hand, they filled potholes, providing a smoother ride for the frequent trucks and not so frequent campers. In return, they received water, food, or a few córdobas from the drivers. Every item imaginable was transported by bike or on the locals' heads. Colorful, historic cities like Leon and Granada were crumbling. At the top of Volcán Masaya a giant cross watched over us as we hiked the trails. It protected us against the evil spirits of the underworld.

And against unknown forces trying to tear Mark and me apart, I hoped.

One of the highlights in Panama was watching the comings and goings in the Panama Canal from a viewpoint over the Miraflores locks. The Panamax ships, named for being the largest ships to fit in the locks, had inches to spare as they maneuvered from the Atlantic to the Pacific – or vice versa. The sailboats in their wake looked minuscule in comparison. Mark volunteered as a line handler on a 53-foot cruising boat transiting the canal and cherished being "on the other side" of things. A Panama Canal crossing is a bucket list item for many sailors.

🌊🌊🌊

RVers have two options after they're done with Panama: load the camper on a container ship to South America (or elsewhere), like Sabine and Michael, or turn around. The Pan-American Highway does not connect the American continents. The road dead-ends in the Darien Gap, an extremely dangerous area. *Lonely Planet* mentions drug runners, poachers, guerrilla fighters, poisonous animals, deadly diseases, heat exhaustion, and disorientation. Building a road from Panama to Colombia would make drug trafficking easier and is therefore avoided.

Never having planned to come this far, we neither had the money nor the desire to extend our trip into the next continent. In the Spanish-influenced town of Portobelo, a haven for sailors, we made a U-turn. On the northbound journey, we hoped to visit places we missed, but reality proved to be different.

One by one, we passed the Central American countries in reverse order. We braved the potholed roads in Costa Rica. Tractors and bikes passed us on a 27-mile (44 kilometer) stretch of road, which took us four hours to complete. The contents of our camper were rattled and so were we. The long days in the car, the tough roads, dust, heat, and humidity, the same company, lack of progress, and absence of homely comforts were taking their toll after ten months on the road.

What do you talk about when you spend 24/7 together?

My visit to Manuel Antonio National Park along the Pacific coast came as a welcome mini-break. We didn't find electricity to run our AC and leave the dogs in the camper to explore this popular Costa Rican park together. So, Mark took Kali and Darwin to a shady beach and waited for my return from wildlife heaven.

It's better to do this alone anyway. I won't feel self-conscious about taking my time, looking for animals and snapping tons of photos.

More and more I felt as a burden to Mark whenever we'd go for hikes or explore new territory. I like to walk at my own pace and stop frequently to be immersed in my surroundings. With my short-term memory, taking photos is important. Seeing monkeys, agoutis, raccoons, iguanas, and a sloth up-close gave me satisfaction. Taking in the expansive views and scenic beaches made me happy. Doing this six-hour daytrip by myself instilled the confidence I needed for my self-worth and declining sense of adventure.

Why is it that we become more dependent when we are in a relationship?

The sights didn't matter as much as how I felt on the trip north. Mark ignored me and avoided exploring areas together. His new habit of criticizing me in public when catching up with friends in Nicaragua lowered my spirits and heightened my fear about our relationship.

Then, we reached Lago de Yojoa in Honduras, a beautiful, quiet camping spot between a picturesque lake and a pineapple plantation. The place where my life collapsed.

Mark and I are the only visitors. Two little specks in a massive universe. *Insignificant.*

It's the first time I see a pineapple plant.

It's the first time I'm dumped.

It's the first time I'm stranded by myself in a foreign country, entered as a couple.

I do not enjoy the view of the mountains and the lake. I do not appreciate the nearby waterfall plummeting into a ravine, its mist creating colorful rainbows. I do not enjoy this camper life, nor my travels through Central America.

I will never enjoy anything anymore and I will never be happy ever again.

Mark's crushing words had hit hard and sunk deep.

༓ ༓ ༓

Despite the memories, the good intentions, and the love I possess for Mark, there is nothing I can do to change this predicament. He's done with me. I cry. I dwell. I feel miserable. I reminisce. I promise to be a better girlfriend. To not act as a mom.

Am I to blame for this turn of events?

I am weak – insecure. I need comforting arms around me, the presence of a real friend, a phone call with my *oma*. Impossible. All I can do is stare dumbfounded at our dogs. His dogs. They lick the salty tears off my hands. The same tears I smothered them with when I broke up with Karl and waited for my new love to come home, that day I moved in without notice.

I gather my leftover wits. Sadness turns into stubbornness. I'm not spending a dime on a plane ticket, giving Mark *carte blanche* on his trip north. This camper belongs to both of us! I'm not making this easy for him by disappearing out of his life. Yet. And maybe, just maybe, there's a chance we get back together before we return to the United States. Who knows what can happen on 2,000 miles of road to the Texas border?

What does happen is the most difficult time of my life. Not that I regret my decision to stay aboard, but heartbreak, expectation, false hope, inexperience with certain emotions, and impulsiveness don't mix well.

What was I thinking? That it would be a joy or even manageable to be cooped up with an ex-boyfriend who I love dearly, but who's ready to move on? Who takes the dogs on walks by himself, leaving me utterly alone at home, wondering what he's up to? Who goes to the bar every night for drinks with new friends in Placencia, the only town we both thought we could settle? Who meets an attractive female tourist and is ready to date again? Who's looking forward to these encounters and exchanged email addresses? Seeing one of her notes pop up when sitting at our shared computer rubs salt in an open wound.

Why do I expose myself to this? Why don't I hop on a plane and out of this hurtful situation? Why am I stubborn, resentful, and holding on? Why don't I find a guy to comfort me?

My female mind works in mysterious ways.

Have I changed that much? Where is my sense of independence, of being strong and adventurous? Would the old Liesbet stay in Belize and start over?

A swift and rainy trip along the Caribbean coast of Mexico takes us to interesting cultural sites and along not-so-interesting beaches. Once inland, we drive by colonial cities, remote ghost towns, abandoned deserts and, eventually, we cross the border into Texas. There, my US visa re-sets. The B1/B2 stamp allows entry for up to six months.

Do I even need it this time?

We're back. Together, but apart – the opposite of what is called a *LAT-relatie* in Belgium, Living Apart Together. We've returned to the United States with our dogs, experiences, and memories, but without the bond we left with.

We need a base after finishing our Latin American adventure. To re-group, or better, split up permanently. What better place to figure out our future than at a dear and hospitable friend's home in Austin, Texas? We park our truck camper in the driveway. Our host welcomes the four of us with open arms. His own dog, Caesar, has sadly passed away, but he has a girlfriend, a blossoming career, and a comfortable one-story house where we can stay as long as needed. I move into his spare bedroom; my ex-companions remain in the camper.

Every evening, I long for the dimly lit vehicle outside my window. I go to bed, alone and heartbroken.

Inevitably, a week later, I say goodbye to my one true love and the two dogs I have come to adore and treat as my own. Tears roll down my cheeks when the camper reverses from the driveway, turns onto the street, and Mark, Kali, and Darwin drive out of my life.

I stand there for what feels like eternity. Ignorant to the fact that the generous guy I'm currently staying with must have felt exactly the same, two years ago. When he was the one driving away with his dog towards an unknown future without me.

His name? Mr. Cute, aka Karl.

Chapter 3

Trying Anew

I miss Mark, Kali, and Darwin. My stomach feels twisted. Despite Karl's soothing words and well-intended distractions of new girlfriends, I yearn for my old companions. I cry and mope for three days. Then I decide to get back on my feet. Maybe this breakup is a positive thing? I don't need men! Being without a partner means more freedom, less restrictions, fewer compromises. Wasn't I happy, confident, and free when I backpacked through Southeast Asia by myself? There is so much I can do – walk dogs, write articles, crew on sailboats, volunteer abroad, translate texts, teach ESL in Asia. I make a list of all the potentials and start researching.

I'm better off on my own.

🌀🌀🌀

Mark calls from somewhere in the Texan desert. Remorse. Regret. Resolve.

"I miss you," he says. My heart skips a beat.

"Really?" I ask. *What just happened?*

"This last week has been tough. Life in the camper doesn't feel right without you. Kali and Darwin miss you, too."

"I guess you needed distance and some time alone to figure this out?"

"Apparently," he admits. "I thought I'd be happier alone, but I'm not. Will you take me back?"

"Yes!" I squeal, after a few moments of silence. I don't want to play too easy to get (back). He's damn lucky I fall for it and haven't moved on completely. Imagine if I would have stayed in Belize...

I hate switching back and forth when it comes to my future, my emotions, my intentions, or anything else, but I'm convinced getting back together is the right move.

When we see each other again, the tears are from happiness. Kali and Darwin, once again, come running towards me, tails swirling in circles. I receive their licks and embrace them. It's funny how the dogs always come first. Mark and I hug and get lost in each other's eyes and arms. The reunion makes me walk on clouds. The sex is out of this world.

ᗰᗰᗰ

"Do you really think I act like your mother?" Mark and I sit side by side on Karl's couch. We need to talk about our differences in order to improve our relationship.

"Maybe not exactly like my mother, but you're constantly asking what I'm doing, and you always try to help and tell me what to do. It's suffocating," he says.

"You're right. I should stop hovering so much," I admit. And I mean it. I usually cringe when I see other women boss their partners around. They often get what they want, because the man habitually gives in or chooses to avoid conflict. I don't want to be one of those women. I fell for Mark for who Mark is, not who I wished him to become.

"Thank you," he sighs, squeezing my leg. I know this conversation is necessary, despite it resembling a business negotiation. We both need a satisfactory outcome.

"You could be sweeter to me. Or show a hint of love once in a while, like in California." It's what I've missed most.

"I'll try," he offers. I knew from the beginning that Mark is not an overly romantic soul, smothering his girlfriend with kisses and attention, but there was a better connection between us in the beginning. I desire some affection instead of just knowing that I'm loved and cared about.

Jealousy rages again when I remember his interest in that female tourist in Belize.

"What happened with that girl in Placencia? Did you two kiss or do anything more?"

"No. Nothing happened. We just chatted and had drinks together. We're not even in touch anymore."

I believe him. He isn't the liar or cheater type. I hope our reality check will bear fruits.

Maybe couples should occasionally split up to improve their relationship?

"Okay. We'll see what happens. We can only change our behavior if we believe in it. But next time, it's my turn to dump you!" While I don't expect us to separate again, I am not ready to forgive him for the pain this breakup caused. At least I have a list of "potential personal pursuits" now and believe I can handle a future on my own, if needed.

🌊 🌊 🌊

Mark, the dogs, and I sleep together in Karl's guest room. We shop, cook, and clean when our host is at work. Kali and Darwin provide entertainment and company. Karl appreciates it all; he still misses his own dog. I had received the news of Caesar's passing a few months earlier, while on the road. I'm glad we remained friends.

Mark and I are glued to our computers. I attempt to write articles and a book about our recent overland travels; he's looking for a four-door Toyota Tacoma. We're moving to our favorite Central American country and this car is the cheapest to import in duty-heavy Belize.

One month turns into three. We sell our F-350 truck easily – this is Texas, after all – but the camper, still in Karl's driveway, has no takers. Mark can't find the right Tacoma and I don't make headway with my writing. Our moods become sour. We bury ourselves behind our laptops until, eventually, we find our Toyota and a shell for the pick-up bed. All our belongings fit and stay dry. Kali and Darwin have their own doors and the entire back seat. Our move to Placencia is imminent.

Being constantly online creates a different conundrum. It doesn't take long before I find out why Mark's time behind the computer – and his excitement – has increased.

"I was looking at used catamarans again," he begins, "and they're cheaper than before."

"Really? Do you want to go cruising again?" I had no idea he's still interested in sailing the world, after our last misadventure.

"Well, since catamarans have two hulls, they are much more stable, comfortable, and roomier than monohulls. I think you and the dogs would like them better."

"Maybe, but there's no way we can afford one, even secondhand."

"You never know. We might find a desperate seller. Or bargain someone down enough."

The thought of owning another sailboat lifts his spirits.

"Or we can live in Belize for a while and find a catamaran there when we want to go sailing again." I hold my ground, yet suspect this small country isn't the ideal place to boat shop.

Mark remains quiet.

"What's wrong with a comfortable, settled life in an exotic Caribbean location? Do we always need to make everything more complicated? Why can't we just stick to plan?" I complain.

At the same time though, the idea of sailing in the tropics touches an adventurous nerve.

Trouble!

Finding, purchasing, and moving on a sailboat will be more tricky, expensive, and time-consuming than driving to Belize. Yet my curiosity is piqued.

I make a list with the pros. I love lists. Catamaran or Belize? Both are equally attractive; each represents something new (sailing or settling in the Caribbean), something old (owning a sailboat or returning to Belize), and something blue (the ocean under our keels or at our feet). Both promise excitement, fun, and adventure.

While I know deep down what our hearts desire, I want to be fair to my list.

As an expat in the tropics, I can be a travel writer – but living on a sailboat offers continuous explorations. Every time I write something positive in the second column to balance the scale, my eyes bounce back to the first one. A catamaran promises more wildlife encounters, peace, and cultural immersions. The boat column grows. It's one of those moments where an important decision must be made – a fork in the road. We can't possibly know what's right or wrong. Thrilled about one option, I immediately fear it will be the wrong one in the long run.

Back and forth it goes.

"What do you want to do?" I ask Mark. I *love* talking about new possibilities and adventures. Life makes sense again. But it's time to choose. If there's anything I hate more than making decisions, it's having regrets. And there's still that camper in the driveway.

"If we want to try cruising again, this is as good a time as any and the East Coast is the best place to hunt for a sailboat," Mark determines.

"Let's go sailing then. Belize can wait!" I decide or *chop the knot* as Dutch-speakers say.

The boat column wins. We're ready to give sailing a second chance, with the assumption that a catamaran is more comfortable than a monohull.

But is this the right time? Can my boyfriend afford a catamaran? I sure can't. Will the dogs get used to this boat? Is there even a chance we'll find the right one? How long will it take? Can our relationship survive another period of insecurity about the future?

The only way to find out is to pursue our new goal.

We've never sailed on a catamaran before. Neither have Kali and Darwin. We send a reader's letter to *Latitude 38*, our favorite sailing magazine on the West Coast, asking whether anyone in Texas is willing to take us on a test run with their cat.

"Glad to read you guys are setting out again," magazine owner Richard emails back. Knowing from experience, he adds, "You'll love cruising on a catamaran." He hasn't forgotten the commotion we caused when informing the sailing community about selling *Four Choices* and why. A readers' debate started between "Good for you to put the dogs first. We're animal lovers as well..." to "I can't believe you're selling your boat instead of getting rid of the dogs!"

Nothing comes of our inquiry and we want to get a move on. We put our camper on consignment at an RV store, transport our gear from Karl's garage into our Belize-approved pickup truck, and, after four stationary months, hit the road again.

"How about giving it two months?" I suggest. "If we haven't found the right catamaran by then, we can hang out with your friends and family in Massachusetts for the summer and head to Belize afterwards."

"Sounds good to me," Mark responds.

Off we go, our lives contained in a single vehicle. The covered pickup bed shelters our camping gear, clothes, dog toys, bedding, cooking utensils, heavy-duty tools, and a cheap printer/scanner/fax, intended for our fictional office in Placencia.

We have one objective: find a suitable, affordable double-hulled home soon. The truck is our transportation device and closet; the three-person tent our bedroom for four. The tailgate acts as a table, bench, and shade provider for the dogs. We use a plastic sun shower to wash up and – without a fridge – buy fresh food every day. Our small camping stove delivers one-pot meals.

After an unsuccessful month on the road, we arrive in Maryland to give our search one last shot. We meet Tommy, a yacht broker in Annapolis we had contacted via email. The catamaran we're interested in is no longer for sale. We lose all hope. But we're not done yet.

Tommy's sense for originality and business strategy surprises us.

"I've been contacting catamaran owners who aren't thinking about putting their boats on the market," he says. "Many people have a boat they never use; it's just costing money. Selling that financial burden might not have crossed their minds, so I'm offering that option."

He has our attention.

"Anyway," Tommy continues, "there is this guy who might be interested in selling his Fountaine Pajot Tobago. It's 35 feet long and well-built. I can contact him. What's your budget?"

"Around 120,000 dollars," Mark answers. Tommy raises his eyebrows. Most 35- to 38-foot sailing cats are being sold for much more in 2007.

"I'll see what I can do," he says. "Where are you staying?"

"At the Greenbelt National Park campground. It's near Washington DC, Baltimore, and Annapolis. Good for sightseeing, but not ideal for boat shopping," I respond.

He nods, and then adds, "My uncle's best friend, Tony, owns a farm on the edge of Annapolis. He's a wonderful man and I know other people stay there. I'll ask him if you can pitch your tent on his property. Oh, and feel free to take a shower in my office any time."

Tommy is a godsend!

The following month, Mark and I live on Tony's farm, joining the ranks of characters already in residence. Jay, resembling Santa Claus, lives in a small room, part of a hangar on the grounds. This structure contains a usable toilet, robust sink, and antique, full-size fridge, which we all share. When it's too hot outside, we find relief inside. Jim, another hippie-looking guy, is a carpenter occupying a small motorboat on a trailer parked at the farm.

Our little family moves to a secluded spot in a field unoccupied by miniature horses or cows. Tony has mowed a path through the long grass and a square patch for our tent. A junked file cabinet has the perfect height to place our sun shower on. Behind us are acres of forest, minutes away from downtown.

Mark and I are content with the location, the company, and the assurance that our broker-turned-friend handles our boating interests in town. With some convincing, our offer of a slightly higher price, and the Tobago owner willing to sell, owning a catamaran becomes tangible.

Chapter 4

Big Trouble

The lines at US Immigration are short. I'm used to much worse in JFK, Dulles, or Miami, where I often had to run to make my connecting flight. While my B1/B2 visitor visa theoretically allows a six-month entry, I'm antsy for the stamp to confirm it. Especially now, those six months are important. Mark and I have to prepare our new sailboat for a journey to the Bahamas, get the dogs used to the catamaran before setting out, and – most importantly – depart after the hurricane season. Going to the tropics before November 1st would be dangerous.

It's June 8th, 2007. I'm in a bind, but I've been here before. I know what to expect. I just have to be polite, honest, patient, and compliant. I *need* that six-month stamp.

"Good morning, sir." I start on a positive note.

"Good morning. Where are you coming from?" the not unfriendly official asks.

"Brussels, Belgium." I smile.

I'm in Dublin, Ireland, on my way back to Massachusetts after a two-week stay in Belgium, visiting friends, family, and doctors. My friend Rosy also married her long-term boyfriend Peter, an additional "excuse" for my trip.

It had been a unique ceremony, followed by a Spanish-themed party. Over Cava, I had reminisced with An, a mutual friend of mine and Rosy's, about her wedding, years prior.

"How about you and Mark?" An had asked, while we watched the newlyweds lock eyes.

I had shrugged my shoulders. "You know me. I don't want to get married. I like my freedom. Besides, Mark and I went through a rough period recently."

I didn't want to get into our breakup. Instead, I took another sip of my aperitif to the upbeat tunes of the Cuban band and added, "But if I ever marry, I want my wedding to be full of love, friends, and fun. Like this one."

I wish I could've stayed longer in my home country, that I didn't have to run around so much, trying to fit everything into a tight schedule. But Mark's parents have their 50th wedding anniversary coming up in two days and I don't want to miss that. *Fifty years of marriage!*

Mark is helping his brother, Tim, and soon to be sister-in-law Kris with the preparations for the party. I'm looking forward to celebrating Carol and Stan's big event with their best friends and family. It will be the last time we're all together before Mark and I leave. The boat paperwork is complete and, after the festivities, Mark, the dogs, and I will return to Annapolis to move onto our new Fountain Pajot Tobago.

"What were you doing in Belgium?" the Immigration officer wants to know.

Why am I being questioned by US Homeland Security while on a layover in Ireland? I want to know.

"Visiting friends and family." I keep it simple.

"How long are you coming back to the US for?" he asks.

"Six months," I say. Six months should suffice to prep the boat and leave. My answer makes him look up from the computer. Few tourists ask for that much time.

How could I have dealt with that question differently?

"Come with me, Miss," the official commands, holding onto my two Belgian passports and boarding pass.

Here we go...

My heart skips a beat as I follow him to the secondary Immigration area. This is where the illegal entrants are held and alleged criminals in handcuffs temporarily detained. I'm ordered to sit down among a scary-looking group. I feel out of place. The waiting starts, and the real questioning hasn't even begun yet.

I used to love flying. Until I started coming to the US of A in 2003. Blame 9/11. Each time I arrive by plane, Homeland Security questions me in the back room, suspects me of *something*, and holds me for ages. They refuse to understand my nomadic lifestyle and how I travel so much with so little money. My explanations sound too crazy to be made up. When they are eventually confirmed during hour-long interrogations, incorporating the right amount of bullying, the border officials let me in. I suspect that's exactly what will happen next.

"Miss Collaert?"

"Yes."

"Come forward, please."

I enter a small office with a counter. A different, stern-looking officer greets me from behind the desk: "When was the last time you were in the United States?"

"Two weeks ago."

"Why did you go back to Belgium?"

"To see family and friends."

"Why do you need six months in the States, again? Are you working here?"

"No! My boyfriend and I bought a boat and we need to get it ready to leave the country."

"How do you afford to stay that long?"

"We have savings to be able to travel around."

"Traveling is expensive. What's your profession?"

"I am a teacher in Belgium." *That was a good move, "am" a teacher and not "was" a teacher.* Theoretically, I am still a teacher, connected to my last school, just not a practicing one.

"How can a teacher take this much time off?"

"I'm on a sabbatical." I don't mention that I get a monthly stipend for opening my position up. That would make everything even more complicated.

Maybe I should have mentioned the stipend to make the money conversation smoother? It's hard to say the right things.

"You're taking a lot of *sabbaticals.* And spending lots of time in the US. Why?"

"I come here to be with my boyfriend and travel around. We're planning to leave to the Bahamas in a few months. I've never done anything wrong in the US."

I'm pretty sure I haven't.

"We'll see about that, Miss. Please, go back to the waiting area."

I go outside. The door closes. I sit in the plastic chair. I look around.

Everything will be fine. I've never done anything wrong.

I stare at the clock. Fifteen minutes pass. The door remains shut.

"Miss Collaert?"

"Yes!" I walk back into the small room. The door closes behind me.

"How many times have you been in the United States?"

"What?"

"You need to tell me exactly how many times you've visited the United States in the last four years. The dates, every port of entry, the length of your stays, every port of exit, and the reasons for your visits."

"I don't remember all that!"

"Well, you better remember, Miss, if you want to get on that plane to Boston!"

My face turns pale. Without my passports, which lie in front of the official, it's hard to recall each visit. He has a computer to check this data as well. I have no help whatsoever. Based on my memory – which is nothing to be proud of – I add up my different trips into and out of the US. I'm warned not to be mistaken, while the man compares my answers to a computer print-out.

"Why did you go to Canada for four weeks?"

"To get to Alaska with our camper."

"So, from the US straight back into the US. You realize that those weeks in Canada didn't count towards leaving the country, right?"

"I wasn't aware of that at the time, but they told me at the border in Alaska."

The man frowns. I begin to realize my stay in Belgium has been too short.

"It appears to me that you're living in the US illegally."

"That's not true," I stutter and swallow. "I've been exploring the US in the past and now my boyfriend and I need to get our boat ready to leave."

"Please, step outside, Miss."

Now I'm in trouble.

I walk back to the waiting area. This doesn't bode well. It's all taking too long.

I will miss my plane! What's going on? Could they refuse me entry into the country?

I am neither here nor there. Not in the US, nor in Belgium, where I could have stepped outside and taken the train back to my parents to let everything sink in. The waiting room has emptied. I'm the only person left.

Maybe these guys are bored and decided to frighten a defenseless, innocent tourist?

Fifteen more minutes pass.

"Miss Collaert?"

"Yes!" I rush back into the interrogation chamber. I have no more time to lose.

"I see you applied for and received an extension in the beginning of 2005. Why?"

"I was done with my travels in the US and ready to leave, but then I met my current boyfriend. We needed the six-month extension to wrap up his life in California and prepare ourselves for an RV trip to Mexico."

I don't go into our failed cruising attempt on *Four Choices*. The story already sounds too far-fetched.

"Where is that extension?"

"What do you mean? It was a stamp in my old passport; the one with the cut-off corners and my B1/B2 visa. Isn't it in there? Can't you check it in your computer?"

If Belgian passports didn't expire every five years, I wouldn't have to travel with two in the first place.

"I need proof of that extension from two years ago. You have to show me the document."

"I don't remember a document. I don't have any documents on me right now."

Was there a form I received? Where would it be?

I draw a blank.

"Please, go back to the waiting room and find proof for this extension. If not, I'm afraid we'll have to keep you in Dublin."

I wobble back to my chair in a daze.

This can't be true. The only proof is the stamp in that passport. Who could I call? I don't even have a phone.

There's nothing I can do to get out of this nightmare.

These powermongers know it. They must have the proof in front of them but decided to make me sweat. I'm waiting this one out.

I have patience; the airline doesn't.

"Miss Collaert?" The door opens.

"Yes." Another ten minutes have passed before I make my way back into the office. The Aer Lingus plane to Boston leaves in less than half an hour.

"We found the proof of your extension."

"Oh, great." A sigh of relief.

"That doesn't mean you're home free. In fact, you've done something illegal when you left last month. You overstayed in the United States."

I look at the stamps he shows me in my passport. My US visa expired on May 20th. I'm 100 percent sure that's the day I left. There is no exit stamp to prove this. Returning the tear-off part of my white I-94 form, filled out when entering the country with a B1/B2 visa, had been the only requirement. The entry stamp of Belgium displays May 21st, one day later. Belgian officials usually don't stamp the passports of citizens, but I had wised up over the years. I request a stamp each time I return home, because US border patrol always gives me a hard time. I want proof for my stories. Today, this stamp is biting me in the butt, thanks to the official's ignorance.

"See, you didn't get to Belgium until after your visa expired. You over-stayed a day."

"That's not true!" My face turns red and tears well up. Is this what they want? For me to cry; to submit to their power?

Are they unaware of red eye flights or is this yet another test?

"I did not overstay. I left on the 20th and it was an overnight flight. The time difference in Belgium is six hours with the East Coast. That's why I arrived in Belgium a day later." I can't convince them and seem to make things worse by opening my mouth.

How can I get out of this?

"You've been in the United States way too many times and way too long. In the last ten years, you've been there more than me!"

Does he want me to feel bad for him?

The official sends me back to my familiar plastic chair. I guess Mr. Homeland Security has been stuck in Ireland for a decade against his will. Unfortunately, he's the one deciding my fate. He's making me pay for living a freer life than him. It's all about who you get at the border, and in what kind of mood that person is. I'm out of luck. This guy got out of bed on the wrong side. I should be happy I never encountered one of his kind earlier.

Through the glass wall, I see passengers walk to the gate and disappear. One by one, they board the plane to Boston. Minutes pass by. I stare at the closed door of the office. The gate personnel wraps things up. It's now or never. I need to get on that plane. Mark will be waiting at the other

end. He has no idea about what's going on here. The gate is about to close.
I want to scream. A flight attendant walks over.

"Are you on this plane to Boston?" she asks.

"I hope so. My luggage is. But they're not letting me go." I point at the
shut door.

"I'll talk to them," she promises. "They will let you go."

She makes her way into the Immigration office to see whether I am to
board the plane. Then, she steps outside and leaves.

No!

The stern official calls me.

"Miss, we're going to do you a huge favor, thanks to my supervisor
here." Serious looks all around. "We will let you on the plane to Boston.
You can enter the United States."

A big sigh. *I knew it.*

"We're allowing you into the country for one month."

"One month? Oh no, I need more time!"

"Miss, you're lucky we are letting you in at all. You have one month
to figure things out between you and your boyfriend. After that, you have
to leave the country for at least six months." My eyes widen. "You're not
allowed to file for another extension, and don't even think about hiring an
Immigration lawyer. You won't succeed. Do you agree with this decision?"

I can't believe it. One month... that's nothing! I'm on a layover. I can't
stay here. What am I supposed to say? I need to get to Boston. I have to see
Mark and talk to him. I'm either getting on this plane now or never. I don't
have another choice.

"Yes." I submit to higher powers. His stamp lands on my passport
page. Instead of relief, I feel dread. *30 days*, he scribbles on it. Then, in red
letters *NO EXTENSIONS ALLOWED*. This note goes into the computer
as well, so I don't get any stupid ideas. My fascination about being in a
multi-cultural relationship is wearing off quickly. I fight back my tears,
grab my passports and boarding pass, and enter the full plane, avoiding
the annoyed stares of the other passengers.

The last time we tried to go sailing, it didn't work out because of the dogs. Now it won't happen because of me. Mark doesn't have the slightest clue about what looms over our heads. And, at 36,000 feet, all I can do is replay endless variations of "Now what?" My mind goes crazy with should haves and could haves, while I continue to block my tears. This isn't a good time to get dehydrated.

Mark's smile disappears when he notices my pale face at Logan Airport. I wait until I'm in his arms to let it all out. I cry, and cry, and cry. Incoherently, I explain what happened in Dublin. And after my arrival in Boston, 30 minutes earlier.

Against protocol and signage, desperate to find a solution, I'd diverted from my easy path out the door to talk to another Homeland Security official. I'd explained my predicament ("I need more time in the US to work on our new boat and get it ready to go." "What? You're *working* on a boat in the United States?" "No! I meant we have to prepare our boat to leave this country but that's impossible in one month. I need more time.") to no avail. There was nothing this Boston officer could do for me.

We are utterly screwed.

Our last resort is to make an appointment at a Boston Field Office of the US Citizenship and Immigration Services (USCIS).

The Monday after Stan and Carol's anniversary party, a sunny, inspiring, and social event with Mark's two siblings, their families, and the couple's friends, the two of us drive into the city for our scheduled meeting with the USCIS. A friendly official calls the grump at Dublin Airport, who's responsible for my conundrum. Unfortunately, the Boston folks can't change a thing. It's the discretion of Homeland Security officers at the border to decide how long a visitor can stay in the United States of America. Our jaws drop, our stares turn blank.

"So, this is it? There's nothing we can do about her being able to stay here for 30 days only, actually, 26 at this point?" Mark asks.

"Not really," replies the male officer.

"Why don't you get married?" his female counterpart suggests.

Let's see... because it's illegal to marry for immigration reasons. Because we got back together a mere few months ago. Because I have little interest in getting married. Unless, maybe, if it were to be romantic, with friends and family, preceded by a sweet proposal, and followed by an exceptional honeymoon.

The mood is grim as we pack, load up the dogs, and head south. At least we have something to talk about on the long drive to Annapolis, where our new floating home awaits.

"I can stay here illegally until we're ready to leave," I offer. If millions of people manage to remain undetected every day, it couldn't be too hard.

"With the Coast Guard becoming part of Homeland Security and us living on a boat in coastal waters, the risk you get noticed is too big," Mark counters.

I imagine being boarded and handing over my passport with the fat red letters. At least now I know when I need to leave. If caught illegally, they immediately kick you out and the chance of coming back is probably slim. With an American partner, whose family lives in the US, it's not a good idea to cut all ties.

"I could try applying for another extension. That would buy me a few months. I'm allowed to stay until they decide the outcome of the request."

"It might give us another month or two, but from the moment they deny your application – and we're pretty sure they will – you'd have to leave immediately. Then what?"

"An Immigration lawyer costs thousands of dollars, money we don't have. Apparently, that wouldn't get us anywhere either." I sigh. There's only one option. But we don't talk about that. Some wounds never heal. Mark is still on trial with me.

The Annapolis area offers enough distraction from our predicament. We have three weeks to come up with a solution. Why not stick to plan in the meantime?

Our new catamaran is called *Big Trouble*. Suitable for the current events, but inappropriate for a home that deserves more and for the adventure we have in mind. Mark and I pick her up and move her to a haul-out facility; high and dry, hot and humid, buggy and troublesome.

The first thing I do is remove the word *Big* from her bum. That's better. We know there's trouble now and trouble ahead, but the boat's own issues shape up after Mark's attention, care, and capabilities. My name removal helps. Especially when the word *Trouble* disappears into the trash as well.

We work hard for a couple of weeks to make the neglected interior livable and the systems usable. The underside, through-hulls, and saildrives (which resemble shafts of outboard engines, but bigger) receive the most attention, as they require maintenance in dry surroundings. Since we don't like being on a boat out of the water, out of the breeze, out of privacy, out of fridge or toilet facilities (seawater is needed to operate those), we want to finish those jobs as soon as possible. The rest can wait until we float again.

We give our catamaran a new name: *Irie*. It means "all good" in the Jamaican Patois language. Our link to Belize. When you're *irie*, you're at total peace with your current state of being. The term is used in reggae songs and we loved it from the moment Mark's brother-in-law Brian suggested it. He was a quintessential hippie growing up in the Sixties, with an expertise of all things *irie*. With such a boat name, what can possibly go wrong?

Chapter 5

Only If I Must

Clerk Robert clears his throat.

"We are gathered here in the presence of this witness to join Mark and Liesbet together in matrimony. The contract of marriage is a most solemn one and not to be entered into lightly, but thoughtfully and seriously, and with a deep realization of its obligations and responsibilities."

I throw a quick glance at my boyfriend and smile. I wonder whether this court guy has any idea why we're doing this.

"If anyone can show just cause why they should not be lawfully joined together, let him speak now, or else forever hold his peace."

His peace? That sounds like a sexist statement. Women are not allowed to speak up?

This is the material of movies. The lyrics sound exactly like on TV.

How romantic!

I look at our one witness, Jim from the farm, summoned in a panic since – last minute – I thought it would be nice if someone could be here and take photos of our wedding day. He remains quiet; nothing like in the movies. I melt and embrace every second.

"Mark, will you take Liesbet (*correctly pronounced!*) here present, for your lawful wife?"

"I will."

"Liesbet, will you take Mark here present, for your lawful husband?"

"I will." I beam.

Then, Mark repeats after Robert: "I, Mark, take thee, Liesbet, for my lawful wife, to have and to hold, from this day forward, for better, for worse, for richer, for poorer, in sickness and in health..." It sounds sweet, convincing. I have no idea yet how true these words will ring.

It's my turn to copy the words. I concentrate. This man has a Southern drawl. "I, Liesbet, take thee, Mark, for my lawful husband, to have and to hold, from this day forward, for better, for worse, for richer, for poorer, in sickness and in health, until death do us ... *what*?"

He said something about death, but I missed the last part. This sentence is new to me. My English isn't as good as it ought to be or I haven't watched enough romantic comedies. It's like those English songs we sang along with as teenagers, not understanding the words, making lyrics up with similar sounding gibberish. I don't want to make up words here.

"Until death do us what?" I interrupt the service.

"Until death do us part." The clerk unsuccessfully hides a smile.

"Until death do us part," I finish my statement. *It must mean the same as "Until death separates us." Why not use that? This isn't a poem.*

Robert ignores the step "with this ring, I thee wed." We told him he could skip that part and start his weekend early. There is no ring. There is not much of anything on this Friday, July 6th, 2007, at the courthouse of Annapolis. I preferred the event to take place on 7/7/7, easy to remember for both of us without mixing up the month and the day, but the building is closed on Saturdays.

As an afterthought, on the way to our ceremony, Mark had stopped the car at a mall, after noticing a flower shop. He felt I needed a bouquet.

"Just wait here," he'd commanded.

I had no idea where he was going and fretted about not making it in time to the courthouse. It had been a busy day already.

In the morning, I dealt with a health exam for my green card application. The wait took longer than expected. We'd been running late ever since. Lunch consisted of three items each from the Dollar Menu at Wendy's. We will always be on a budget. Forking out $260 to be declared healthy had hurt. Then, we settled Kali and Darwin at a dog-friendly motel, another last-minute arrangement.

The right frame of mind came to me only yesterday, when I thought it a better idea to spend our wedding night in a hotel room with a King-size bed, instead of a mosquito-infested, hot, humid, facility-lacking boat bunk. Rushed, we had summoned the dogs to lie down in the comfortable air-conditioned room while we both took a shower. Mark put on a long-sleeved maroon shirt, tan shorts, and his trusted flip flops. From cubbyholes in the boat, I had gathered a khaki, hippie-looking skirt, a baby-blue top with spaghetti straps, and my favorite silver necklace. Black flip flops complemented my attire.

"Here you go." Mark's eyes twinkled as he handed me a lovely smelling bouquet of white and red roses.

"Where did you find those?" I asked.

"Well, I saw that florist, but the owner only sells funeral flowers. I told him my predicament and he came up with this. Aren't they pretty?"

"They're perfect," I answered, clutching my unusual wedding bouquet.

The two of us did make it to the courthouse without further delays. Jim was stuck in rush hour traffic. Mark and I held hands and waited on a wooden bench, almost as nervous as the pregnant teenage couple next to us.

At 3:45pm, our unwashed friend showed up, straight from work, right on time. Long grey hair with a beard to match, sweat dripping from his face, he was stopped at security. After handing his Leatherman and carpenter tools over, he joined us with a wide smile. I gave him my digital camera and prayed he knew how to use it. Excited to "give me away" as my substitute father, he hooked my arm as we walked into the courtroom, ready for our no-nonsense ceremony.

"By the power and authority vested by law in me as Clerk of the Circuit Court for Anne Arundel County, Maryland, I now pronounce you husband and wife," Robert concludes.

Then, to a vague click in the background, Mark and I kiss the most romantic, meaningful kiss to be kissed. Sweet, soft, and slightly wed. I mean, wet. I look into my husband's eyes. I imagine mine sparkle just as much. We are married. In all of five minutes.

People don't often marry anymore in Belgium or they live together for a long time before tying the knot. Sometimes they seal the deal for practical reasons. A bit like us, I guess. Taking your husband's last name is not a practice either. Mail is addressed to both last names, separated by a hyphen. If Mark and I were to live in my home country, envelopes would mention "Familie Kilty – Collaert" as the addressee.

Even when considering or having children, marriage has nothing to do with that decision. Why do you have to be married to commit to each other? What's the difference when you love somebody, and you plan to be with him as long as you're happy?

I never understood the urge of American women to marry immediately after graduating from college. How do you know he is *Mr. Right*, if he's only *Mr. One* or *Mr. Two?*

I'm 32 and the concept of marriage still daunts me. Without expecting – let alone planning – we had done it.

I thought about Rosy's wedding in Ghent, only weeks ago. Who would have guessed I'd be next, and so soon? Life has a funny way of throwing curve balls.

My stubbornness about not marrying had to give. My dreams of a romantic wedding with friends and family in a tropical setting had to go as well. A honeymoon where romance trumps adventure? Highly overrated, I'm sure. As for my desire to marry for love, that one stands.

Jim congratulates us and returns my camera. I'm thrilled to discover that he does know how to take decent photographs. And that is that. I am ready for a fun evening. All we have left to do on Monday is pick up my tuberculosis results at the doctor's office and drop the green card application, including a fat check, into a mailbox.

Jim, *my husband* Mark, and I walk to an upscale bar at the circle. Our yacht broker-turned-friend Tommy joins us. What happens next is a blur of drinking, laughing, and companionship.

As always, I'm at a loss in an American bar. There are no drinking menus to browse. I need to know the prices of everything before I buy something, whether we're in a grocery store, a restaurant, or a bar. It drives me nuts not having any idea of what something costs. Maybe it's because of incidents in less-developed countries where locals try to take advantage of "rich" tourists by overcharging them; maybe it's because I'm used to price tags and menus everywhere in Belgium; or maybe it's because of my incorrigible frugality, but ordering a drink in the States stresses me out. Asking the waitress how much a certain beverage costs is usually received with an empty stare. She either doesn't know or the question takes her by surprise.

It must be nice to not worry about money and order whatever you want.

"I wonder how much a Cosmopolitan costs?" I whisper to Mark. I'm curious to try one.

"Order whatever you want," he replies. "It's your wedding day."

Good point. After two sweet martinis, my worries about the bill dissipate. Tommy suggests we move to a tiki bar at the waterfront. He's promoted to taxi driver and smoothly transports us around his town. We feel like royalty, minus the clothes, wealth, and entourage.

More rounds of drinks later, we realize a fancy meal at Annapolis's best seafood restaurant would be a waste of money in our current state. We cancel our reservation and postpone that treat to when a better appreciation for well-prepared food prevails.

We bid Tommy and Jim farewell and order a greasy portion of fish & chips in a pub. I hold Mark's hand across the sticky wooden table and glance at my wedding ring, created from a paper napkin earlier in the evening. My bouquet of funeral flowers rests between my cup of ice water and glass of red wine.

"I love you, husband," I say, as I lock eyes with my brand spanking new partner for life.

"I love you, too, dear wife."

Chapter 6

Let's Go South!

Work on *Irie* as newlyweds should be easier and faster, or at least more romantic.

It's not.

The only thing our constantly dripping, grimy bodies desire is a cold shower. I'm glad our wedding night involved a comfortable motel room, where the sweating was caused by something other than humid air. Those memories will have to hold us over for a while.

The good thing is that we're not in a hurry anymore. The application for my permanent residency went into the mail on the date my visa expired. The postal stamp made our request official in the nick of time.

Once you apply for a green card, you're allowed to remain in the country until the verdict. So, for now, I'm legal in the United States of America.

Take that, grumpy, stuck-in-Ireland macho man!

Even if my request to become a "legal resident alien" were to be denied, it buys us enough time to get our sailboat ready to leave US soil. The only step left is the dreaded, media-hyped interview, where – according to popular belief – officials grill the married pair to find out whether they know each other through and through. We don't have to think about that yet. If red tape in the US is anything like in Belgium, we have plenty of time.

Mark and I work hard in Maryland's summer heat and humidity to get the out-of-the-water projects finished. We scrape, sand, rinse, and paint the underwater part of our cat, after fixing blisters by opening them up, drying them out, and filling the holes with epoxy. The engines receive a lot of attention and so do many other parts of our floating home.

While Mark dives into the technical aspects of the ship's systems, I install lifeline netting on deck to provide a safer environment for our pets. The days are long. We focus on the boat forever. I feel neglected.

This is quite the honeymoon.

One of these years we'll have a party to celebrate our marriage in style, with family and friends, good food, maybe a ring, and definitely... romance.

Tying stubborn pieces of string around metal wires under a beating sun is a far cry from bridal bliss. The harder we work, the sooner we get back into the water and into the breeze. Kali and Darwin relax underneath our bridge deck, which provides a slight flow of air and ample shade for an improvised workshop and lounge area with camping chairs; an unexpected advantage of owning a catamaran. The dogs prefer lying inside the boat under their rotating fan, but dread walking up the wobbly, steep ramp we created to get them on board. Kali slips off twice. At nine years old, she's not as agile as her "little brother."

How did this yard visit turn into four weeks? A rookie mistake of optimism, naivety, and lack of experience. We learn to multiply the expected time, cost, and effort of a future boatyard stay by three. That helps rein in overconfidence and disappointments.

But everything ends, even living without our own toilet, shower, and fridge in filthy conditions.

Early August, *Irie* is launched into the Chesapeake Bay. We find an affordable slip in rustic Pier 7 Marina and continue our seemingly never-ending preparations for an extensive cruise. We focus on the projects to get her shipshape and in rudimentary living condition and will finish the to-do list underway. The sooner we can start sailing, the better.

Despite our good intentions, some tasks are arduous, like installing a horizontal propane tank in the cockpit locker and running the hose to the stove in the galley. After hours of patience, trial and error, pulling and pushing, scraping skin, and lots of cursing, Mark's frustration reaches an all-time high. He hits poor *Irie* with his dominant fist. She's hard as fiberglass and doesn't take abuse lightly.

After a trip to the emergency room, Mark's hand is in a cast. Broken. Defeated by his subject of affection.

There goes the plan of leaving Annapolis any time soon...

Refusing to let his handicap slow him down, Mark becomes a pro in one-handedness. He installs a heavy inverter and alternator in the engine room and learns to use his left hand for all things essential. If nothing else, we're going forward as a more productive team, strengthened by a physical *and* lawful bond. Our combined efforts get the jobs done and I take over the cooking. Love making becomes challenging, but we appreciate new approaches to just about anything in life.

Summer passes.

After work, we socialize at our dock-turned-Tiki-bar, with plastic palm trees and Caribbean decorations, courtesy of a floating neighbor. I have multiple ideas for stories, but no time to produce articles. This is to be a recurring theme. Just like Mark's frustration with boat-related issues and our dogs' stubbornness about not doing their business on deck.

The leaves turn color, Kali and Darwin become reluctant to swim in the river, and warm clothes replace shorts and T-shirts. It's mid-October – time to head south.

After three and a half months, we fixed the imminent problems, installed new electronics and gear, and cleaned *Irie*. She forgave Mark for hitting her. He learned his lesson, wearing a cast for five weeks.

On our last days at the dock, we sell our Belize-friendly truck to someone who has no intentions to drive it there. We provision, load up spare parts, and wash and brush the dogs to look extra pretty when wagging goodbye to our Annapolis friends. We trust our lives and future to *Irie*.

She's our home, our transportation, our safe haven, our irritation, our support, our biggest curse, and our greatest treasure. Our family sets sail into the sunset to live happily ever after. I start my blog *It's Irie* to document exactly how we do that and envision sharing frequent updates.

🌊 🌊 🌊

Mark and I have one mission: get warm.

After a bit of sailing in the Chesapeake Bay, failing miserably at catching fish for dinner, avoiding crab pots as if it were a sport, and testing our anchor in a few less-developed areas, we enter the Intracoastal Waterway (ICW), the "highway" for boats. The ICW is an enclosed network of rivers, canals, and bays. This boat is new to all of us and I'm a novice sailor and navigator, so we choose this protected, relatively straightforward, and slow passage to get used to *Irie's* quirks.

We follow the waterway to Florida, passing historic towns, smelly swamps, national parks, wildlife reserves, cute cottages, immense mansions, busy docks, quiet anchorages, massive properties, rickety fishing piers, majestic shrimp boats, funky yard statues, festive house decorations, and countless channel markers with osprey nests on top. We smile at a fake giraffe, camouflaged hunters and boats, a "ski lift" with golfers crossing the channel above us, silly boat names, and inappropriate conversations on the VHF radio.

Having to stay in the marked channels restricts progress to daylight hours, when we can see what we're doing. Finding a comfortable place to spend each night also requires time. None of this has to be taken into consideration if sailing longer, non-stop stretches in the ocean. Going slow is part of our intentions to understand our boat and get it – and ourselves – ready for adventures further afield. Plus, we have to take the dogs ashore every morning and evening.

There are more obstacles to run into than on the ocean, but there are advantages as well. On the waterway, I don't get seasick. Kali and Darwin are comfortable. We see fascinating sights and sleep well on flat water. Our favorite places for the night are tucked-away anchorages. To be surrounded by nothing but cypress trees and peace (so quiet you hear the leaves fall) is magical. Our only requirement for an anchorage, other than adequate protection and good holding, is a spot to land the dogs. Sometimes it's a small beach or a wide-open field, other times just a tree root or a mud bank, but, apparently, it beats having to go on *Irie's* trampoline.

We rise early in frigid temperatures, take the wheel, test the autopilot, follow day marks and buoys, look at charts, check our depth, observe the chart plotter, and shiver non-stop. We pay attention to the route, take photos, get in line for bridge openings, and stick to a schedule of eight to ten hours on the go.

Never cut corners. And never follow a catamaran unless you're on one!

We anchor, take the dogs to shore for a walk, watch sunset, make dinner, and turn in exhausted and fully-clothed; only to repeat the same routine with slightly different scenery the next day, and the next, and the next.

꩜ ꩜ ꩜

Motoring for weeks becomes monotonous; the humming of the engines, the exhaust smell, the evening anchor rituals, joining a boat string of snowbirds. Our cat remains flat and steady, ideal circumstances for dog naps. Except when a *real* powerboat passes us, and its wake disturbs the peace. It gets bumpy. Kali retreats inside the saloon and hides on her blanket. After the excitement, she returns outside to join Darwin under the helm seat.

Human entertainment is provided by a rogue crab pot near Titusville...

Irie has a delightful day, sailing along at eight knots in perfect conditions. Mark's in heaven; the dogs point their noses into the wind, sniffing a hundred miles an hour. I savor the moment. Suddenly, we slow down. Wind speed and direction haven't changed. Something is amiss. I look behind. A fluorescent monster follows us! The port hull is trailing a gigantic cage.

Mark immediately starts the other engine and we lower both sails. With a boat hook, I pull the heavy item in from the bottom transom step. The cage is empty. No free dinner. I cut the rope, sinking the ballast.

That'll teach the crabbers to not put these obstacles in the middle of the channel!

Then, we search for the buoy that marked the trap. It must be caught near the saildrive or the rudder. Hopefully, the rope isn't tangled up. It's good to have two engines in situations like these. With one usable engine, the starboard one, we anchor awkwardly. Mark braves the water to unwrap the line from the rudder. It's cold, dark, and choppy. We're fortunate the snagging happened while under sail. Running the port engine could have caused major damage.

Since crossing the border of Florida, our bodies can breathe again. The sun envelops us. Jackets, hats, and socks are stored. Past Melbourne, the wake of relentless, inconsiderate, rule-disobeying powerboats drives us mad. The constant motion is a good test for my seasickness, while the unexpected maneuvers of the culprits challenge our reflexes, patience, and seamanship. Southern Florida is Boating Central.

We park ourselves in Stuart and rent a mooring ball for $10 a night. This includes the use of showers, internet, and a lounge. The climate, the company, the conveniences; it's all *irie*.

We mark remaining items – like installing solar panels on a cross bar between our dinghy davits – off the list; wait for our scheduled green card interview; celebrate Christmas and New Year's Eve with other boaters; and go on a giant grocery shopping spree. We listen to stories from old salts who claim the Bahamas are their favorite cruising grounds in the world. We find that hard to believe since they're only a stone's throw away – just across the Gulf Stream.

We enjoy being in Stuart, but it's time to move on and conquer that channel.

Except, we can't.

I need a green card – or a deportation note – to leave the United States. *The irony!* When I want to stay for a certain amount of time, *they* don't let me. And now that I want to leave, *they* don't let me either. I hope nothing happens to my *oma* in Belgium. She's my favorite person and not the youngest anymore. If she becomes sick, or fate forbid, is dying, I have to be with her. Even if it means abandoning my application. Luckily, it doesn't come to that.

Early January 2008, six months after I applied for permanent residency, Mark, Darwin, Kali, and I find ourselves in a rental car on the way to Boston. Pet-friendly motels, crowded highways, the Jersey Turnpike, tollbooths, snow on the ground. We reverse the track we did with *Irie* and extend it, 20 times faster than by sailboat.

The interview appointment is upon us.

"You must be Mark and Liesbet?" A man approaches.

Mark and I look up from the room filled with immigrants, their lawyers, and their translators. After hearing anything but English for half an hour, the question comes as a surprise.

How does this guy know who we are? How did he pick us out of the crowd?

"Yes, we are." We stand up.

Is this our interviewer?

"I noticed your yellow sailing jackets hanging over the chair and thought 'this must be them.' Please, follow me. I'm in charge of interviewing you today."

"Great!"

How fortunate to be assigned to an official who likes sailing, or at least recognizes foul weather gear.

Our nervousness dissipates as we follow him into a cubicle. We take a seat and swear to tell the truth and nothing but the truth. What follows is not "What's the brand of your spouse's toothpaste?" or "What's his favorite color?" but questions about our lifestyle and awe about the path we've chosen.

Not once does our interrogator ask why we got married days before sending off the application or what our intentions are in the United States. The answers about our love for this country might not have been as satisfactory as the proof of our love for each other. The interview is relaxed and our documents, photos, blog posts, emails, testimonials, and supporting material provides enough evidence that our marriage is truthful and legal. We walk out the door with a handshake and a smile and put our yellow "winter" jackets back on.

Shedding clothes along the way, we return to Stuart. Sunshine blesses our bodies and minds once again.

After heaps of paperwork, biometric evidence of finger prints and mug shots, physical exams and health records, a 2,800-mile road trip, a total cost of $2,000, and another two-week wait, I'm the proud owner of a state-of-the-art ID with a green tint – the dream of potential immigrants.

Now, I'm allowed to reside in the United States of America, work here, and stay forever; to build a life and indulge in the American Dream. Instead, my companions and I leave the next day.

Bahamas, here we come!

Chapter 7

Just Across

T he sand is so bright it hurts my eyes. I blink and blink, and wish I'd brought my sunglasses to shore. Azure water laps onto the white sandbank. The sky is dark blue. The sun warms our exposed bodies in a more than pleasant way. I can't wait to get tan like the other full-time cruisers. The dogs don't care about their complexion. All they do is run around and splash in the water.

I smile at Mark. His eyes sparkle when he throws the ball into the deeper part of the bay. "Go get it, Kali!" She sets out eagerly, followed by a barking Darwin. He loves chasing her. We haven't seen our pups this happy in a long time. Maybe they reflect our moods? Kali tries to get rid of her younger buddy, with a snap and a growl. He continues to annoy her and steal the ball.

It feels wonderful to wade through the clear Bahamian waters in our bathing suits.

Irie is parked 50 feet away. The current is strong in this area, so we deployed two anchors off the bow. One is set as usual and the other will grab the sand once we turn direction and fall back. This way, we're always hooked on the bottom, whenever the tide changes. This practice is aptly called a Bahamian moor. So far, so good. We couldn't have picked a more scenic spot than Double Breasted Cays in the Abacos as our introduction to the islands.

Because of our shallow draft, we can anchor close to beaches and therefore need less anchor chain than our monohull peers in deeper water, who also have to take slightly different routes to navigate the Bahamas. Maneuvering the Bahama Banks in water so clear that you see every rock and coral head pass under the keels is nerve-wracking. You expect a crunching noise any time and don't believe the depth sounder.

On the bow, looking down to gauge the depth of the water, I constantly ask Mark, "How deep is it here?" and register the answer. After a while, I estimate the depth and Mark confirms or corrects.

Being able to "read the water" is extremely important in archipelagos like the Bahamas, where navigation aids are absent and GPS waypoints aren't always accurate. The higher the sun in the sky, the better your visibility of the water. Ideally, the sun is behind you or directly above. On cloudy days, navigating becomes even trickier. Every color – from black and brown to deep blue and bright white – has a meaning, ranging from safe to dangerous to "too late." While we gain confidence and improve our water reading skills, we still hold our breaths in certain areas.

"I swear I can touch the bottom here with the boat hook!"

"Impossible. It's ten feet deep," Mark responds. I let it go. For a few minutes.

"Are you sure?" I stare at a sharp coral head approaching swiftly.

"As sure as the depth sounder."

Needless to say, our progress over the banks is slow.

With a first night passage under our belts and welcomed into the country by a spectacular sunrise bursting in all tints of orange, we feel like different people. We left the United States behind with a "have green card, will travel" attitude and entered a new world, mentally and physically.

From the East Coast of the US, the Bahamas are the obvious destination when desiring a cruise in an idyllic environment or trying out island life by boat. It's quiet here, beautiful and serene. And it's just across the channel.

Because of the Gulf Stream's reputation – you have to be careful when you cross the narrow, north-running stretch of water – we waited for the right weather to avoid a "wind opposing current" situation. We bashed into the waves under motor and took turns at the helm every three hours. Staying awake in complete darkness was hard, but we made it to the other side safe and sound. Without dogs mistaking walls for floors or me getting sick. Hurrah for cats!

Now that we're here, our stress about crossing the Gulf Stream dissipates. We're stocked up and well-equipped. We swim, we eat, we play with the dogs, we explore by dinghy, we sip cocktails in our cockpit.

I could get used to this.

We're in a new place; on a new adventure. We take it step by step and have no idea how long we'll stick to this lifestyle. "We will continue as long as it's fun or until the money runs out," we say, when people ask about our plans.

This is the last year of my Belgian stipend and Mark has a minimal amount of savings left after purchasing our floating home. We'll manage and find solutions if need be. As a frugal couple from the moment we met, we're careful with money and avoid unnecessary material goods. We never budget; we just spend as little as possible to eat and live comfortably.

In the Bahamas this is easy. Everything is so expensive that we only buy the bare minimum of fresh produce and meat. And local rum. We register our cheapest months ever.

🌊 🌊 🌊

"Not again!" I object.

"Yes, again," Mark mutters. "Let's pick up anchor and move."

He listened to the weather forecast. Another cold front is arriving from Canada. This brings strong, clocking winds. Beautiful anchorages, with a stretch of white sand in front of you and open water behind you, unfortunately don't offer enough protection from a storm. During winter, the enjoyment of a perfect place in the Bahamas is frequently cut short because of the weather, which necessitates moving. We have to sail or, more often, motor to an all-around harbor, where the wind and waves will have no effect on our life aboard.

In the Abaco chain, that place is usually Marsh Harbor. The good thing about a stop here is the opportunity to go fuel, water, and grocery shopping. Plus, we get to meet up with friends, since finding protection in a safe bay is exactly what everyone does in these circumstances.

Cold fronts restrict our freedom; we are slaves to the weather. So be it.

Once the storms pass, we leave the busy, comfortable harbor and are on our way again to less popular, more seductive places. Slowly, we follow the necklace of low-lying, palm-absent islands southeast, touching most of the island groups. The effect of past hurricanes is visible on the beaches, where palm trees have been reduced to broken trunks or plain nothing. It's difficult to find shade. Darwin and Kali dig holes to lie on the hard-packed parts beneath the scorching white sand and swim a lot to stay cool.

We leave the Abacos and meet my parents in Eleuthera – another arduous plane journey to see their daughter.

My dad, who was in the Navy for two years in the Sixties, when the military draft was still mandatory in Belgium, loves standing behind the wheel and sailing *Irie* from bay to bay. My mom, who I inherited my seasickness from, is less of a boating fan. They join in the daily errands, like gravity filling our freshwater tank with five-gallon jugs and learn about wrong weather forecasts first-hand.

The combination of extremely windy conditions and an antipathy for being on the water the entire time has us exploring Eleuthera overland and taking it easy for a few days. However, the best way to experience the beauty of the Bahamas is by boat.

Going on a side-trip to the Exuma Cays shows my parents some of the most fabulous sites and experiences of these islands. At the end of their stay, we bring them to Nassau for more shore-time and a long flight back to Belgium. I wonder if they'll ever visit us again.

In the capital, beaches and shrubs are replaced by big buildings and even taller cruise ships. We try to get onto their WiFi networks for internet but fail.

Days prior, boats had been broken into.

The anchorages are frightening places to stay, with bad holding, lots of wake from passing boats, funky currents, giant ships maneuvering everywhere, debris on the sea floor, and little protection from the wind. There are also the city nuisances: traffic noise on bridges, honking cars, booming night clubs, the overflow of tourists from multiple cruise ships every day.

But Nassau cannot be avoided, for logistical reasons and the necessary projects and provisions.

One evening, the wind shifts. We turn as well but notice that we're not falling back far enough. We're stuck on something. It was bound to happen here. Closer inspection reveals that our anchor chain is wrapped around something heavy on the bottom of the harbor. Three times.

Mark gives directions from the bow, while I master the helm and the engines to carefully drive *Irie* around the culprit. Three times. Hopefully in the right direction. We fall back so far that we end up on top of a mooring ball. We move once more and re-anchor in the fading light.

Of course, we didn't plan for this and soon it's pitch-black. Unable to watch shore and our surroundings to confirm the anchor is set properly, we hope we won't drag. With his thoughts still on the anchoring chaos, Mark forgets to hook the grill up to the propane tank before opening the valve. Seconds later, propane gas spews into the cockpit. When the barbecue finally lights, there is so much leftover grease on it that the unit catches on fire. Flames surround the grill. Luckily, the cushion in front of it, which we use to block the wind, survives. We use the last of our energy to extinguish the fire, have canned food for dinner, and let the dogs out.

Mark's brother, Tim, is getting married to his girlfriend, Kris, in Massachusetts. Because of our furry family members, only one of us can attend. That person would be Mark.

I stay with the dogs in Nassau at a cheap marina to make those single days easier. While I enjoy a good party, I'm happy waiting here on my own. I'm ready for some privacy and quality time with Kali and Darwin, without my other half.

I thrive and feel self-confident, an emerging flower in spring. I'm more social, make decisions, and do exactly what I want when I want. I sleep in, take the pooches for a morning walk, eat breakfast, rummage around the boat, write, eat lunch when it fits *my* plans, and explore the area by foot at *my* pace, on *my* agenda. I take my time running errands, get projects done, and shoot hundreds of photos. I don't miss Mark at all.

Does this mean I don't love him? Would I be better off without him?

That train of thought scares me.

Maybe it's normal to not miss a spouse when living together 24/7?

Mark carries a long list of boat items back in his suitcases. From spare engine parts to ropes to a 20-pound aluminum anchor and chain, 25 feet of it. When he arrives, we have our work cut out, and I'm happy to see him... bringing lots of edible goodies.

We return to the Exumas and follow the string of islands, stopping for windswept hikes, a snorkel session in the wake of James Bond at Thunderball Grotto, and the curious sight of swimming pigs at Big Major Cay. Every little town has its sun-blessed charms, bright cottages, and multitude of white-washed churches.

🦋🦋🦋

While Mark learned from another cruiser how to open conch shells and remove and clean the ugly creatures inside to make delectable conch fritters, our fishing success has been non-existent. What are we doing wrong?

After Mark and I dinghy back and forth to Georgetown all day to get water and other provisions, we sit in our cockpit for dinner. Mark digs into the last pork chop and contemplates finishing the last baked potato as well. I have potato skin (Belgians don't eat skin) and pork fat (no fat, either) left on my plate and throw it overboard.

"Wow, Mark, look at that! Fish are eating the scraps. They're big! Get your gear, baby. They like pork."

"Hand me that last piece." Mark gets his line ready. He puts the bait on the hook. Within seconds a fish grabs it. Mark lifts the animal out of the water. It escapes. *Huh?* The commotion startles the others. I throw more pig fat overboard to change their minds and lure them back.

"Let's try again," I suggest.

"We're out of pork," Mark replies.

"How about a piece of potato? This one is undercooked. Easy to hook." I hand Mark a sturdy piece of starch.

"Fish don't eat potato. Grab the net, just in case." Mark hangs the line off the boat again. This time with a piece of baked potato.

"We caught one! Get the net! Quick, get it in the net!" he screams after three seconds.

"I'm trying. This thing is big." *What do I know about catching fish? With or without a net.*

We trap it in the webbing. The fish wriggles so much that it wraps itself around the material. We don't know what to do. So, we both press the bulging net against the transom steps and sit there. Thinking. After a few moments, I let go, grab the bottle of rum, and pour liquid in the bouncing gills. The fish keeps moving. I try vodka. We love rum and cokes too much. Our catch refuses to die. I don't like this at all. When the creature finally calms down, we put it in a bucket. Each time I step over it, the tail jerks and startles me. Still alive! This is bad. And stupid. We need to find a quicker way to kill a fish, if we ever succeed in catching another one.

Half an hour later, the animal doesn't budge anymore. We stretch it on the cockpit floor. Kali and Darwin show no interest at all.

"Now what?" Mark asks. It's 9pm and dark. So much for some rest after a tiring day.

"Can we call anybody on the VHF for help?"

"Not really." It's late and we'd sound like idiots.

"What kind of fish is it? I sure hope we can eat it, so it didn't die in vain," I say.

I check our pocket guide *Corals & Fishes in Florida, the Bahamas, and the Caribbean* and deduct it's a horse-eye jack.

"They don't exceed three feet," I read. "Wait, there's an asterisk."

On the bottom of the page, the asterisk explains: "Large specimens may be poisonous to eat." We measure the jack. Two feet. With "large specimens" the fish connoisseurs must mean closer to three feet. I take photos; in case someone finds our dead bodies later and investigates. Mark cuts the head off, guts the body, and stores the meat in the fridge. It barely fits but we can't remove the tail. We need a sharper knife. We're still ill-prepared to be fisher(wo)men.

The following evening, we invite friends over for our first self-caught, home-cooked fish dinner. As with the small barracudas Mark caught off the beach in Belize two years earlier, butter and garlic make this fish edible. It's a start.

🌊🌊🌊

We don't die in the Bahamas. But here in Georgetown, we have to make an important decision. The cruising season is ending. *What to do?* So far, we enjoy the watery lifestyle and are happy taking it day by day. If we want to return to the States, this is the turnaround point. The alternative is continuing towards the Turks and Caicos Islands and spending hurricane season in the safe harbor of Luperon in the Dominican Republic. All I know about that island is that it's a popular and cheap last-minute holiday destination for Belgians. Cheap sounds good and so does spending time in a comfortable, protected harbor without having to move because of the weather. Do we have what it takes to keep going, to sustain ourselves? And not just financially?

As hurricane season approaches, we zigzag further down the necklace of sandy jewels, discovering off-the-beaten-path islands, bays, and beaches, like appealing Long Island and the outstanding Acklins.

During an extremely flat and hot motor trip, we rinse ourselves and the dogs with buckets of salt water to keep cool. Mark notices dolphins in the distance. They come closer and closer to *Irie*. All six of them, in formation, glide between our hulls, and swim in front of the catamaran. The clearness of the water reveals every single detail on their bodies and their big smiles. Only common sense tells us that they're indeed in the water and not above it. Belly down on the trampoline, I can almost touch them. The dogs sense our excitement and join in the fun. That's too much for our performers. They leave as quickly as they came.

There's no turning back to the States now. We're committed to continuing, without a chance to linger. The out islands don't have decent protection and June is around the corner.

Hurricane season in the Atlantic officially starts on June 1st and runs until November 30th. September and October are the peak months. Not much activity is predicted for June, so a visit to the Turks and Caicos Islands on our way to the Dominican Republic is in the cards. While thoroughly enjoying our explorations in the tropical Bahamas, we barely scratched the surface of its more than 700 islands and cays.

Despite running from winter storms and needing wetsuits to snorkel, we agree with the old salts in Stuart: the Bahamas are a magical place, conveniently located "just across."

Chapter 8

Hurricane Force

Four weeks of bay hopping in the little-visited Turks and Caicos archipelago morphs into a growing temptation to be settled. That and the increased likelihood of hurricanes have us on the move again. The conditions for our 80-mile voyage to the Dominican Republic aren't ideal, but the next favorable forecast, called a *weather window*, wouldn't happen for another ten days, so we take our chances.

We steer as close to the wind as possible to stay on course as best as we can. The autopilot helps. Mark and I take turns at the helm. *Irie* charges forward, pounding along the waves, which slam onto the bridge deck. We've gotten used to the heavy sounds and vibrations underneath when hugging the wind.

A bright moon keeps us company during the quiet night. She reveals a vague border between sky and sea. Her reflection in the water is the only light to be seen. Kali and Darwin handle the movements well. I don't get seasick. Our full sails keep pushing the boat up and over the moderate waves at a steady speed.

At 4am, we're 15 hours into our crossing from the Turks and ten miles off the Dominican coast. A penetrating smell fills the air. *Dirt!* We haven't smelled that in ages. We stare at the horizon. It's too dark to see anything.

An hour and a half later, the fragrance of flowers wafts into our cockpit. We're getting closer. Giant contours appear. *Mountains!* Ever more distinguished as dawn arrives. While the sun and the temperature rise, lush surroundings materialize. Green hills, palm trees, grass, and flowers are revealed. Such a contrast with the flat, barren land and beaches we left. We start the engines. The wind dies, facilitating our arrival.

Daybreak and a reliable GPS guide us towards the entrance of Luperon Harbor.

From the moment we enter its mouth, the water becomes as flat as a flip flop. Slowly but surely, we follow the guidebook's directions for a perfect approach into the safest of harbors. We weave our way through the murky water, among the flotilla of boats already moored for the season. Tired, we drop anchor in the middle of the long bay, not too far from town.

After a couple of tries and an hour of digging the anchor into the mud with our engines to make sure we don't drag, we call ourselves settled. We clean the boat up and take Kali and Darwin to shore. We check into the country, get our paperwork in order, and learn about the steep fees. Once numerous officials have visited *Irie* and a substantial amount of money has changed hands, we're officially based in the Dominican Republic, our summer destination.

🌊🌊🌊

The anchorage is calm. Dark brown, dirty water, with a lot of algae growing, but as flat as we like it. Soon enough, the first ripples shall appear. They'll turn into chop and before anybody realizes it, white caps take over Luperon Bay. But not yet.

It's 7am. We have time left to move about on the water without getting wet. This is also the perfect period to do work higher on the catamaran or under it. Early starts are important, before the wind and waves shake everything up.

Our dinghy creeps towards town. We have to save gas.

In this part of the world, a gallon costs about $6, the same price as a bottle of rum or a small Taino painting. The sun already beats down. She and her friend, Humidity, make us sweat from the moment we get up until we fall asleep and sometimes even at night; our bedroom fan offering little relief. We swat mosquitoes and no-see-ums – the wind will take care of those soon – and marvel at the green hills.

We tie the dinghy to the crooked floating dock near the concrete pier and walk by a security gate. We greet the group of officials and other Dominicans hanging out here and continue on.

Luperon slowly comes to life. Some stray dogs are up and about, while others still sleep, spread out, dotting the sidewalks. A herd of short-haired sheep wanders by in search of food. A young girl approaches one of the strays and pets it. A guy comes out of his shack to brush his teeth above the gutter. He's not totally dressed yet. Toothpaste joins the wastewater, garbage, oil, and dog poop stagnating along the street.

Further up the road, a stream of blood is on its way to join other substances. Fresh chickens are now ready to be sold. We hear cows in the distance. A baby cries. A few people leave their modest houses. We wish them a good day. Their response: "Bueno dia!" No pronunciation of the "s" here.

Most restaurants and stores are still closed, but the vegetable truck is in town. We join the chaos of locals and browse the merchandise displayed on the ground. Two pineapples, a melon, a pound of tomatoes, peppers, onions, potatoes, a head of lettuce, and... is that broccoli? Our piles are weighed, extra items thrown in, and we pay. Six dollars.

We talk to fellow cruisers and try to find other goods in the stores. This proves to be time consuming, especially when boat parts are needed. We walk along noisy traffic, get offered rides by *moto concho* drivers (motorcycle taxis), and avoid potholes and broken sidewalks.

Smiley, the town's friendliest dog, approaches with a smile, a wagging tail, and a personal greeting that sounds like a bark, yawn, and cry combined. She deserves all the love we provide. Villagers now roam the streets or sit in the shade in front of their homes. Later on, they'll play dominoes, visit neighbors, or shop. When we return to the dinghy, our clothes are drenched in sweat.

The wind has picked up substantially. To get home, we head straight into it and the waves, with even wetter clothes as a result. Salt from sweat or salt from the bay, what does it matter?

The most beautiful quality of the harbor appears at night. The water is dense with phosphorescence, creating a wonderful display when disturbed. Driving the dinghy illuminates the area under and behind the engine in such a way that it blinds us. All around, fish shoot in every direction and become green flashes. The tops of the waves whipped up by the wind glisten and glow, an explosion of brightness in the dark.

Another advantage Luperon offers is its social scene. Being the safest place in the area to hole up during hurricane season, it brings in a fair amount of cruisers to share boat stories, plans, and experiences. Expats provide useful information and services. Many arrived by boat years ago and never left. There's also a group of *in-betweens* who live here semi-permanently. They organize activities while figuring out whether to stay or continue on. If they ever get their anchors out of the sticky mud.

Naturally, there is the local community. By visiting the small businesses, sitting at a loud bar, trying chicken, rice, and beans in the *comedores*, watching a baseball game or joining one on Saturdays, or just taking in the village scene, we immerse ourselves in the Dominican culture.

$$\mathfrak{I}\mathfrak{I}\mathfrak{I}$$

If there's one time I thought my plane would be delayed, it is now: the summer of 2008. An approaching hurricane and a stop-over in Jamaica on my way back to Luperon have me at the edge of my economy class seat. After the layover, we're still on schedule. I have hope to defeat the weather (g)odds.

Ever since watching the forecast for the Dominican Republic on a visit to my parents' house in Belgium, I feared Hurricane Ike would beat me to my floating home. He's predicted to arrive within hours. I sigh when my plane touches the tarmac in Puerto Plata. Right on time. What's more, my important cargo makes it into the country: abbey beers, quality chocolate, delicious waffles, mosquito rackets to electrocute the little bastards buzzing about, and miscellaneous parts for the boat all survive the trip and the checkpoints.

I drag my five heavy pieces of luggage outside the airport building and instantaneously sweat.

Where is Mark?

Nowhere to be seen. My smile evaporates in the hot sun. Relief becomes disappointment. There's no time to lose. Hurricane Ike will soon swallow the blue skies and affect everything in his path. I envision making it back to Luperon by public transportation with my load, sweating like crazy. My precious chocolate will most definitely dissipate on the long, three-part journey.

My non-challenging life of the past weeks is a distant memory already, even though I just returned to the tropics.

When August arrived in those tropics, I had been more than happy to leave and more than ready for a break in a Western country. It was easy to adjust to the luxuries of a house. I savored showers, flush toilets, a comfortable bed, not bumping my head walking out the door, jumping on a bike or going for a stroll within minutes of putting my shoes on, and casually opening the fridge, grabbing whatever I wanted. I lounged on each comfortable chair in the house, used electricity as I pleased, and sat behind my laptop to write or check the web whenever. Getting online was stress-free. The weather was cold, grey, and rainy – a terrible Belgian summer. I didn't care. The only thing I wanted to avoid was sweat. That and having a headache from the heat every single day. I succeeded. The temperature was half of what I was used to, and I actually enjoyed wearing socks, shoes, trousers, and sweaters and sleeping in flannel sheets.

As long as it was temporary.

In the midst of my contemplations, a tall guy with a scruffy beard and a huge smile runs towards me. I receive him with open arms and lots of kisses. My annoyance melts away and my good mood returns. After one more hug, we jolt back to reality.

"We have to get going." Mark urges me towards the car.

The wind blows steady and the clouds increase with every minute. In my moment of excitement, I'd forgotten about Hurricane Ike.

"Of course."

We drag half of my bags to the trunk and stuff them next to a pile of groceries. The rest goes onto our laps. Mark rented a car and driver with our friends LeeAnn and Gray to shop in Puerto Plata before picking me up. Because it's Saturday and a big storm is brewing, the check-out lines at the supermarket had been extremely long, causing their delay.

We rush back to Luperon. Everybody's eyes are focused on the sky. Mark fills me in about the situation in the bay, where hurricane preparations have been in full swing. Most of the boats are tied off in the mangroves. The harbor is a mess of lines, anchors, and vessels.

Since it's dark by the time we arrive, I don't get to see any of it. Yet.

Mark quickly transports the luggage to *Irie*. She's securely attached to the mangroves with five heavy lines and held in place by three anchors on the opposite side. My sweetheart disappears into the darkness and the chop, without help. There's no room in the dinghy for me and we need to act fast.

As he heads into a direction unfamiliar to me, I feel disoriented, helpless, and in a different world. Was it only this morning that I woke up in a comfortable bed and bright room? The wind howls. I have no control over anything. All I can do is hope that nothing and nobody falls overboard while Mark is on *Irie*. We are a team. We usually do things together.

Mark returns after a long while – he had to adjust the lines that keep *Irie* safe – and reports that my belongings are safe and dry aboard. The wind had shifted to the west, contrary to the eastern trades, and the rain holds off. A lucky combination.

The wind strengthens; the clouds grow darker. I pick up Darwin and Kali in the rented apartment of LeeAnn and Gray. They relaxed there in comfort during the afternoon. Kali is happy to see me; Darwin is ecstatic, flying over the barrier that our friends had put in place to separate the animals from the kitchen.

In the meantime, Mark makes more trips to the boat to drop off our groceries. As the wind picks up, so does the rain. Within minutes, the storm arrives. A torrential downpour follows. The dogs and I take shelter under the thatched roof of the marina bar with a group of other sailors and wait.

I hope Mark is okay.

Gusts of wind push the rain inside. We move closer to the wall. Mark shows up, completely drenched. He helped another friend re-secure his boat. It's awe-inspiring how everybody has been lending hands, moving and securing boats, providing assistance where needed. The cruising community at its best.

We sit, wait, and smile at each other. People around us discuss the storm and the predictions. It's all they've been talking about for days. Now, everyone is ready for Ike and hopes for the best. Mark looks exhausted. I'm tired as well and can't wait to get to our house on hulls. We're trapped on shore, however, until the first break in the rain. Once that happens, we rush ourselves and the dogs to *Irie*. Kali is terrified of the thunder and lightning. By 10pm, we finally climb aboard. It's good to be home.

I unpack my bags. My captain continuously checks our shorelines for chafe. The boat remains calm, while wind and rain batter the shell that protects us. Mark removed everything that could blow off the deck and cause damage. Our spare bunks are cramped with the bimini, sails, and grill. While Ike passes over, I give the dogs special treats, display my goodies, and present Mark his Belgian favorites: dark beer and fondant chocolate.

My stories are interrupted by heavy wind gusts, line inspections, and messages over the airwaves. Our VHF radio stays on through the night. People give updates about the weather every half an hour and call each other to stay awake. It's a distraction, but a good precaution in case something dramatic happens.

The storm is stealing my thunder.

"*La Vie Dansante, La vie Dansante*, this is *Tatia*." The radio chatter doesn't stop. I turn my attention back to Mark and ignore friends' conversations. Our tender kisses become intense.

"*Irie, Irie, Irie*, this is *Tatia*."

Why did I come home on a night like this? Why does this stupid radio have to stay on?

We don't answer. Dave will have to find someone else to socialize with.

He calls Frik's boat next: "*Desire, Desire, Desire*, this is *Tatia*."

Now that's more fitting.

Mark and I eagerly touch each other's naked bodies, craving long-missed intimacy. I zone out the radio and get lost in the moment, unaware of anything else around me. It's all reduced to background noise. We make love like we rarely do, tender and passionate at the same time. I moan. Mark grunts. Darwin howls. Kali chimes in. They do this each time a climax is reached.

"*Irie, Irie, Irie*, this is *Desire*."

My moaning turns into groaning. *Bang, bang, bang*, the halyard screams. No rest for the weary. Or for the lovers. Mark throws me a grin and a kiss. He puts his swim trunks on and fixes the halyard, followed by another check-up of our safety lines and anchor rodes (ropes and chain). The rain pounds on deck. The wind shrieks through the rigging.

We're well-secured and intermittently make electricity with the newly installed wind generator; one of Mark's projects while I was away. We fall asleep grinning, bodies intertwined. We're safe in each other's arms and in our spider-like nest.

What a homecoming.

I wake up to a peaceful morning. The water is murkier than usual and full of debris. We're surrounded by sticks, leaves, tree trunks, and garbage. The air is crisp, the strength of the sun bearable. The sailboats around us lie where they're supposed to be, scattered, facing different directions because of the way they're secured. Nobody dragged.

I take a dinghy ride in the harbor to get a feel for what's going on. It's tricky to get around floating tree logs and garbage bags aiming to foul the propeller.

We never checked our cockpit instruments, but hear the wind peaked at 50 knots that night. We don't believe it; not where we're located. Sailors, like fishermen, are known to exaggerate. The fortunate thing is that we were situated just outside Ike's path. He hit poor Haiti twice and turned south over Cuba, leaving devastation behind. If Ike would have altered course, things could have turned out differently.

We leave the stagnant, bug-infested mangroves to relocate to the middle of Luperon Harbor. It takes days to clean the muddy, barnacle-covered lines, spare anchors, and chains. They make a mess on board and change our skin from bronze to grey. We dress *Irie* so she's not naked anymore: mainsail, jib, grill, canvas for the bimini, flags.

The storm brings cooler weather. The dogs don't pant; we feel energetic and sleep without sweating. Life in the DR turns back to normal.

Soon, Hurricane Ike is forgotten. As if it never happened. Like my vacation in Belgium. It's weird to travel between continents, time zones, dimensions. When you're in one familiar part of the world, your other life feels like it has been a dream all along.

🌊🌊🌊

"Hi, I'm Ed." Mark and I look at the sun-tanned stranger with suspicion.

What is he doing on Yankee Zephyr?

He must have read our thoughts.

"I'm a friend of Graeme. He asked me to keep an eye on his boat while he's away."

We relax and introduce ourselves. Ed continues, "He said I'd enjoy meeting you two."

That's all it takes to have another peer added to our collection of new friends. Something about him affects my heart and intrigues my psyche. Is it his smile? Or his good looks? His intense eyes?

The active social scene makes our five-month stay in hot and humid Luperon bearable, even fun. Life in a small community is like a soap opera, unraveling intrigues ranging from love stories to gossip to drunken events, blackmailing, and hooker encounters. The smorgasbord of characters – local and imported – keeps us entertained. Even I become involved in the new dynamics of a micro cosmos that organically ripples into existence. My role is small and behind the scenes; a secretive scenario with one other actor unfolds.

꒰꒰꒰

When not having gatherings on boats, our family of four spends the hot afternoon in the shade of the Puerto Blanco Marina drinking hole. With a slight breeze, it's the coolest place in the vicinity. Kali and Darwin like the tile floor and stretch out. We meet friends for games and chats.

I glance at Ed. Again. He stares back with his captivating eyes. They're blue, like mine. His eyelashes are sexy, his bronzed body and curly blond hair attractive. He reminds me of a quintessential California surfer dude. Our gazes meet. He smiles.

Am I flirting? Are we flirting?

I wonder whether he saw me peek at him through our porthole earlier today. He buzzed by in his dinghy, stretched out, in no hurry, with no worry.

Dreamily looking out over the water with Ed's appealing body floating on it, I had imagined myself at his side on his boat, *Nini*, caressed on deck by his soft hands, relaxing in his hammock, eating his incredible curry, making love under the stars. Just the two of us, slowly sailing the world seas and hanging out on the beach, smoking a joint. No stress in the world. It sounded alright in my head.

I tried not to think about being married. Sometimes, it feels like Mark and I aren't spouses at all. I am still annoyed with the way it happened; no leading-up time, anticipation, eagerness, or excitement about getting wed. I always thought *if* I was ever to marry, it would be a fabulous, entertaining, and memorable event. Memorable in a *good* way.

And I haven't told anyone but my parents and *oma* in Belgium about that event.

I purposefully keep our relationship status hidden, so we can have a *real* wedding in the future. I fear that if my friends and other relatives know I'm married, they won't fly in for the party. Whenever and wherever that might be.

Secrets are okay.

Like the concealed thoughts going through my head this very moment.

Since I met Mark, I've felt responsible, organized, and uptight. I miss my former *laissez-faire* attitude. My personality could have been enhanced another way if I had bumped into a different guy. A guy like Ed.

I wonder whether Mark and I chose the wrong boat name. Being *irie* is a trait obvious in Ed's attitude. That this comes with downsides is not part of my thought process right now. I have a crush, with hurricane force. I dream about him at night and imagine lying in his arms.

I crave romance in my life.

There we go again. Ed has got to be a romantic lover. *Sigh.*

Each of my three serious relationships lasted three years. That's usually when I get antsy for something new, like backpacking Southeast Asia after Tim, flying to Indonesia with a one-year ticket after Andy, and leaving Karl after a long-distance relationship and overland travels. Mark and I have been together three and a half years; a personal record.

Could it be called the three-year itch?

Well, there was our *little* episode in Honduras that devastated me. I have neither forgotten, nor forgiven, what happened. Maybe this is my revenge? I did tell him it would be my turn next to break up.

I can't believe I'm having these thoughts.

I struggle for weeks. Emotionally and physically. I'm drawn to this exotic, South African man. I'm enchanted by his accent, his pleasure in the little things, his relaxed approach to every situation. I enjoy playing games with him, talking until late at night, exchanging sarcastic comments, staring deep into his twinkling eyes.

Does Mark notice?

I wish I were single. That I had met him on one of my backpacking trips. I'd love to visit South Africa. I'd love to wander the oceans without bad moods.

I plan a three-day weekend in Santo Domingo, the capital, without Mark. He's not interested in exploring further afield. I ache for Ed to join me. It would be a bad idea. But the thought of being with him exclusively, the excitement of giving in to passion... that instant when you find out the other person loves you back. This feeling is stronger than reason.

It's dangerous, it's off-limits, it's fluttering, and it's impulsive.

Then it happens. An unexpected turn of events.

A female arrives in the Dominican Republic to crew on the boat *La Vie Dansante*. She's 25, blond, attractive, and big-chested. She's passionate about sailing, has an amazing personality, is active and cheery, and loves to have fun. She's a head turner from Britain. And she's single.

My status as the only woman in a group of slightly horny men ends. The attention of the crowd shifts and so do the dynamics in our circle of friends. There's new blood in the harbor. The single men vie for her attention. Even Ed. My feelings alternate between jealousy and relief.

Emily saves the day. She saves my marriage. It doesn't take long before the two hotties are an item and she and I become close friends.

My solo excursion to Santo Domingo offers plenty of time and reflection. To get back to reality. To come to terms with the happiness of the new lovers. To reassess my feelings for Mark and my commitment to our relationship. Sometimes, you need a shock – a wake-up call – to appreciate what you have and to realize what you'll miss if it's gone.

Chapter 9

Disaster in Puerto Rico

I
t's our last day in the Dominican Republic and – together with our friends Al and Gail from *Our Lil' Chickadee* – we use Punta Macao as a jumping off point to cross the challenging Mona Passage to Puerto Rico, a trip of around 20 hours.

The Mona Passage is a body of water getting squeezed between the two countries. The Caribbean Sea narrows down into the Atlantic Ocean here, or vice versa. The current and shallow areas influence the surrounding water and cause turbulent, unpredictable seas, only to be battled in decent weather.

We take Kali and Darwin to shore at 5am, unable to estimate the size of the waves crashing on shore. It's pitch-black. We attempt beaching our dinghy in synchrony with the waves to avoid capsizing. Mark times it right. We're not too soaked upon landing or when launching towards *Irie* again.

We take the engine off the dinghy and haul both onto the pitching boat. Then, we wait for a sliver of light.

At 6am, we lift anchor and head out of the turbulent bay, in the wake of our friends. We have to motor over a shelf, where the water is shallower.

While not an issue when we arrived, now the waves are breaking here. We crash through them. *Irie* bangs up and down. This is the first sign of an unpredicted rough sea and heavy winds. Do we continue or do we return, defeated? We picked this weather window for a reason. What if it's worse tomorrow? Al and Gail decide to turn back to Punta Macao. They're experienced sailors.

We stick to plan, staying in radio contact with our boating buddies.

For another hour, we plow through the water, hoping conditions will improve. The wind blows 20 knots, the waves are seven feet high. Our prospects: being uncomfortable for 20 hours, wasting a lot of fuel, and beating up the boat. Things *will* break on a journey like this. We need to be smart and patient.

We follow *Chickadee*'s example. We turn around, unfurl the jib, and sail – fast now with the wind pushing us – back to Punta Macao. It takes half the time. Of course, we have to pass the shallow bank again, with following waves. One of the breakers picks us up and thrusts us deep into the bay, towards shore. *Irie* is surfing! We have no control over the boat. It's exhilarating for me; frightening for Mark. We're doing 12 knots. The bay deepens again and the wave carrying us mellows out. We don't end up on the beach. Over the VHF radio, Al asks how the heck we got back already. Catamarans fly!

The weather turns on us. The predictions get worse the longer we wait. Punta Macao is a relatively unprotected anchorage. We don't want to be trapped here. The swell is forecast to come from the north later on, a dangerous proposition for this bay. It might be safer in the ocean.

We have to make a decision soon.

The next day, we leave, hoping the NOAA weather experts are wrong. Al gets in touch with friends in Luperon through his SSB radio, the only means of long-range contact, and transmits to us over the VHF: the Mona Passage is "open" for another 36 hours; decent crossing conditions should be had. It's a go! *Chickadee* follows us six hours later, minutes before the anchorage turns life-threatening.

Mark and I are relieved to be back in a US territory with beautiful beaches, clear water, mysterious mangrove channels, deserted lighthouses, and easy online shopping, but new problems arise.

Puerto Rico isn't the greatest place for Kali and Darwin. Stray dogs are aggressive, most beaches don't allow dogs, and in Ponce we almost get fined for not having muzzles on our pups while walking them, on leash, through a pedestrian zone.

I start exploring areas by myself. Not a bad thing since lately our relationship is strained again. The list of boat projects is never-ending and each new issue is discovered and approached with cursing and yelling. When Mark is in these frustrated moods, Kali and Darwin cringe. I feel their anxiety. We all lower our heads and tuck our tails between our legs.

Ideally, we hide as far away from the captain as possible, but there's nowhere to go. So, we let the explosion of complaints wash over us, unable to do anything else but sit and wait until the mood improves.

I offer suggestions and solutions, but nobody listens. My words seem to have the opposite effect and make him even madder.

Are my ideas stupid? Is Mark sick of me? Should I just shut up and suck it up?

These moments are unavoidable and dreadful. They make me feel minuscule. I worry about having children with this man. What if he were to yell at them? While I realize Mark is not technically screaming at me – I didn't do anything wrong, it's the situation he's annoyed with – it feels personal when he hurls the words at me. His brother, Tim, has similar tendencies, yet he's a great dad. Maybe there's hope for my husband? He *is* awesome with our dogs.

I wanted to make up my mind by the age of 30 about ever becoming a mom. *Yes or no?* That didn't happen. We were busy selling a sailboat and changing gears to become gypsies on the road to Central America. Who'd think about children then? And who'd think about them now, when juggling life on the water, errand runs, dogs needing shore breaks, failing boat systems, and opposing winds to get to the Eastern Caribbean?

I still have time. I'm 33.

But if I want kids, it has to happen before I turn 40.

🐬 🐬 🐬

It's Christmas Day 2008. The four of us are on *Irie* near Dewey on the island of Culebra, Puerto Rico. We've almost made it to the US Virgin Islands, the *real* Caribbean. Mark and I unwrap our modest gifts. Darwin and Kali watch curiously, before ripping theirs apart as we cheer them on. The harbor is filled with boats on anchor, bouncing in the strong winds. I think about today, while cooking a holiday breakfast of toast, eggs, and bacon.

We should do something special on our first Christmas in the islands.

Mark just returned from taking the dogs to shore by himself, which was challenging with the heavy chop.

"I figured out what I want to do for Christmas." My voice competes with the sizzling fat.

"What?"

"I'd like to move the boat to the west side of Culebra, where the water is calmer and clearer. Much easier to take the dogs ashore. It should only take an hour to get there and settled. In the afternoon, I want to snorkel on the reefs and hang out with Kali and Darwin on the beach. And we could go out for dinner from there. That has been a while."

It's the perfect plan.

"Sounds appealing, but there's still too much wind to move. Maybe we'll motor over there in a couple of days. We can take the dogs to the beach from here as well. Going out to dinner sounds good." Mark is more careful and realistic than I.

We have a wonderful breakfast. Darwin eats his food. Kali doesn't touch hers. This worrisome behavior has been going on for a few days. She started to eat less a month ago. We thought she didn't like her new food or that it was too hard on her teeth. We've been mixing it with wet dog food or boiled rice. She was fine with that, until now. Maybe it's too hot inside, despite the fan at dog-level?

In St. Thomas we plan to take both dogs to the vet for their annual check-ups and see what's going on with Kali's appetite. Mark pours the cooled bacon grease over her food. Nothing happens. *Weird.* Usually, when we give her this special treat, she gobbles it up.

"We need to bring her to a vet, right now," I conclude.

"It's Christmas Day. Where and how is that going to happen? Let's take her first thing tomorrow morning."

Mark is the one with the brains. Luckily, there is no such thing as our Belgian "Second Christmas Day" in this country.

We search in books and online for what could be wrong with Kali. We have no idea.

Mid-morning, a neighbor invites us over for a Christmas meal around 2:30pm. Mark and I accept the invitation and come up with a dish to take.

"We better load the dogs in the dinghy and head for the beach if we want to give them time off the boat today," Mark suggests, after our early dinner contribution is prepared.

Without further delay, we pile into the inflatable and drive through the choppy bay, under the drawbridge, and into calm water on the west side of the island. From the moment we reach the beach, Kali jumps out and embraces the shallow water. She strolls through it, wagging her tail, barking excitedly. She looks for rocks to paw. Sometimes, she moves them closer to shore and carefully picks them up with her mouth, head under water. That's what she did the previous day in a bay further north. Here, no rocks are to be seen.

"She likes the other place better," I mention to Mark, still hoping to move the boat there. Darwin tries to play with his sister, but she shows no interest. Her age is catching up with her. Mark and I watch Kali while we sit on the sand.

Dogs that don't eat are sick. Is something serious going on?

I brush the thought off. She's so happy and such a special creature; more than *just* a dog. She loves people and leaves an impression on everyone she meets. We've both noticed how she has a harder time jumping in and out of the dinghy and climbing on the back steps of the boat.

"I hope she doesn't have cancer," I say.

"I don't think so," Mark answers. "We would have noticed that on her body. My guess is it's her heart. Hopefully, the vet figures out what's wrong."

She wags her tail, as always, when we come home from the Christmas party right before dark. We take our pups to shore one more time. Both enjoy the walk and do what's expected from them. Kali is a little slow. Before we go to bed, I pet our girl and let her know how much we love her. My heart is heavy. I don't know why. I give her kisses on her nose. I hold her head. I sniff her ears. Sweet as honey. It's her smell.

The next morning, Mark and I locate the house of a Humane Society member in Dewey. We explain our problem and learn that there's no vet on Culebra. Marsha is a huge help to us. Since we don't have a phone, she calls her vet in mainland Puerto Rico, to confirm his clinic is open today. She arranges transportation for us in Fajardo and finds a dog cage for the ferry ride.

"Are you coming with us?" Mark asks me, back on the boat.

"I probably should. It would make things easier, but somebody will not be happy." I look at Darwin, who has never been without his mate.

At noon, we help Kali in the dinghy and take her to shore, a challenging feat with the high waves. Darwin stays on *Irie*, alone for the first time in his life. We pick up the cage. Marsha accompanies us to the ferry dock, where she wishes us good luck. We're early and wait in the shade dreading the afternoon ahead.

From the moment we enter the transportation building, Kali is required to enter the crate. Mark and I carry our caged 70-pound dog to and onto the passenger ferry. She's not allowed in the air-conditioned section. Cargo goes outside, in the back, partly in the sun, on top of the roaring engines. I can't believe it. We protest, to no avail. Mark and I keep our pup company during the hellish ferry ride. The noise is unbearable, the sun hot, the boat rolls back and forth. Kali is trapped. We can't even comfort her. She doesn't deserve this. Poor girl. We are mad and feel helpless. Hopefully, we find a better spot on the 4pm boat back.

As soon as the cage is off the ferry, we release our dog. A taxi is waiting and takes us to the animal clinic.

It's quiet at the vet, the day after Christmas. Within minutes, the doctor calls us in to examine Kali. Mark lifts her onto the observation table. We talk about her symptoms, while the vet checks her out. When he reaches her stomach, he feels a big bump. Are we sure she barely ate this morning? *This is not good.* He wants to take a scan and do blood work. Mark's eyes fill with tears. We hold Kali while the doctor draws blood. Then, we put her back on the floor and sit with her. She stretches out on the cool floor and relaxes. We talk to her, pet her, and hug each other. We hope that whatever this is can be removed.

When the vet returns, he starts with the good news: the blood work seems fine, nothing out of the ordinary. The scan, however, shows two massive growths near her abdomen. The photos in his lab don't lie. One tumor is the size of a baseball, the other as large as a football. With growths this size, the chance of the cancer being spread is high. Kali is not in pain, but the masses keep her from eating because they're pushing against her belly. More tears well up.

"What do you recommend?" Mark asks.

"I can't recommend anything," the doctor says. "I can only give you options."

We stare at him, unable to grasp the situation. We can take Kali home and feed her wet and liquid food until she becomes too weak and needs to be put to sleep. Or the vet can perform exploratory surgery and remove the tumors if not spread out, and Kali will heal. If the cancer is too bad, he can either sew her back up or euthanize her right there and then. His words hit like a lightning bolt.

An avalanche of thoughts floods our minds. Back in the examination room, Kali rests comfortably on the tiles. Her tail sways back and forth, slapping on the ground, when she notices us. Three times. It always makes me happy: *thump, thump, thump.* Not a dog to show much emotion, it's one of her few expressions. We sit back down with our baby. The tears flow.

"I'm not ready to let her go. Are you?" I'm losing my senses even asking this.

"Of course not!"

Disbelief. More tears. Ten and a half years is too young for her to die. She needs more time to play in the water, eat steak on her birthdays, and surround herself with balls. We must take her home. It's too soon to say goodbye. Mark and I talk through the options and understand she's extremely sick.

How could we not have noticed before?

There's a possibility the tumors can be removed. We have to take that chance. Her blood work is fine. Maybe it's not that big of a deal? Maybe the doctor can cut the bad lumps out and that's that? Think positive.

Hoop doet leven. Hope creates life.

"Let's go ahead with the exploratory surgery," Mark tells the vet. We need to know what's going on and this is the only way to heal her. If the cancer is too far progressed, we will take Kali home and give her everything she desires for her last days or weeks. While the vet prepares for surgery, we spend more time with our sweet girl.

Does she have any idea what's going on?

We cherish her, pet her, communicate with her, using sentiments only she recognizes. I smell her ears, make her do one more trick, absorb her intent look. Mark gives her a butt rub.

"Be strong, baby. You survived Parvo. You can do this," he whispers, his voice breaking.

She and her daddy have been through a lot. They have a special bond. We ask her to get up on her leash. She walks to the door, the one to the exit. She wants to go home. *Enough of this,* she seems to think. We have to pull her away and send her through the other door, the one to the operating room. She keeps looking back, her gaze asking "What's going on? What are you doing to me?" I want to hold my sweetheart while the doctor anesthetizes her. It's not allowed.

During Kali's surgery, Mark and I walk around the block. We talk about her life and what she means to us. Taking her back home if the cancer metastasized doesn't sound like a possibility anymore. With a stitched-up belly, she can't go in the water – her favorite activity – or even walk around in comfort. Taking her on and off *Irie* will be painful, almost impossible. She'll be in worse shape than before.

For the first time on this sailing adventure, we wish we lived in a house. We push away the thought of leaving her behind. This can't happen to our girl.

We sit in the waiting room when the assistant calls us in. The vet stands in the examination room with bloody hands. He tells us what's going on.

"When I opened her up, it looked promising. Her spleen is full of cancer, but I can remove that. Dogs can live without a spleen. I was hopeful. Then I checked further. Her liver is completely covered with masses. It's in bad shape. You can have a look at the images if you want. My guess is that the cancer has entered her lungs as well."

Another shock. More tears. More disbelief. Nothing can be done. We don't need to look at her liver. We believe him. He gives us a few minutes in private. We don't have much time to decide, since our girl is lying in the operating room. Mark and I hug each other. There's only one option left. We have to let her go.

Kali is stretched out sideways on the table, a towel over her body, an IV in her leg. Her eyes are open, her limp tongue clipped out of her mouth, so she doesn't choke.

This must be a dream. A nightmare. We stand next to her cute face, touch her, talk to her. She can't hear or feel anything. She's already somewhere else. The vet gives her the fatal injection. Its effect doesn't take long. Words cannot describe how we feel.

For the last four years, the four of us have been together 24/7. She's a family member. *We can't lose her!* The machine monitoring her heart rate stops beeping. Our baby is gone. She is no more. She just lies there. Motionless. Dead.

Our world collapses.

The doctor leaves. Mark can't stay in the room any longer.

It's just me and Kali, my sweet girl. *Poor baby.* I pet her soft head. It's wet from our tears. I kiss her nose, smell her ears one last time, tell her we're so sorry.

We failed. We should have noticed earlier that something serious was going on. We should have taken her home when she showed us to the door. She could have had some happy last days. With her brother.

I can't stop crying. I allow my whole body to shake and mourn for minutes. Reluctantly, I leave the room.

Looking at our peaceful dog through the doorway, Mark and I ask more questions and obtain as much information as possible. The vet tells us we made the right decision. "Now I can say this," he adds. Kali was in bad shape. Cancer symptoms in dogs show up at the end, when it's often too late to do anything about it. She wouldn't have lived longer than a few days.

It was 3pm when we arrived at the vet to figure out what was wrong with Kali. At 5pm, she's gone, and we leave without her. The cab picks us up. We put the empty crate in the trunk.

"El perro?" The driver asks about our dog.

"Muerto." *Dead,* I answer in a daze. My eyes run again.

The ride back to Culebra is a trip from hell. The Christmas winds are blowing like crazy. It's pitch-black outside as we catch an evening ferry to the island. We head into the waves and get thrown back and forth. *Kali wouldn't have liked this at all.* I'm cold and seasick.

On shore, Marsha is waiting for us.

"I heard what happened. I'm so sorry." She gives us a hug. I burst out in tears once more, joined by the others. We hand over the cage – *that awful cage* – and thank her kindly for her help.

Back on our boat, Darwin has been by himself for nine hours. He greets us profusely. His tail almost falls off. He looks around. Something is missing. Mark and I feel terrible. He didn't even get to say goodbye to his friend. Neither did we, really. *Imagine I would have stayed home today!* We sit down with our boy. It's quiet on *Irie.* No more Kali. No more triple-thumping on the floor. No more intent puppy eyes. No more high-pitched barking from shallow waters. No more digging up rocks. No more whining when Mark and I have an argument. No more funny barks when we make love.

Kali's blanket remains empty.

Chapter 10

The "Real" Caribbean

Kali's passing not only fills my eyes with sadness, but it has also opened them to how fragile we are as human beings, as a family, as participants in an unpredictable life. When you're young, you're fearless. You think everything will work out, no matter how you behave. As an adult, you become more cautious, but you still need to believe something better is around the corner when things go wrong.

In Dutch, the expression is *Alles komt op zijn pootjes terecht – Everything lands on its paws.* Just like a cat.

Everything will be alright. Irie.

It took me until now, at 33, to learn that everyone is vulnerable. I'm finally growing up. Losing Kali is a reality check. We have to deal with it and whatever else. During this sailing adventure, I've looked forward to numerous opportunities that never materialized because of weather or other factors beyond our control. Anticipation leads to disappointment. Better to take it one day at a time.

Mark, Darwin, and I cherish each other as 2008 peters out. Still, Mark's depressed tendencies are contagious.

Maybe that's part of maturing as well?

After dipping *Irie*'s bows into the northern bay of Culebrita – the uninhabited little sister of Culebra – and experiencing similar circumstances to when we surfed back into Punta Macao, we leave.

The lure of anchoring close to a gorgeous beach dissipates when we see massive waves crashing on shore. We settle on the west side instead, where we find free mooring balls and peace. Nobody else is around. The sand is white and pristine. *Kali would have loved it.*

One afternoon, taking Darwin ashore for playtime on the beach, we bring Kali's belongings. We find a shady spot above the high water line and bury her food bowl, favorite ball, and tags. We pretend it's her last resting place. While we had to leave her body at the vet's clinic, her aura is with us. We sit, contemplate, and are with her in spirit. We loved her so much. We will miss her even more.

Kali's death brings a period of continued depression. Mark and I can't shake our foul moods and blame each other for everything that isn't going right. We decide to leave Culebrita on New Year's Eve, knowing that if we stayed, we would mope day and night, straight into the new year. Our plan is to go to Charlotte Amalie, the capital of St. Thomas in the US Virgin Islands. We're bound to meet people there and be surrounded by activity.

We leave Puerto Rico with mixed feelings, tears rolling down our cheeks.

🌊 🌊 🌊

We made it to St. Thomas in the USVI. The *real* Caribbean. In Belgium, we're not familiar with this part of the world. It's relatively far away, across the Atlantic. The Dominican Republic and Cuba are the only popular destinations because of affordable package deals.

"Where does the Caribbean region actually begin?" I had asked Mark, months ago.

"Probably in the Bahamas, but when Americans talk and think about the Caribbean, they mean the Virgin Islands and farther down," he had told me.

We're finally here. With three instead of four family members. Distractions abound. From the moment we arrive in the giant harbor, we hear the noise of a jet above, a sea plane lands around the corner, ferry wake ruffles our boat, and sailboats dot the bay.

Ignoring that Darwin isn't fond of fireworks, we spend the last night of the year in hectic Charlotte Amalie. Kali was the one who really hated the bangs. *She wouldn't have liked this place*, we remind ourselves, trying to feel better about her absence. We buy fancy groceries and cook a wonderful meal on the boat. After drinking a bottle of wine, we feel too tired and unmotivated to party in a bar. We snuggle up under a duvet on our trampoline and fall asleep.

At midnight, the fireworks wake us. We watch the spectacle. Darwin trembles close by. We're engulfed in an explosion of colors and sounds above the bay and in our own minds.

Despite our fights, Mark and I have grown closer this last week. We spoon before falling asleep and are still embraced when we wake up. We alternate great sorrow for Kali with great love for Darwin. We shower him with attention. He seems okay, all things considered. Maybe he thinks his sister will return?

Cancer sucks. It destroys everything, internally and externally. It's a monster, looming around the corner; invisible, yet present. *Cancer is the disease of the future.* I'm convinced it's how most of us will die; we just don't know when.

We take Darwin to the vet for his annual check-up. A tumor discovery in his abdomen! It needs to be removed. When the doctor sees the fear in our eyes, he promises the surgery is simple. These circumstances keep us in the area longer than planned, so we explore town, fill our tanks and fridge, and do laundry.

We also need a signature on Darwin's health certificate, for which we have to travel to the other side of the island. The only mode of transportation is an expensive taxi. We decide to hitchhike. When the vet overhears our plan, he promptly hands over his car keys. Yes, we completely trust him to operate on our boy.

Darwin's tumor is benign. We take the stitches out a week later, after making the small hop to St. John, where everyone's wounds start to heal. Mark and I like the eclectic island and the national park, where anchoring is prohibited, and moorings cost $15 a night.

This trend, in a more expensive fashion, continues in the British Virgin Islands. The popular bays there are littered with mooring balls and extremely crowded. Anchoring is allowed, but seems only possible in the outer, choppy parts. Not a comfortable alternative and a long dinghy ride to shore. Mark and I play the card of stubborn, frugal cruisers and refuse to pick up a mooring ball the entire month we spend in the BVI. We take advantage of our catamaran's shallow draft and zig zag around the moored boats towards the shallow areas in front of the pack, where we tuck in for free.

The three of us meet up with Ed and Emily. We rendezvous in the most attractive bays, go for walks, and enjoy sundowners together. Food and drinks in popular beach bars are expensive. We prefer a cocktail in our cockpit or grab a drink from our fridge and watch sunset ashore. Happiness and love radiate from our friends' faces. They cheer us up.

It's hard to ignore the beauty of the Virgins, especially the magnificent Baths on Virgin Gorda. Witnessing several sailboats race to claim the last empty mooring ball is almost as entertaining as exploring the gorgeous trail to Devil's Bay. We meander through walls of rock, under massive boulders, in clear water, and along white sand beaches.

My ex-boyfriend Karl joins our group for ten days. There is never an awkward moment as we, the crews of *Irie* and *Nini*, follow the island chain, crossing each other's paths.

Another positive effect of being adults?

Sailing in the British Virgin Islands is close to perfect. The trade winds allow *Irie* to elegantly make her way from island to island on flat, protected waters. The different destinations lie within sight and do a charter vacation justice. Clear, turquoise water. Decent snorkeling. White sand beaches, with or without palm trees. Balmy days and cool nights. Colorful people and a relaxed atmosphere. Beach bars with the sounds of reggae. The BVI has it all. And it's still possible to seek out less-visited bays and call certain coves and beaches our own for the day.

On Tortola, a cute stray dog hangs out with us and follows Mark, Darwin, and me to the dinghy dock, where I pet him goodbye. He sits down and watches us disappear. We stare back until he becomes a black dot on the white sand. It's too early to replace Kali, even though Darwin might enjoy a companion. We're still impressed that he's not showing signs of missing his sister.

🐚 🐚 🐚

To get from the British Virgin Islands to St. Martin, we have to cross the Anegada Passage. The 80-mile night crossing is anything but enjoyable. The wind blows straight on the nose. The high seas create an uncomfortable ride. *Irie* is not happy. Neither is the crew. After 20 hours on an angry sea, we check into St. Martin, on the French side.

The island consists of two distinct parts. Sint Maarten is a territory within the Netherlands and Saint Martin is an overseas collectivity of France.

On the Dutch side, people speak English and pay with dollars, even though prices are marked in Antillean Guilder. Sint Maarten also has its own flag and license plates. Resorts and condos tower over mega yachts in marinas. On this side of the lagoon and in Simpson Bay, boat owners pay a fee to anchor and get through the bridge.

On the French side, people speak French besides English and pay in Euros *or* dollars. The flag and license plates are the same as in France. The building code is stricter, but traffic is as congested as across the country line. Mooring in Marigot Bay costs money but passing under the French bridge and staying in that part of the lagoon are free.

Guess where most of us anchor?

The Dutch side is cheaper on shore and has attractive happy hours, a concept less heard of on the French side. There, bread, pastries, wine, and cheese are affordable, irresistible, and oh-so tasty! Marigot, the capital, has more charm than its counterpart Philipsburg, but sports homeless people, the smell of urine, and dog poop. Practically, cruisers shop and go out on the Dutch side and venture into France for specialty items and chic boutiques.

Confused yet?

Where do France and the Netherlands border each other? would make a great Trivial Pursuit question.

A day before my parents, Jacques and Agnes, arrive for a three-week vacation, the heat exchanger in our starboard engine breaks. Luckily, we're immobilized inside the lagoon, and therefore protected from bad weather. The timing of this incident is less fortunate. It's our first big boat problem, just when we planned a week-long cruise around the island with guests. With only one functioning engine we can't go through the narrow bridge, let alone pick up anchor and drop it again, seven days in a row.

The cheapest and fastest way to obtain a new heat exchanger is to have Mark's parents, Carol and Stan, bring one from the States when they visit. My parents arrive safe and sound and live with us on the boat in the lagoon. Their flexibility is appreciated. We go on daytrips by bus, dinghy, and rental car. Sometimes Mark and Darwin come, but mostly it's the three of us, yapping away in Flemish (a dialect of Dutch) and exploring what the island has to offer.

Orient Beach, the ruins of Fort Amsterdam, Oyster Pond, the capitals Marigot and Philipsburg, Pic Paradis (the highest mountain with spectacular views); there are enough land sights to keep us occupied. We stroll along attractive beaches and lounge on Maho Bay, famous for its location at the end of the runway. Massive planes take off, creating blasts that kick up clouds of sand and have the potential to throw the unsuspecting tourist into the sea. I hold onto the chain link fence enduring the force of KLM's

747. My sunglasses effortlessly and unsuspectingly disappear into the blue beyond.

The heat exchanger arrives in St. Martin with Mark's parents, but not without the attention of the Customs department. Doubting the availability of laundry detergent on the island, Carol brought her own white powder. Packed in a Ziploc bag and conveniently stored inside the heat exchanger, it had been mistaken for something less benign. Nobody was sent to jail, but the suspicious substance was confiscated.

The parents settle in their respective hotels on opposite sides of the lagoon, in different countries. Near stores with laundry detergent. Carol, Stan, Agnes, and Jacques meet each other for the first time, after four years of Mark and I being together; a highlight in itself.

The two of us work out the logistics to see everybody in equal amounts *and* fix the boat.

From the moment our starboard engine operates, we arrange a day sail for the entire family. Mark maneuvers *Irie* through the narrow French bridge. Before long, we glide through the turquoise waters of the Caribbean Sea. Such a difference from the murky lagoon. We stop at a group of rocks near Grand Case to snorkel and have lunch on the boat. My mum suffers from seasickness, so I bring her and my dad to shore. They'll return to Simpson Bay Lagoon by bus.

The remaining party sails along the north coast of St. Martin. We cross the invisible border with Anguilla and gaze at the contours of Tintamarre and St. Barth, future destinations. The weather is wonderful and the sailing superb; a nice outing before we return to our protected neighborhood.

Mark's parents leave ten days after they arrive; my parents stay a little longer. Everybody had a good time, and everything *landed on its paws* in the end, despite our boat issues and worries. My mom was probably glad she only went sailing for one hour instead of seven days.

Mark and I value the efforts of our parents flying long distances to see us. Maybe we're a good excuse for a distant holiday and an encouragement to see different places. But deep in their hearts, they'd like us to stay put *somewhere*, ideally within reach, and live an ordinary life.

Chapter 11

Good Idea?

Mark grabs his backpack and puts his computer and electrical cord inside.

"Do you want to join me ashore? I need to send emails and do research online."

"Sure! I always have something to launch into digital space, like another blog." Since we started cruising in October 2007, I have been able to regularly post stories, photos, and updates on *It's Irie* about our life aboard.

I consider the windy conditions. Darwin will be left alone and the holding of this anchorage is questionable. Weeds cover the muddy bottom.

As long as the wind doesn't shift and Irie *doesn't drag again, we have nothing to worry about.*

I frown, remembering that embarrassing event. Until then, our trustworthy anchor dug into the lagoon's floor splendidly. We had meandered backwards, without realizing it. *Knock, knock, knock.* A hollow sound from the hull caused Darwin to bark ferociously and us to jump out of bed and up the stairs.

"I tink you arrrre goin' away," a French cruiser exclaimed from his dinghy, holding onto *Irie* at the crack of dawn. Before we deciphered his words, we noticed that the island in front of us had become smaller. We were dragging!

We thanked our observant neighbor profusely, picked up anchor, and discovered that it clutched a pile of seaweed. During a wind shift at night, the fluke had scooped up plants and the tip became saturated with greenery, keeping it from digging in again. Mark and I returned to the same general area and re-anchored, pulling back on the chain, making sure we didn't budge.

This spot, our home for the time being, faces Grand Ilet, also called Explorer Island by the locals, or Dog Shit Island by cruisers. We like it here because there's a small beach for Darwin to play on, and it's quieter than elsewhere in the popular lagoon. Less attractive is the long commute to shore, usually upwind.

Today, we choose an internet destination downwind.

I hope the dinghy ride back won't be too wet, so our computers don't get ruined.

I step into the cockpit and shut the door. We slip into our dinghy and drive to Turtle Pier, packs strapped to our backs. It's the closest place with WiFi and a popular cruisers' hangout.

We pick a table in the corner and focus on our tasks, confident that the connection works, a reason to smile.

Many quests for internet have ended in disappointment, either because the bar we find is too expensive, the restaurant promoting WiFi wants you to purchase a meal, the shack on the beach has no outlet available, the internet café charges exorbitant rates, or you aren't allowed to use your own computer. That, or the establishment has an unreliable connection, a problem with the router, or a password that doesn't work. Sometimes, frustration gets the better of us and we return home, having accomplished nothing.

Loud music distracts me. So does the waiter, inquiring again whether we want something else to drink. My blog post is finished, but my juice is not.

Maybe I should Skype my parents? It's not too late in Belgium yet...

Happy to hear ma and pa's voices, I'm aware of other customers getting annoyed by mine. The connection breaks up. I detect my mom's increased annoyance when repeating herself. Seconds later, I promise to call again another day and hang up. Soon after, Mark and I leave.

The dinghy scoops up liberal portions of murky lagoon as we fight our way into the wind and waves. Mark tries to keep us dry by anticipating the chop, swirling left and right along the wind waves, but saltwater splashes into our faces each time the bow hits the surface. The smile has long rinsed off my face. The contents of our bags stay dry, but we need to wash off the salt.

"I can't believe people do this every day to get online," I whine.

"They don't," Mark says. "There are plenty of products on the market to pick up a WiFi signal from your boat."

"Really? Why don't we have one of those?"

Mark sighs. "I've looked into it, believe me, but the available systems are either too expensive, or they aren't well-made. And they're not waterproof, even though the manufacturers claim they are. The marine environment is harsh on products, you know that, and I want our gear to last, especially when spending hundreds of dollars."

"So instead, we have to go ashore and be frustrated every time we want to be online? It might be cheaper to get one of those systems, if our laptops don't survive these rough rides."

I wonder why these wet trips bug me so much now. Because we decided to stay put for a few months of work and maintenance and it has been windy?

I can't wait to leave and explore.

"Maybe I can try to build something myself," Mark says.

"Sure, why not? This anchorage is comfortable enough and importing boat parts to Sint Maarten is cheap and straightforward, apparently."

Lately, Mark has been assisting cruisers with computer problems to make some money. A few captains of big yachts asked his help to configure their onboard WiFi systems. Those expensive units are difficult to set up and maintain; only network engineers manage.

This realization encourages Mark to come up with a better solution: a system that's affordable, well-built, and easy to use. He researches the best way to put a WiFi product together and orders the most durable materials and highest performing components he can find: the best antenna, chip set, waterproof box, cables, and hardware.

When the parts arrive by plane, my single-focused husband gets to work. The result looks homemade but, once installed outside, picks up multiple WiFi signals, one of which is called "Turtle Pier." We have internet on board, thanks to our marine-grade, affordable, and easy-to-use system! To get online, all we have to do is plug the USB-cable of our WiFi device into our laptop. The signal isn't strong enough to make Skype calls, since Turtle Pier's router is located behind concrete walls, but emailing and browsing websites pose no problem.

We're both ecstatic. I'm proud of my hubby's skills.

When we tell cruising friends about our new invention, they're in awe. They, too, are sick of the risk, time, wetness, hassle, and money involved going ashore for internet. Sailors want to communicate with friends and family, research boat projects, and check the weather from the comfort of their boat. They want... what we have.

Could we make a few more of those?

Mark and I are surprised our peers want to pay for this product instead of building one themselves, but why not? First, we're going on a vacation, or shall I call it a business trip?

Sitting in the dirty lagoon for weeks, focusing on boat projects, makes us forget we're on a tropical island in the Caribbean. I crave new horizons.

To remedy our succumbing to daily routines and boring environs, Mark and I sail around Saint Martin/Sint Maarten for one week. We want to be tourists without work responsibilities or errand runs. We failed to do this cruise with my parents and are curious about the anchorages surrounding the island. We sail up and down wind, take Darwin for walks on pristine beaches, sit in the cockpit with cocktails, enjoy unobstructed sunsets, read a lot, and do absolutely nothing.

One of the goals during this circumnavigation is to test the new wireless device we put together. The prototype works splendidly. We can call with Skype over WiFi from every place, except "remote" Tintamarre. Here, we don't even try to connect but just swim in the clear water and play with Darwin on the deserted beach once the day-trippers have left.

Upon our return to Simpson Bay Lagoon, we're convinced our WiFi solution for boats works. Mark orders parts to build ten units and together we turn them into waterproof systems. *Exciting!*

The body of the product is a Pelican case that contains the electronics. Pelican is a high-quality brand that has been making robust waterproof cases since 1976. We'll provide three colors (maroon, blue, and yellow) to match people's canvas or add extra flair. The grey Alfa unit inside the box is the brain. A marine-grade antenna on top completes the device. We water test each one in our sink under the running tap and collect the liquid in a bowl to baptize more units. Fresh water is precious on a small sailboat; we need to conserve wherever we can.

Mark and I bring the ten finished products to the weekly cruisers' meet-up at Turtle Pier to promote them. We ask $225 for each long-range WiFi unit, a fair price, set to fit the cruising budget and provide us with pocket money. A week later, we've sold every one of them.

Maybe we're onto something?

Using our own prototype, which has become indispensable, Mark orders parts for 20 more units. The investment puts a dent in our savings.

"We should come up with a name for our product," I suggest.

The brainstorming begins. I'd like to incorporate our boat name. A light bulb goes off.

"Why not call it The Wirie?"

Mark thinks it sounds funny but doesn't dismiss the idea.

I explain: "You know, *irie* means 'it's all good' and the 'w' stands for 'WiFi,' so 'wirie' means 'wireless internet that's all good.' Who would not want one?"

We have a name and the ball starts rolling. We advertise The Wirie on VHF channel 14 during the daily cruisers' net, organized by Mike, aka Shrimpy. People are curious. They ask questions at the weekly happy hour or come by our boat for more information. We create and print Wirie brochures. Our "Belize" color printer/scanner/copier comes in handy! Customers are pleased with the performance of The Wirie. Word spreads.

🜩 🜩 🜩

It's May 2009 and our cruising life is about to change. The weeks are busy and focused on our invention. We realize we should put a website together to provide potential customers with information about The Wirie. Handing out a website address is easier than a brochure.

As a software engineer, not a designer, Mark wonders how to go about this step. We ask our web-developer friend in Austin for help. Rachel and I became fast friends during that broken-up period I'd like to forget. I'd written an article for her and she'd been eager to return the favor.

"Send me the logo and the information about the product and I'll see what I can come up with," she emails back.

Logo? I guess that'll be the next project.

We want something colorful, quirky, happy, and reggae-ish. I write the word Wirie on a piece of paper. The dots on the 'i' could be eyes and the 'r' looks like a nose.

"Why don't we put an arc underneath those letters to create a smiley face?" *Yes!*

We experiment with colors and fonts in Word. We opt for red, yellow, and green, the reggae colors. *Irie* is a Jamaican word and we should stick to its roots. We pick the Croobie font.

Two hours later, we have an attractive logo to send off. Once the foundation for www.thewirie.com is laid out by our skillful friend, Mark makes a few adjustments.

We have a website!

Wait a minute. Why have a website if we can't sell anything on it?

One idea morphs into the next and we keep working.

"It would be ridiculous not to sell The Wirie through our website. How can we make that happen while sailing in the Caribbean?" I ask. It's one thing to import parts, build units, sell them from our boat, and promote them locally. But to invite cruisers all over the world to buy our product and distribute it internationally...

"We might be in luck," Mark says. "My brother is out of work right now. He could probably use some income and distraction. I can ask him to become part of The Wirie crew."

"Great idea!"

Tim, like Mark, has a degree in computer science and, like Mark, is skilled with electronics. He already owns a small company and, excited about the idea, incorporates The Wirie into his freelance business.

There's no turning back now.

⫸ ⫸ ⫸

Mark and I need to make money to keep cruising. Most of his savings are tied up in *Irie*. While we're frugal spenders, dollar bills disappear without being replaced.

The Wirie is a wonderful concept, especially now that it is turning into something, but the money we make doesn't cover our living expenses. I feel pressure to pull my weight.

With the help of our new device, I send out resumes and get hired to write lesson plans around meaningful books for students in the US. I take the job seriously and enjoy the process. That I only make $200 for the 40 hours I invest in each of these instruction booklets is less important.

Another idea I expand upon is writing walking tours for Visual Travel Tours. I pick Marigot and Philipsburg as my destinations and set out on foot for the umpteenth time in these intriguing towns. I spend hours visiting sites, taking photographs, and scribbling notes. Back on the boat, I create comprehensive visual tours with text and photos. The assignments are fun, eye-opening, and educational. It's satisfying to combine my two passions: exploring and writing.

I've always imagined that being a travel writer would be the perfect job for me. The extra income buys us groceries and happy hour drinks for a week.

Now that we're in business, the peace on *Irie* is forever gone. We are busier than ever with our new initiative, taking Darwin to shore, keeping up with boat projects, and maintaining our floating lives.

The VHF radio vomits noise on Channel 14. Non-stop. We have to leave it on in case someone calls *Irie*. Then, we answer the radio, switch channels, and converse. Sailors come by with questions about The Wirie or to purchase a unit. Friends jump aboard for a chat or invite us to a social event. "We're not going today" is an answer we use more frequently, unwilling to start the next morning with a hangover.

The days of going to every event and joining gatherings galore are over. Work gets in the way.

꧁ ꧁ ꧁

We slide into a fluid business routine. My brother-in-law Tim builds Wiries in his workshop and ships them worldwide. Mark and I import parts from the US and build and distribute completed units in the Eastern Caribbean. Mark takes care of customer support. I help with text and edits wherever needed. Without our own Wirie, these tasks would be impossible.

There are more steps involved than we ever anticipated. Running a business is anything but easy. We have a superb product that competes with other companies' higher-priced WiFi systems of inferior quality, but we still have a long way ahead to become professional.

Imagine we created a product that allows us to combine work and travel and make enough money to keep cruising for years...

This is a goal of many non-retirees and a dream of anybody *not* in our shoes. Most younger couples have income from rental properties or they have enough savings to last a while. The alternative is making money while sailing or inventing a marine product to sell from your boat in the middle of nowhere.

We start the process of accepting credit card payments online. Then we add a page with refund and warranty information, and another one with unsolicited testimonials. We assemble and print Quick Start Guides and compile a comprehensive user manual, which we burn on DVDs. We create the first press release and research the cheapest ways to market our product.

Time catches up with us.

We're ready to leave the lagoon. Darwin, slightly neglected for weeks, would like to get the attention he deserves, swim in clear water, and run on white sand beaches again. Our boat is also more than itching to go. She doesn't like to sit and collect barnacles, and we have no intention of exporting them or carrying "dead weight." So, after our four-month stay in the dirty lagoon, we scrape *Irie*'s bottom. Removing the living shells is an ordeal; it's physical, gross, and time consuming. Cleaning the waterline is the easy part since we anchor in four feet of water for the job. I can walk around the boat and scrub the sides as if washing a terribly stained car.

Despite our achievements, I am on this boat to discover the islands.

By the time we head south for hurricane season, everyone and everything is in order. We have a sound, finished product and enough stock to build and sell units underway. The initial excitement of our invention leads to a new focus that alters our cruising lifestyle and influences our decisions in ways we never imagined.

Chapter 12

Shifting Priorities

On a well-prepared and equipped *Irie*, Mark, Darwin, and I conquer the rest of the Eastern Caribbean. We enter Anse de Columbier in the French island of Saint Barthélemy, also called St. Barth or St. Barts. The uninhabited bay with inviting blue water, turtles, remoras, and an attractive white sand beach offers free mooring balls. They prevent anchor damage to the ocean floor and make it easy to get settled and enjoy the tropical view.

There's a 20-minute walk to the small town of Flamands, where we pick up baguettes or hitch a ride into Gustavia, the capital. The pretty beach is more than adequate for Darwin. To cool off, he opts for a swim or digs a hole in the hard-packed sand. It's the perfect place to relax for a few days after our hectic time in St. Martin.

As we follow the most popular route down the Eastern Caribbean chain, we explore the islands of Guadeloupe, Dominica, Martinique, St. Lucia, Grenada, and Carriacou. I research dog regulations for each island, contact the appropriate officials, and gather information to bring Darwin in legally. Following the rules, collecting health certificates before arriving in an ex-British country – usually by hitchhiking to vets with Darwin in tow – and making sure his rabies documentation is in order, we manage to go everywhere we want, although some countries make that harder than others.

Like Antigua.

It's an early morning in July 2009, when Mark, Darwin, and I approach Jolly Harbour, ready to check in with our dog, his health certificate and extra rabies vaccination in hand. While these vaccinations are valid for three years, Antigua requires one that is less than a year old. There was one other test request according to our email from the Antigua Agriculture Department, but we knew Darwin didn't have Lyme disease. We never needed this test before and we figured we could deal with it upon arrival, if truly necessary. We also assumed we'd need a temporary import permit for him once we got there. That usually doesn't cost more than $10.

The sail to Antigua was bumpy and uncomfortable, so we're exhausted. Mark and I lower the dinghy, put its engine in place, and drive the mile to the Customs and Immigration office. There, the officials tell us we have to move *Irie* to their dock for check-in. Back to the anchorage we go. We lift anchor and motor to the Customs dock with our big boat. The Immigration officer gives us a bunch of forms to fill out. We can't officially check in until a vet inspects Darwin.

Maybe we shouldn't have mentioned him?

Of course, we're not comfortable smuggling him in, so we wait. For four hours. Then the fun begins...

The vet jumps aboard and wants to test Darwin for Lyme disease and examine him. Lyme disease mainly exists in the northeast of the United States and Darwin hasn't been there for two years. That doesn't matter. Darwin doesn't have Lyme disease symptoms. That doesn't matter. Also, Darwin was examined in Gustavia by a vet just two days prior and received a clean bill of health. None of it matters.

"Then why did we have to spend $50 to get him a current health certificate, if this doesn't mean anything?" I ask.

"You only spent $50 in St. Barth? What a bargain," the vet responds.

More discussions prove that the test is unnecessary, but what throws us off most is the price: for this little joke, we have to pay the equivalent of $50. After that, we'll be issued a temporary dog import permit for another $50. If we'd known this ahead of time, we could've sailed straight to Guadeloupe, a much nicer sailing angle.

If we want to visit Antigua with Darwin, we have to fork over $100 to this vet and the Agriculture Department.

In other countries we've visited, we never paid more than $15 per dog. Most of the time a permit is free, not required, or about ten dollars, including the vet visit. This vet, who already has an attitude, gets annoyed with our objections. He suggests we leave the country instead. We agree. He storms to the Immigration officer to tell him we're not allowed to stay in Antigua.

Now what?

We're tired after this night crossing and it's 2pm. We can't make it to Guadeloupe, mentally, physically, or by nightfall. Staying in Antigua isn't worth the extra money. Our initial excitement to visit this new-to-us island has evaporated.

After the incident, witnessed by all officials present, we have a friendly chat with the Immigration officer. He's sympathetic to our situation and allows us to stay one night, anchored in the harbor, to get some sleep.

Back on the ocean, we're happy about our decision. Too bad we don't get to explore Antigua, but we'll spend our money in places where our dog is as welcome as we are.

With a different destination on the radar, the elements agree with us. The sun sits bright in the sky and the wind blows a perfect 15 knots, propelling us at an average speed of 7 knots.

Look at us now! Conditions like these don't happen often, but today you can all envy us.

Mark and I are in a good mood, despite the change of plans. We join hundreds of flying fish, flying south. In a swift seven hours, we arrive in

Deshaies, Guadeloupe. Checking in is free and takes five minutes. One sheet to fill out, no stamps or permits required, and Darwin is more than welcome.

When I discover that fellow international dog owners are surprised our pet is allowed in the ex-British islands, I write articles for *Caribbean Compass* about facts and experiences we gathered. I've always enjoyed writing and sharing adventures with others, so I create destination pieces and send them off to the two Caribbean boating publications. Based on the readership, the style, and my mood, I contribute my pieces either to *All At Sea* or *Compass*.

Now, I can call myself a freelance writer, which comes in handy when asked about my profession on forms.

"I don't know why you keep writing *teacher* in the occupation field," Mark said at an Immigration office recently. "You haven't taught for years and it only raises questions as to why you're not in school right now."

He's right. It's been so long since I was standing in front of a classroom that I don't even feel like a teacher anymore. Except when working on my lesson plans for *Book Rags*. And when reading typos in books on the New York Times Best Seller List. Of course, I make them myself, thus this habit becomes even more annoying, if not hypocritical.

We stay on the leeward side when passing the islands, which means the wind is finicky and we have to motor frequently. The dolphins don't mind. Their company is delightful!

The hierarchy on *Irie* has changed since we left St. Martin. When we started cruising, Mark's attention was focused on: #1 The weather #2 Darwin #3 *Irie* and #4 Liesbet. Now, The Wirie business stands as a strong number two. The weather remains in the lead – everything depends on it. Otherwise, The Wirie rules. Commitment to our company is the guiding factor on this new path. The rest of us have dropped down one position, with Liesbet still at the bottom.

"The wind finally settles down." Mark listens to the daily Chris Parker report on our portable SSB radio. "We'll leave first thing in the morning."

"Okay." I'm not sure anybody heard me.

"I would really like to stop *there*. I've heard it's a magnificent anchorage," I often say as we sail to the next location. Once we establish there's enough protection, the first consideration used to be "Is there an accessible beach to take Darwin?" Now, that's replaced by "Can we get online from the boat?"

Of course, we don't know the answer until entering a harbor and trying. We get settled; I salivate over the pristine surroundings. At times, we're in luck and stay. More often than not, we pick up anchor and move elsewhere.

"This is such a beautiful place." I try again.

"It doesn't look like anybody lives here," Mark objects and we continue on.

Quiet bays used to draw us in. We like to be on our own, with a rewarding view of the coastline, the beach, the forest, the mountains. It's difficult to find WiFi in places absent of houses, marinas, bars, and restaurants. Our desire for peace makes way to our desire, or shall I say *need*, for internet.

Darwin appreciates his walks on the beaches, but it doesn't prevent a change in his behavior. Maybe it's from dropping down a spot on "the list of importance" or maybe Kali's passing is finally dawning on him. At some point, he realizes she's never coming back and loses his patience and jolly attitude. He develops a serious form of separation anxiety. Mark and I can't leave him alone on the boat anymore. He'd chew his tail until it bleeds. Plastic cones, no matter the size, don't contain him. Most of the time he joins us ashore, as usual. He loves being at parties, getting extra cuddles, or lying at our feet under the table.

Shopping becomes my job, as well as other chores off the boat, like laundry and errand runs. Mark is busy on *Irie,* with physical or mental occupations.

I don't mind being out and about. It gives me purpose in this work-orientated life and I prefer visiting stores by myself: nobody to criticize or rush me when I browse. If Darwin can't come on outings like island tours or snorkel trips, one of us has to stay home. Despite the inconveniences, we love our boy to death and would do anything to make him happy.

꩜ ꩜ ꩜

"When was the last time you were in the United States of America, ma'am?" The Homeland Security officer at San Juan airport scrutinizes my green card and passport.

Mark's sister's only child is getting married in Boston. We plan to attend. Mark will return to Grenada soon after and I'll tag on two weeks in Belgium to see friends and family. I especially look forward to catching up with my *oma*. Our German friend Angie is staying on *Irie* to take care of Darwin. They adore each other; we couldn't have picked a better caretaker.

I try to remember when we left Puerto Rico on our boat. Oh yeah, soon after Kali passed away, the end of 2008.

Why does this matter, anyway?

"Hmm. About ten months ago." I look at the officer with no worry in the world. I should know better.

Am I supposed to be away this long, longer, not as long?

I have a permanent resident card and am married to an American. Despite my stubborn denial of this matrimony, that should count for something. Mark is not allowed to join me at the desk, where I'm bombarded with questions. As usual, Immigration pulled me aside – in Puerto Rico – on a layover to the mainland. I was confident my green card would prevent this heartache.

Nope.

Luckily, Mark was granted entrance at the second security checkpoint. I can feel his eyes on my back, wondering what the heck is going on.

What did I do wrong this time?

The official's stare is cold. He waves the green card before my eyes. It makes me dizzy.

"You don't deserve this," he screams, still wagging the plastic inches from my face. "You are supposed to live in the United States for six months a year. You're a *permanent resident!*"

I gaze back. While this information is new to me, I'm not impressed and certainly not intimidated.

"I had no idea." I use my friendly voice.

The vigorous shaking of my "priceless possession" continues.

"Do you know what people would do for this? Do you know how many people want this card but can never get it?"

I tilt my head.

"You need to treat your residency with respect. It's a privilege. If this happens again, I will take it away from you!"

I am careful to not actually shrug my shoulders. I don't know what benefits me anymore, having this card or not. I never seem to do the right thing. First, I'm in the US too much as a tourist and now I'm not there enough as a resident. When I visit with a green card, my mantra should be *I live here and I'm returning from an extended vacation.* When I visit on a B1/B2 visa, I ought to remember *I live elsewhere and I'm only here for a short vacation.* I have to keep these perfect answers straight. Yet, it's still "hit or miss" when dealing with Homeland Security.

I take my valuable ID back and walk towards Mark.

"What was that about?"

"I'm supposed to live in the US for at least six months every calendar year. What are we going to do now? My green card is invalid if I don't actually live here."

"That's why it's called a resident card, I guess."

"It does make sense. Luckily, I'm only visiting the States for a week. Wait a minute, maybe that's a bad thing? Staying longer might be better." I try to grasp the situation. "Should we surrender my green card? Apparently, I don't deserve it. We won't move to the US, right?"

This revelation throws us for a loop. Most of our time in New England is, yet again, spent researching the internet for information about permanent residency, citizenship, and the rules and regulations involved. It's all logical, just not nomad friendly. What fits best in our current situation? Are we willing to throw away the effort, time, and money invested?

We mull over the possibilities for weeks. We contemplate dividing our time between Puerto Rico and Grenada: six months in the US territory to work and sell Wiries, and then southward bound for hurricane season in Grenada, like this year. It fits our sailing plans and benefits the cruising kitty.

After three years of this, I could apply for citizenship.

By 2012, I could be an American citizen, never to be hassled at the border again.

It sounds promising and straightforward. Except for one slightly important factor: I don't want my future defined by Homeland Security. Not again. I want *us* to decide when we sail where, as much as that's still possible. I want *us* to mold our own lives, independent of laws and red tape. The government already forced our marriage. I won't be pushed onto a particular path for years, while this might not be what we would choose to do. Three years is a long time.

Mark agrees.

So, I give up my precious green card. I write a nice letter to the USCIS, explaining that I want to pause my permanent resident status, because at this time in my life I cannot commit to living in this great country, and therefore, I do not deserve this card. *The guy at the border told me so.* (I don't add this last bit.) We hope the USCIS appreciates our honesty and files this letter. Just in case we pick up the paper trail for residency again in the future. When everything is over and done, I take a deep breath and inhale my freshly acquired freed... I stall halfway. No green card means no more income from US sources. I grudgingly write a letter to *Book Rags*, explaining why I can't create more lesson plans. Then, I apply for non-US freelance jobs.

🌊🌊🌊

"What do you wanna do for your birthday?" Mark asks when the end of November nears.

Last year was a bust in Puerto Rico, where nothing he planned worked out. Not that he had planned much. He failed to buy a birthday gift and when we tried to go out for dinner and drinks, none of the restaurants in Salinas allowed dogs. Stubbornness won over hunger and – more out of principle than out of frugality – we returned to *Irie*, defeated and starving. Mark cooked up the only thing we had in our fridge: a whole chicken that took two hours to roast in our unreliable oven. I had my birthday dinner at 10pm and was not merry.

Surely, Mark would do better this year.

"I'd really like to go to the Tobago Cays for the day." Since we had been in a hurry to reach Grenada two months into hurricane season, we'd skipped the Grenadines.

"It's your birthday!"

So, on November 28, we make the short trip from Carriacou to paradise: the pristine islands of the Tobago Cays. We pick up an empty mooring ball and pay the fee for the marine park to a ranger passing by. I sit in the cockpit and revel in the view of sandy beaches, waving palm trees, and turquoise water, while having a tasty lunch. Mark sends Darwin to me. Our precious boy carries a gift on a string around his neck. When I open it, my eyes sparkle as much as the piece of jewelry inside: a black pearl necklace from the Pacific. Mark puts the gorgeous gift around my tan neck, like in the movies, the romantic ones. The three pearls reflect the colors of the sky, my eyes, and the ocean.

I read the sweet birthday card my husband wrote and give him a hug. It's signed "Mark, Darwin, and Kali, wherever she may be." I shake off the twinge of sadness and focus on this blissful moment. Darwin rests his head on my lap and Mark kisses me tenderly. Then, he cleans up the dishes and we slide into the water with our snorkel gear. As long as Darwin can see us from the trampoline, he'll hopefully stay put and not attack his tail.

Moments later, we float and watch several turtles underneath us. They feed on grass in the shallows. We follow one, then another. When they swim, we have trouble keeping up. We can always fall back and choose another photo subject to observe.

When the light fades, we take Darwin to shore for his evening walk.

His tail is wrapped with a new bandage, since he pulled the old one off during our snorkel expedition. He runs, rips coconut husks apart, and digs his head into the sand. His nose is covered. Mark and I sit together on a sarong. We watch the sun dip behind the horizon, illuminating the sky in 50 shades of orange and pink.

I smile.

Chapter 13

Back to the Office

In St. Martin, it feels like we have returned to the office. A loud, busy, and wobbly one. Roaring planes, wake-creating dive boats, plowing ferries, passing tenders, buzzing jet skis resembling oversized mosquitoes, and sailing dinghies practicing for local races make up our neighborhood in Simpson Bay Lagoon. The contrast with previous islands couldn't be bigger.

Our last stop – in remote Barbuda – was as peaceful as one could imagine. We tried to last as long as possible with our provisions, but when our toothpaste was finished, we only managed a few days using a mixture of baking soda and salt. The third ingredient to substitute toothpaste flavor – peppermint extract – proved indispensable.

This will be our home for a few months again, and even though getting back here is somewhat of a shock, we knew what to expect.

Like last year, we anchor off Grand Ilet, one of the quieter places in the lagoon.

When cruising through, two weeks on St. Martin is enough: one week to fix boat issues and provision, the other for sightseeing, beach bumming, and city roaming. However, if you plan on running a business, you need to stay longer.

Mark and I are here to work, and we take that task seriously from the moment we arrive.

Instead of spending an hour or two daily on our Wirie business, Mark now sits behind the computer the entire day, communicating with Tim, researching ideas and products, advertising, improving the website, understanding the competition, reacting to unethical statements on forums and message boards, communicating with journalists, and providing support. He also deals with customer issues, credit card issues, and internet issues for others, as well as for us.

The list goes on.

Nobody said owning a company was easy, let alone from a boat in the Caribbean. I'm not sure how he'll keep up once we leave St. Martin. Life is hectic and demanding, partly because we're extra responsible, responsive, and caring. It's difficult, but we focus on the now and don't think about leaving again. We just arrived.

The last few months, between Grenada and St. Martin, Mark and Tim worked diligently on The Wirie business. Positive changes have been made to the website and the daily operations. We produce a new wireless product. We grow. We improve. We need to stay abreast of the technology market, which is constantly changing.

Mark is not happy with the newest heart of our product and contacts the company. For the next four months, he develops software he's comfortable with and communicates with Alfa Networking on a weekly basis. Every Wednesday evening, while the rest of us are at the bar, Mark sits on the top step of a nearby building, while planes fly overhead, and talks to the chief engineer in Taiwan over a flaky internet connection. The noise, occasional rain, poor English of his peer, time difference, and culture barrier make these business calls difficult.

Three times a week, I work eight-hour shifts as a bartender in Lagoonies on the Dutch side for $5 an hour. Customers rarely tip. I can't blame them.

As a Belgian, I was never one to tip on top of paying for my meals and drinks. I prefer the European system, where everything is part of the price on the menu. Americans tried to explain that tipping is part of their culture because employees get paid less than minimum wage in the hospitality sector. Now that I'm on the other side of the counter, I understand the value of tips. Standing on your feet and running around for eight hours straight is hard work. At the end of the day, I go home with 40 dollars, maybe 45, if people were generous. Every bit helps.

Until it doesn't anymore.

After six weeks, I quit. Mark needs help with The Wirie and writing articles doesn't require a long ride to shore, which is expensive in gas and leaves Mark without transportation. Plus, in its current shape, our dinghy could falter any time. Having to be rescued by a competent bronzed knight might sound romantic but is slightly embarrassing. We need that engine fixed.

Every other weekend, we break the routine and the collection of barnacles on *Irie*'s bottom by sailing to a more attractive harbor and indulging in the beauty of the Caribbean. After these two-day outings, it's back to our familiar spot in the lagoon.

When the captain of the biggest sloop in the world, *Mirabella V*, hears about The Wirie, he decides to buy two. I take advantage of our acquaintance and request a tour of his ship. The answer is affirmative.

A week later, Mark and I explore the decks and interior of the massive *Mirabella V*. I write an article about the ins and outs of the sloop. It becomes my most popular story published in *All At Sea*. I'm getting the hang of article writing and grow fond of working from home.

With our small income in 2010, we almost break even at the end of the year. Boat projects, insurance, and haulouts still take a chunk out of the savings account, but we hope to resolve that in the future.

🐚 🐚 🐚

After weeks of work behind the computer and on the boat, I need an outing. My nagging to stop in dramatic Saba on our sail north was met by deaf ears.

"It's too uncomfortable to moor along Saba's coast. There are no good harbors." It was the undeniable truth, expressed by my captain. "Besides, even if we stop for a few days and survive living in a washing machine, how will we take Darwin to shore for his potty breaks? There is no good beach, only waves crashing against the rocks."

To reach land, one needs to climb a stairway of 800 steps in Ladder Bay or take the dinghy over two miles of ocean to the main dock in Fort Bay. Even I had to admit this didn't sound appealing. But a seed was planted in my head.

I was going to Saba with or without Mark.

After two months in St. Martin, it turns out I prefer without. I need a break as much from my other half – who's turning into a stress ball, lacking patience and sweetness – as from the routine of lagoon life, chatter on the VHF radio, and endlessly repeated activities and chores.

Sorry, cruising kitty, part of my well-earned money goes to Saba with me.

Ferries are expensive and their schedule is inconvenient, so flying is the better option. Not only do you get to Saba in 15 minutes and hassle-free, but the experience is a thrill. The plane is loud and shaky, the views marvelous. Before you realize St. Martin is behind you, the giant mountain of Saba looms ahead. In the front, you almost have a pilot's perspective. I'm up and close to Saba's spectacular scenery from the moment we approach the shortest runway in the world. With a quick drop, the wheels touch ground and the shrieking brakes stop the plane in seconds, at the ocean's edge.

After my first encounter with Saba's climbing roads and steep steps, I check into rustic El Momo Cottages. At $50 a night for one person, more than a day's work in the bar, it's the cheapest room on the island.

By 10am, I'm ready to explore. I observe a glass blowing demonstration at Jo Bean's Gallery and venture into the town of Windwardside. The whitewashed gingerbread houses with red roofs and white picket fences instill a friendly feel, which is also reflected in the people who live here. The town is quiet and peaceful, with a few churches, a museum, a couple of grocery stores, and a handful of bars and restaurants. Goats roam freely.

The atmosphere is serene and Dutch. I reconnect with my native language. It's lovely to be on my own and divide my short time here the way I see most fit.

Saba overflows with hiking trails; you can walk around the entire island and rarely touch concrete. Mt. Scenery, with its 1065 steps, is the biggest challenge. When the weather is nice, the 360-degree ocean views must be amazing, but I happen to visit on a cloudy weekend.

It takes a few hours to climb the steep steps cut out of rock. They love their stairs on Saba, which is nothing more than one massive boulder. Taking photos is a good excuse to catch my breath. Moist jungle plants, green elephant ears, banana and palm trees, colorful flowers, and chirping birds surround me. The air is wet and chilly. Everything is veiled in mist. I keep hoping for a miraculous breakthrough of the sun, until I stand on the highest point of the Netherlands, with the whistling wind and obscuring white clouds as my only companions.

Going back downhill happens fast. Maybe a bit too fast, since one of my knees explodes in pain with the first step down the stairs of my cottage the following day.

Not good!

My plane to St. Martin departs late afternoon, on the other side of the island. I'd planned to hike to the airport, the long way around via trails. It's a fantastic plan, so I stick to it.

What am I thinking? I don't even have my knee brace with me.

I check out, strap my small backpack on, consult my map, and begin my arduous trek. The exercise starts at 9:30am, when I once again climb the steps of Mt. Scenery. Descending is excruciatingly painful. I doubt my intentions again. As long as the trail goes up, I'll be okay.

I continue on the main track, pass the sign for Mt. Scenery, and follow the Bottom Mountain Trail. By Saba standards, this one is flat. I enjoy being alone in the wilderness and the pastures, surrounded by wild goats, fluttering birds, spotted lizards, and soundless butterflies.

The worst part of the day, for people with a painful knee, is the steep and infinite path down the mountain towards the road. As slowly as I can, I proceed and focus on the taste of the ripe mangoes that almost fall on my head.

I usually hate climbing, but the upward parts of this hike become my favorite. I yelp with each downward step, glad nobody's around.

When I reach the winding concrete road, I face a dilemma: giving up and turning left, steeply downhill to reach the capital, The Bottom, and hopefully catch a ride towards the airport or remaining strong and turning right, steeply uphill to reach the Sandy Cruz Trail, the most popular one on the island. The painful prospect of going down more and the stubbornness to do this *nicest trail* make me turn right.

At the Sandy Cruz Trailhead, I stop. Once I start this one, there's no turning back. Most people walk this trail the other way around. I find out why when I come across a young couple, five minutes into the hike. They say they've been going downhill most of the time. This means loads of climbing for me. *Perfect!*

After a glimpse over the ocean and the rocky cliffs, a quick snack, and a moment to let my sweat evaporate, I'm ready to continue on – and up. This island is steep. I huff and puff, yet savor the peace, quiet, and beauty of the jungle. It's cooler than in St. Martin.

Behind me, a man appears. He wears camouflage clothes and carries a rifle and a rake.

"Is there anybody behind you?" he asks.

How would I know? And why does he care?

"I have no idea."

The day before, I saw two men in the same outfit, with the same tools, on Mt. Scenery. In front of them lay two dead goats; legs tied; heads cut off. I suddenly realize I'm alone and vulnerable. No crime exists on Saba and I shouldn't worry. Yet, when remembering bloody scenes in the boonies, one gets carried away.

The humidity is high. I stop frequently to breathe and wring my sweat-drenched T-shirt. The incline goes on forever, but my knee feels fine.

At last, I arrive at another split. My choice: taking the All Too Far Trail, followed by the Sulphur Mine Trail, which brings me to Lower Hell's Gate, the town closest to the airport or continuing along this trail into Upper Hell's Gate. The second option promises less distress, so I stick to my track, downhill this time, until I finally reach pavement. The main road winds down, down, down to the airport.

The hairpin turns are too steep. My knees are battered. They can't support my weight without intense pain. I discover I can do this descent with one stretched leg and less agony. I zigzag down a zigzagging road. I develop a robot-like stride downhill and, like the Duracell Bunny, I keep going. After seven hours of hiking, I sink into a chair at the airport. When I get up to soak my face in the restroom, my legs shake. I fall back onto the seat.

On the brief plane ride back, I look at the green, curvy mass of land on which I walked for two days. I made the most of my time here, having captured the beauty of Saba, the *unspoiled queen*, with my camera, my soul, and my poor knees.

Exhausted and sore, I hug Darwin and Mark in St. Martin.

Did I really only leave the previous morning?

Chapter 14

Reality Happens Elsewhere

W hen July 2010 rolls around, we're in Grenada for another hurricane season.

"Where is it?" Rosie whispers, after Mark and Sim left *Irie*'s cockpit to check out the turnbuckles near the mast. We had become close friends on our sail down from St. Martin, after she and her husband bought a Wirie. Mark and I don't like traveling with other boats, but we frequently caught up with a fun group of sailors along the major stops south. We hung out on beaches, as well as met for potlucks, swims, and walks. British Rosie not only sports an endearing accent, she has a fabulous sense of humor, is my age, and – like me – never thinks before she speaks. We hit it off immediately.

"Come with me." I look topside to make sure our other halves are still out of earshot.

During one of our happy hour conversations last week, I told my friend about the mysterious object I discovered behind a stack of books on a shelf in the engine berth. We descend to the starboard hull and squeeze into the space, which also acts as a second spare bedroom. I stretch my

right arm and hook it behind a row of thick volumes about boat maintenance, to retrieve a small black jewelry box.

It's heart shaped.

"I think there's a ring inside." I give it a gentle jiggle but hear nothing.

"You haven't looked yet?" She frowns when I shake my head. "It seems
old. Open it!"

"No. I don't want to jinx it if it's for me. Or what if Mark got this for
someone else?"

"Don't be silly. When did you find this?" Rosie turns the object around
and around.

"Over a year ago. I was cleaning the shelves when I stumbled across
it."

"What? You've known about this for a year and you never told me?
Or Mark? Why?"

As one of the most curious people I know, she's baffled. I remember
when my fingers touched the precious box and I came face to face with it.
Mark and I had been officially married for two years. He knew I hoped for
a real proposal and a wedding party one day. I had felt excited and annoyed
at the same time. Excited because this had to be an engagement ring or
maybe even a wedding ring. Annoyed because I'd found this well-hidden
treasure that surely must be a secret gift. Each time I clean this aft cabin, I
make sure my little heart is still there.

"I hope it's an engagement ring. I don't want to ruin the surprise when
he hands it to me. Obviously, he's never proposed and in three years there
hasn't been a party. Who knows if it'll ever happen?"

"Oh, Liesbet. It might still happen," Rosie sympathizes. She and Sim
married on beautiful, tropical Grenada last year, but have yet to go on a
honeymoon. Like us.

"You have no idea how many times I sat across from him on special
occasions in idle anticipation. At this point, he might not remember its
existence anymore."

"That would be strange. Do you think the previous owners overlooked
the ring?"

"No. We would have found it earlier. We emptied and cleaned this entire catamaran after the purchase. It's a true mystery to me, another boat mystery. I don't want to confront Mark about it in case he forgot to propose to me."

"Have you ever heard of a man who bought an engagement ring, and then forgot to propose?" Rosie snickers. "Something else is going on. You should just ask Mark about it."

"Not yet. I might as well wait a bit longer. Maybe he'll propose on my birthday when we're back in the States." I smile at my friend, probably giving Mark more romantic credit than is due, and put the box back where it appears to belong. We return to the cockpit.

"I had to show Rosie something downstairs," I mumble as we slide behind the table and join our husbands. I resume my Miss Patient stance and change the topic.

When Mark and I sit on the beach with Darwin and talk about our content lives in the tropics, nothing ring-like happens.

When we watch the star-lit sky during a romantic moment on *Irie*'s trampoline together, nothing knee-bending happens.

When we go out to dinner on our last night before flying out of the country, nothing teary-eyed happens.

The jewelry box remains a mystery.

〰️〰️〰️

Like retired seasonal cruisers who leave their boat in the tropics and return to their comfortable land-based home during hurricane season, Mark and I have hauled *Irie* out of the water in Grenada. Unlike our older peers, we separate with our floating home for only three months in the fall and for entirely different reasons. We're back in the United States to take care of Mark's sister, Dru.

A few months ago, while still in St. Martin, Mark received the shocking news that his sister was diagnosed with Stage IV ovarian cancer, one of the most aggressive and deadly of all cancers. The five-year survival rate is less than 20 percent, with an average life expectancy of three years after the diagnosis. By the time this type of cancer is detected, it's usually too late and the disease has spread. This enemy is a vicious one.

Mark and I couldn't spring into action and help the family until we reached a sheltered spot outside the hurricane zone. Packing up a floating home and leaving her safe and secure for months in the Caribbean is never a straightforward feat. Neither is bringing a dog with separation anxiety on the plane with you.

The first thing we do after our arrival is take Darwin to a vet. Unexpectedly losing a pet to cancer is not something we want to repeat. After a full check-up and necessary scans, our pup receives the "all clear."

Next, we put our energy towards Dru.

Every other week, Mark and I make the four-hour trip from our US "home base" at my in-laws in Newburyport, Massachusetts, to Greenwich, Connecticut, where Dru and her husband, Brian, are caretakers of an impressive property. We then spend a few days with her, cooking meals and bringing her to appointments and chemotherapy sessions.

After one of those visits, Mark and I drive home in the borrowed car of his parents. As our stay in the States progresses, we look forward to being on *Irie* again, in a peaceful environment devoid of the commotion, distractions, and traffic of Western life. Back to the basics. We miss nature and being on our own.

Luckily, it's not too busy on the highway.

What I enjoy on these long, easy stretches of road is talking to my other half, away from his computer. Darwin stands on the back seat, head through the window, tongue hanging loose. It's still warm for October. The open window creates a lot of noise, so I wait until Darwin lies down to close it and share what has been on my mind.

I've wondered whether Mark brought the mysterious ring to propose on my birthday but decide not to bring that up. Instead, I broach another unfinished topic.

"I was thinking," I begin, while my heart beats faster, "we still need to throw a wedding party. It has been over three years since we officially tied the knot."

"Has it been that long already? Really? What do you have in mind?"

"Well... I think St. Martin would be the perfect place. Most of our cruising friends are headed that way for the winter and spring. Plus, it's not too far from Massachusetts, or Belgium."

I still managed to keep our official bond secret from my friends and most of my relatives. Of course, my *oma* or parents might have spilled the beans. But would my family spend this much money to come to a celebration in the tropics? Few are familiar with the Caribbean, let alone travel far and wide to attend a wedding event.

"Where would you want to organize the party?"

"Maybe we can rent a villa for a week? We could have some couples stay with us and share the cost. And you and I can take care of everything else, the food, the invitations, the drinks. I need to research this, obviously."

"Sounds good to me. We probably can't do this on the cheap, but work your magic."

That ring will finally find its way to my finger!

🌊🌊🌊

It's nice to have a task while living in the room above the garage of Mark's parents' condo. I research rental places, contact real estate agents, and scour Google for the ideal spot for our event: a re-enactment of the wedding I've always preferred. I need to find a pet-friendly villa, since I'd like Darwin to play a role in the celebrations.

Maybe he can carry our wedding rings around his neck?

Mark is running out of time if he's ever to propose. Did he really forget the mystery ring?

Before we return to Grenada with the news that Dru is doing well, under the circumstances, I book a villa near Baie Rouge on the French side of St. Martin.

Our wedding party will take place on April 30th, 2011. The villa is located on a hill overlooking the water, a block from an attractive beach where we can have a ceremony with rum punch. It offers five rooms, a swimming pool, a sizeable deck for our party, and welcomes dogs. I've been able to haggle on the price, making this venue quite affordable.

Finally, a party that is all about us! If anyone shows up, of course. The future looks bright and I have a 35th birthday to celebrate.

Mark spoils me with gifts, one of which is a state-of-the-art digital camera that's waterproof and shock proof and takes decent above-water photos as well. There's even a "pet function." You enter your pet's name and date of birth and it keeps track of his age with every photo you take. I'll be using that setting frequently. I'm thrilled about the prospect of non-blurry photos when snorkeling among colorful creatures and beautiful coral.

At a Thai restaurant, we eat my favorite food and chat about our return to Grenada and our April party in St. Martin. I don't see any jewelry boxes. After dinner, we hang out with Darwin in our room and shower him with love.

"What's wrong with his eyes?" Mark asks. They're devoid of any color.

"I have no idea." I hope this is a temporary condition. We're leaving in a few days and we want our boy to be healthy for the plane ride. Mark opens Darwin's mouth. His tongue looks white. There's no pink left.

"Maybe he's dehydrated." Mark notices Darwin's belly is bloated. It sends a shiver through our spines. Thoughts of Kali and her life-threatening cancer emerge. It seems unlikely to have two dogs with the same symptoms within two years.

The following days are a blur.

The vet examines Darwin. His gums and tongue are pale; his belly doesn't feel normal. His blood work comes back. The red blood count is low, which explains his anemia. But why?

They keep Darwin for the rest of the morning, take X-rays, and perform more tests but can't figure it out. We are referred to specialists in Portsmouth, New Hampshire. There, a radiologist takes an ultrasound of Darwin while we wait. A couple of hours and hundreds of dollars later, we hear the verdict: our boy has a rare and devastating cancer. He's bleeding to death internally. The news hits us like a bomb. My stomach shrivels. Darwin has three malignant masses, on both kidneys and his liver. His bloated abdomen is believed to be filled with blood, leaking from a ruptured tumor.

It's almost exactly what happened to Kali. *We did a check-up three months ago to make sure he was okay!*

"How could this have happened?" Mark questions the specialist. Our tears run freely.

"Poor Darwin." I look through a wall of water at my sweet pup. He's lying on the cool tiles, stretched out. His tail makes soft thumps when he hears his name. Mark and I hug each other in disbelief. Again.

"How much longer does he have?" I croak.

"It's a matter of days at this point." The answer comes from far, far away.

This can't be true. This is so unfair. This isn't right.

"What else can we do?" I ask. "There must be something we can try?"

"I'm sorry," the vet responds. "There truly is nothing else you can do but make sure he doesn't suffer."

How will we know it's time?

The next day, Mark notices a red dot on Darwin's shaved belly. He immediately calls the radiologist to inquire about it. There might be a chance Darwin's blood didn't clot right; a chance that the blood in his belly, and his anemia, are the result of a clotting problem.

That's all we need to load our boy into the car and drive to New Hampshire again. A sprinkle of hope that this was a short nightmare. Another blood test is performed, only to erase that last bit of optimism. It's over. Disbelief. Pain. Sorrow. Buckets of tears. We're in shock.

If only it was in one kidney... If only he didn't get sick... If only he could be with us a few more years... If only...

Darwin's condition deteriorates rapidly from the moment we leave the clinic. Mark and I spoil him with bacon, steak, brie (his favorite cheese), and homemade treats. He drinks a lot, proof that his kidneys are failing.

His belly keeps expanding. Mark carries him up and down the stairs to our room. He isn't interested in walks and grows more uncomfortable every day. We shower him with hugs, love, sweet words. I kiss him on his nose, between his eyes. My favorite spot to connect with him. I used to stroke him there in *Irie's* cockpit, while his head rested on my lap, until he drifted into a contented sleep.

I don't think I ever cried this much. We cannot imagine a life without dogs, especially on the boat. Everything we did, the choices we made, the kind of boat we have, the way the days developed, it was with Darwin and Kali in mind. The doggy toys and gear we bought to take back to Grenada... to the home he'd never see again. An empty *Irie* for us to return to. Why would we visit beaches anymore? Or get up early? No more licks in the mornings, soft growls or huffs to warn us, a wagging tail to greet us, four-legged company everywhere we go.

Why would we even go back to our boat?

Mark's brother comes over to say goodbye. His parents have red eyes as well during dinner time. Mark and I are speechless. We're not ready to lose yet another member of our family. Darwin isn't even ten. We anticipated him to live until 16. It's not meant to be. We cannot postpone the inevitable. Darwin stares at us with a confused face.

It's time for him to find Kali.

Mark makes the worst phone call of his life to set up an appointment.

"I think he's doing better!" I walk Darwin to the car and he sniffs the bushes before tinkling. "He seems completely healthy. Almost happy. We shouldn't go yet. He can easily live another day. We need to cancel the appointment."

Mark stares at me with pain in his eyes. "We have to go through with this, sweetie. Don't make it harder than it already is." His voice is barely more than a whisper.

"I don't want to go. I don't want to do this!" I scream.

Darwin looks up with sad, inquisitive eyes.

"Do you want to stay home?" Mark asks, not sure what to do about my hysterical mood.

"No!" I'm convinced to be part of this. I need to be there. I need to say goodbye to my dear boy. I need to be there for Mark. He needs to be there for me. We help Darwin in the back of the car for his last ride. He loves cars. He loves everything – as long as he can be with us. Now, it's more important than ever for us to be with him.

After the nurse administers the fatal injection, we're alone in the room with our pup. His head rests on my lap. Mark and I are as close to his face as we can manage. We pet him. We stroke his side, adore his soft head, gently flatten his cute ears. We kiss his nose, whisper favorite words to him, and pour our remaining love over him. Our tears unite on his dying body.

"We will miss you, buddy. We're sorry this has to happen. Sweet, sweet boy. We love you so much."

When Darwin's last breath leaves his body, we can't get up. We sit there, holding our lifeless pet. We don't want to let go.

"Do you need more time?" the nurse asks, her head through the doorway.

"Yes, please." It is quiet, so dead quiet. His spirit is gone.

After a few more moments in silence, Mark indicates he needs to leave. There is nothing more for us here. I give Darwin a last kiss on the bridge of his nose, between his eyes. We pay our bill, get in the car, and drive home. Just the two of us, staring at the tear-stained road ahead.

🌙🌙🌙

On the plane ride back to Grenada, Mark and I are silent. Deep in thought. Half aware of what happens around us, half zombie.

"Darwin gave his life so Dru could survive." I try hard to see something positive in this dramatic turn of events. "Let's not forget that your sister is healing and has a chance to become cancer-free. That's a good thing. And we still have each other."

I attempt a smile. It doesn't sound as convincing as all those years ago on our first boat in Emeryville. With the rate at which our family is reducing, there is no reason to smile.

If there were any optimistic thoughts left, they disappear in the wet-ness, sweat, and grime of the boatyard in southern Grenada where we unpack our heavy bags full of expensive boat gear and colorful, obsolete, dog toys.

We pick up our lives on *Irie*. She's been relocated to a swampy area with mosquitoes and frogs. During the day, we slosh around in puddles. The heavy rains have turned the ground into mud mixed with toxic waste and blue bottom paint. My bare feet are exposed to water and chemicals. The power supply is inefficient and unreliable, and the water pressure is sporadic, especially when needed most.

After long days of heavy labor, Mark and I walk to the showers for a serious clean-up, only to find a trickle of cold water and soiled toilet bowls with no water to flush them. The psychological pain of losing Darwin is soon augmented by physical pain from having to squat all day, since the wet ground doesn't allow sitting or kneeling near difficult to reach areas under the hulls. The mosquitoes drive us crazy.

Darwin would have hated it here.

After a week of this, we pay another exorbitant bill, chase the remain-ing frogs off, take a few fat mosquitoes with us, and sail away with a spar-kling *Irie*. Under the waterline, anyway.

Our sailboat is empty without Darwin. The trips to shore feel incom-plete. Something is missing. We keep looking around. Where is that comfy dog at our feet?

After three and a half years of owning *Irie*, I learn how to lock our door from the inside. We cope in our ever-busy life, which creates the best distraction. The Wirie business thrives and I publish articles. The question on everybody's lips is: "Are you getting another dog?" Our answer: "Not yet." We always told others that if you already have a dog before setting off, make it work. But if you're cruising without and contemplate adopting one – don't, because it makes sailing more complicated.

It is more convenient to have Mark help me carry grocery bags, but after taking care of these errands myself for a year, because we couldn't leave Darwin alone, I miss my me time, no matter how sweaty and back-breaking those days were.

Losing our dog makes me realize something else. I loved having our family of four, and then three. Darwin and Kali were the main reason Mark and I met each other, grew closer, and became a couple through thick and thin. Our dogs meant everything and guided us towards decisions and destinations. How will we pick where to anchor in a bay now, without needing a beach close by for potty breaks and walks?

We had a purpose, we had living beings to take care of, adventures to share, and observations that made us laugh. The joy of seeing our pups chase each other on the beach, fetch a coconut from the ocean, or dig a hole in the sand is irreplaceable. I feel empty.

Does Mark experience the same?

With our dogs gone, is there a reason to stay in this relationship? All those tough times in the past... Mark's frustrating episodes as a boat owner then and now...

Doting on our furballs, I could always cheer everyone up: "Look at our wonderful family. We're together and we can handle anything." Now, it's just the two of us.

Is that enough? A family of two? Can you even call that a family? Is it time to have children? What is keeping me with Mark, and his business that is sucking the pleasure out of cruising? I could be free. No more responsibilities.

The thoughts make me sick.

Chapter 15

Romance in the Caribbean

April 30th and our wedding party are quickly approaching. Life on *Irie* in St. Martin is pretty much the same as the last few months: busy, busy, busy. Mark has been working non-stop to test developments for our new product, The Wirie^{AP}, and has been researching, diagnosing, and rewriting code, while trying his best to communicate with the hardware developers in Taiwan. He does this about ten hours a day, plus often in the evenings because of the time difference. I take care of what resembles our life aboard, write, and run errands.

In the meantime, business is good, and our worldwide sales have picked up. We locate parts needed for our cruise south and complete boat projects. On top of this, we have a wedding party to plan.

Last I checked, the mystery jewelry box was still behind the stack of books. I expect a marriage proposal, silly as this may be. Mark and I are already married on paper. We're busy preparing for our second big day. Not that the first one in Annapolis, four years ago, was that big. We're finally having the Caribbean wedding party I dreamed about. And we're doing it right, with wedding rings, friends, and family.

But what's the deal with the hidden ring? I guess I'll find out in a few days.

Or not.

My first attempt to find elegant wedding rings was met with an answer that rubbed the excitement straight out of it: "No silver on the boat! It oxidizes too easily, especially in this climate." Silver and a salty environment do not go together and that was that. Despite our shopping phobia, Mark and I make a concerted effort to take the bus to Philipsburg, shopping central, and a major cruise ship destination.

We're overwhelmed by the number of jewelry stores.

We humor the salespeople and ourselves for about two hours. We've been looking for something simple, silver colored, and not too expensive. In case it gets lost in an unfathomable hole on *Irie* or the bottom of the deep blue sea.

"What do you think?" Mark asks as we sit on a picnic bench, gazing at the calm, indigo bay of Philipsburg. Tourists mill about jewelry store after jewelry store after souvenir store after jewelry store. Bars sport loud music and restaurant patios overflow. Beach chairs are occupied by visitors in Hawaiian shirts and colorful bikinis boasting pink skin.

"Well..." I sigh. "As always, it comes down to how much we're willing to spend. Do we want rings, or do we want beautiful rings? You don't even wear jewelry."

"Nope, this is all you. I don't mind spending a bit more on rings if you found something you really like. You only get married once. Or twice, in our situation."

"I like those white gold ones from the last store, with their simple design and curved lines. But they cost 250 dollars each." I gasp as I pronounce the amount out loud. "We might be able to get 50 dollars off the total price, but that's still an awful lot of money."

"Of the fancy ones we saw, I prefer those as well. But what if you lose yours? You'll be devastated. I'm okay getting them, as long as you're sure about your decision," Mark says.

"When am I ever sure about a decision? Maybe we should get those stainless-steel ones. They match our personalities and lifestyle better. And our budget."

"We are cheapskates and steel rings are better than no rings, I guess."

"It would be fitting to add stainless-steel rings to our stainless-steel collection of boat parts. It's the only thing that survives in a marine environment and we want our love and our rings to last, right? Let's do it!"

We bargain the price down and spend 80 dollars on two rings, sized to fit our ring fingers and put into ugly corduroy pouches. Proud with our new purchase – the price is right and the material perfect – and relieved the ring buying ordeal is over, we meet our friends Rosie and Sim at happy hour in Lagoonies.

"We did it!" I yell at Rosie, waving the green pouches above my head. She's standing at the bar with her husband. We've enjoyed planning my wedding party together, roaming around the island, walking sandy beaches, swimming in azure waters, and showering in a massive rainstorm.

She had joined me a few days earlier to help find a wedding dress. Like in the movies, we went from store to store to try on dresses. Unlike on the big screen, we settled for a simple white summer dress with spaghetti straps and a relatively flattering bottom part, which flanks my wide hips without grabbing them. For good measure, we picked a grey dress of the same material, in case I wanted to change after the ceremony. Or if I spilled on the white one, which would be more likely. At 20 dollars a dress, I didn't mind getting a back-up.

"Let me see," Rosie demands as we approach the bar. "How did it go?"

"It went alright. We decided to go for stainless-steel instead of the fancier white gold."

I open one of the pouches and put the smaller ring on.

"Why are you putting it on your right hand?" Rosie asks.

"What do you mean?" As I look at her wedding ring, securely fastened around her left ring finger, an eerie feeling engulfs me. My stomach contracts. *Shit!*

"You're kidding! Why didn't that woman in the store tell us we're supposed to wear our rings on our left hand?"

"There are countries, like Norway, where wedding bands grace the right ring finger," Rosie states. "The sales rep probably noticed your accent and thought you were from Northern Europe. Maybe in Belgium rings are worn on the right? What about your parents?"

My face lights up. If that's the case, I'll feel much better.

"My parents don't wear their rings. They are no frills people, like me." I try to remember Belgians and their wedding bands. I'm pretty sure Rosy and Peter slid the rings on left fingers during their ceremony four years ago.

"Mark, the rings needed to fit our left fingers, not our right ones! How could you not know this? You're the one who's been married before."

With a look of *Who cares which finger it fits on?* he turns to me. "I guess I didn't remember. You're the woman. Women should know these things!"

Well, I'm not your everyday woman who cares about typical woman stuff. And I've never been married before – *never wanted to* – or I would have avoided this pickle.

This is his fault.

"You were married for seven years, wearing your wedding ring every day, on your *left* hand. How can you forget that?" I grumble. "What do we do now? The party is in a few days."

"We can either go back and let them resize the rings or we can move on and wear them on our right hand. You can anyway. Wearing jewelry on a boat is asking for trouble. Even off the boat, I don't like it."

Yes, we established that loud and clear.

"You wore a ring with your ex." I mope a bit more, knowing this is not the issue at hand. "We'll keep them like this." I go for the easiest solution.

How can I fatten up my left ring finger?

"I tried wearing a wedding ring on my left hand and that didn't work out. Maybe I have better luck wearing it on my other hand," Mark says to Sim. While our friends laugh out loud, I crack a smile as well.

Maybe he'll wear the ring after all.

🌊🌊🌊

I hope it doesn't rain; that the wind won't destroy our decorations. I hope Eli makes it in time with the side dishes. And brings the two helpers we hired. I hope everyone shows up. That my dad is okay walking me down the improvised aisle. I hope Ed doesn't lose the rings. And that Brian prepared a nice speech. I hope everything goes as planned. That everybody will have fun.

The tables around the pool display sarongs, conch shells, and candles. My mind set on using the eight smelly shells I harvested in Barbuda as centerpieces, it took me and the sun ages to dry and clean them. My parents and Mark's closest relatives join us in the villa. His sister Dru, still going through cancer treatment, remains at home. I invited my entire family – brother, grandparents, aunts, uncles, cousins – but nobody else from my family attends.

Belgian Rosy and her husband, Peter, fly in for the event, as do Mark's friends, Joe and Elsa. All other guests are friends we made sailing throughout the Caribbean. Ed is promoted from former crush to best man and ring master, and British Rosie is maid-of-honor, not that I know what this means or what her job is supposed to be. Luckily, she does.

My other girlfriends decorate the beach for our unofficial ceremony, while the husbands haul chairs and rum punch that way. Sister-in-law Kris creates a beautiful bouquet from the flowers in the garden. She and Tim assisted with the food prep for dinner as well. German photographer friend Axel captures the precious moments.

Mark and I had requested help instead of wedding gifts.

"Do you want me to do your make-up?" Rosie asks. I didn't even think about cosmetics and hope she brought some from her boat. She did. I so appreciate her assistance. Make-up aside, I wear the elegant silver necklace Mark's mom gave me. It goes splendidly with my summer dress. My basic attire is complemented with something old (a white anklet made by Rosie that I've been wearing for over a year), something borrowed (Rosie's perfume), and something blue (bracelets sent from the UK by Emily). The something new is my white dress.

Before I realize it, everyone is gone from the room, and my dad knocks on the door. Not one to care about institutions, celebrations, or gatherings, he agreed to fly to St. Martin, just to see his daughter. He is happiest on his couch at home, deciphering sudoku or crossword puzzles. He's relatively quiet and possesses a sarcastic, dry sense of humor only I seem to appreciate. Yet that's his language – direct and controversial.

"You ready?" His expression screams *I can't believe you made me do something this stupid!*

"Be happy you don't have to join me in a church. Are you really wearing those ugly *sloefkes*?" My dad loves his indoor slippers. Ideally with socks stretched high. Today is no exception. "At least get rid of the socks."

While I – and everybody else – walk around in bare feet, he stubbornly scoops up half the beach as we walk "down the aisle." I urge him to crack a smile. For the photos.

As I approach Mark, everybody hums "Here comes the bride."

How many rum punches have been consumed?

"We're not taking anything back to the villa!" rum representatives Sim and Jon had said earlier, carrying my homemade concoction to the beach.

Mark and I join Brian before the Caribbean Sea.

I hope people will hear us over the sound of the waves. I should have thought about that.

It would be rude to ask Brian to speak up.

As he's about to read his speech from a piece of paper, Mark signals him to stop.

Now what? I look at the small crowd. I look at Brian. I look at Mark.

Out of nowhere, he drops to one knee.

"Liesbet, will you marry me?" he asks. On the verge. At the very last moment.

Did he wait until this day to be sure of the answer?

Still, it's a complete surprise; possibly the only proposal ever, absent of an engagement ring.

"Yes, of course!" The spectators applaud. *Am I on a movie set?* Then, Brian shares his sweet and heartfelt words as only he can. Mark and I read our vows to each other and tear up.

"Dear Mark,

I met and cuddled Kali and Darwin. Then, at a distance, I saw you standin'.
It could be called 'love at first sight.' Our being together felt totally right.
The following weeks flew on by. With confusion and a final cry.
There was anticipation and stuff to do. Following my decision to be with you.
The four of us became a family. The way life is expected to be.
With time and love and some romance. Until we drastically changed our plans.
Since that day we've been on the move. Finding our mutual travel groove.
Exploring countries by land and sea. That is more how life should be.
From the moment we met in 2004, we've been together almost every hour.
24/7 is not easy to achieve. But we manage well, I do believe.
There have been times of sorrow and fun. Of heavy clouds and rays of sun.
We stuck together and held tight, sharing our love, companions in fight.
We support each other in all we do. We share the stress, the joys, the loo.
We follow our sailing and traveling dream. Together forever as a perfect team.
With these words I hope to express, my love for you, more or less.
Together we are meant to be. Because you are the one for me!

Mark,

You are the sun in my sky, the rainwater in my tank. You are the air in my lungs and the fire in my heart. You are the honey in my yogurt, the fruit in my cereal. You are the chutney with my curry and the mayonnaise with my fries. You are the nutmeg in my punch, the rum in my coke. You are the mint in my mojito and the sunrise in my tequila. You are the electricity for my battery bank, the fuel for my engine. You are the wind in my sails and The Wirie for my *Irie!*"

I thought this part was funny, but nobody laughs.
See, they don't hear anything we say.
I return my focus to our intimate scene at the water's edge. Mark's

voice trembles.

"Dear Liesbet,

I love your willingness to try anything. I love your desire for a simple life. I love your love for Kali and Darwin. I love your patience with me. I love your success with your writing. I love your Belgian chocolate and Belgian beer. I love our life together. I love that all your food needs to be eaten in proportion. I love your desire for independence. I love your willingness to scrape all the barnacles off the bottom of *Irie*."

Laugher – ha, they must hear.

"I love that you said 'yes' to marry me."

How was he so sure when writing his text yesterday?

"I love that you don't get upset when I don't shower for four days. I love that I can make you smile and laugh. I love that you don't get seasick anymore. I love your addiction to travel. I love that we get to spend the rest of our lives together. I love your spirit and soul. I love that you are never demanding of me. I love that our world is so small, yet the world so big. I love that you're a cheap date."

Lots of laughter, especially from me.

"I love that you love everything I cook for you. I love your support for me in everything I do. I love the support and help we receive from our friends. I love your family and my new family. I love my family. I love our future together. I love you."

I'm quiet and cherish the moment. I sink into my dearest's eyes. Mark's mom reads her poem about the ebb and flow of the ocean and of love, followed by another poem picked by Kris, which Brian reads.

Our cruising friend Dave on *Tatia* couldn't attend the wedding but composed a song about us to the tunes of *If I had a million dollars*. It's called *They got married in five minutes*. We play it on speakers, while everybody follows the lyrics on sheets of paper distributed by Rosie.

Ed dunks our stainless-steel rings into the ocean for approval from Neptune and to ensure them a rust-free life. Mark slides the smallest one on my right ring finger. I repeat the process with the other one. The gesture must look correct to half of our guests. Besides Belgium and the US, our collection of friends originates in Germany, New Zealand, South Africa, Venezuela, Egypt, and the UK.

The wedding ceremony concludes with a blessing by Mark's father, and a short statement from my dad: "Take her, she's all yours now. My responsibility is finished!"

"You may now kiss the bride." Brian says and laughs.

As my lips touch Mark's, soft and long, the sound of the lapping waves matches my heartbeat in one of the most romantic settings of the Caribbean. The only things missing are palm trees and Darwin. The girls did a wonderful job creating a path with palm fronds, but our sweet boy is irreplaceable.

We join our friends, who cheer, toss rose petals, and drink rum punch. Jon and Sim make sure nothing goes to waste. Axel organizes a variety of photo shoots.

Back at the villa, the balmy evening starts with a first course of smoked salmon, different pâtés, an array of French cheeses, crunchy baguettes, and local plantain chips. This is followed by succulent grilled chicken, beef, and shrimp skewers with a variety of homemade side dishes and French patisseries for dessert. The self-serve bar is assembled in a nook of the patio and contains gallons of beer, wine, liquor, soda, and juices. Despite everyone's best efforts, most beverages have to be taken home to *Irie*, making provisioning for our departure easier.

"It took us four years to have a wedding party. I guess we will go on our honeymoon in 2015. Thank you so much for being here and sharing this special occasion with us."

After I end my speech, our extensive playlist of favorite songs commences; the dinner selection is followed by the party one. During our opening dance of *Burn One Down* merging into *With My Own Two Hands* from Ben Harper, we're joined first by our parents, then by our friends, who dance the night away. More than once, I peek at Ed, wondering what he's thinking. He and Emily broke up a little while ago. I never thought they were a good match, but neither would he and I have been.

Probably.

I feel fortunate about the way things progressed. I have Emily to thank for that.

The day after our "Loyal Wedding," so called because it competed with the "Royal Wedding" of Prince William in Westminster Abbey, we invite our best sailing friends for a swim in the pool and a feast of leftovers.

Being in this villa for a week relieved our stress for the party and created a perfect debrief environment. Not only did everyone have a fabulous time, this one-week wedding celebration might go down as the cheapest in Caribbean history, costing Mark and me less than 3,000 dollars. This includes food and drinks for the entire week, all the alcohol, the party favors, most of the food at our wedding party (Eli provided the side dishes), and Mark and my share for accommodation. We couldn't have had a better time in a better location.

I grab my husband's hand – I have no problem anymore calling him that – and melt into his eyes.

"We did it," I whisper, "and we have wedding rings!" I lift our intertwined hands and show off the simple, single ring. A ring that has absolutely nothing to do with a black jewelry box, hidden away on our boat in the lagoon.

Chapter 16

What's Next?

Our wedding party quickly turns into an unforgettable but distant memory, and our efforts return to the boat and the business. When we leave St. Martin in June 2011, we have a feeling it will be for the last time. Mark and I set out on our longest trip thus far, a 48-hour bash into high seas and winds to reach Martinique before my cousin Griet and her family arrive from Belgium.

Once we clear land and the waves are in full swing, it doesn't take long before I'm hanging over the side with my life jacket and harness on. Mark takes the first shift, while I retire downstairs, tossed around by violent swell and wind chop.

When it's my turn to take care of *Irie*, moving upstairs has me vomit again. Mark sends me back to bed. At 2am, he's exhausted and soaking wet. I'm on watch for three hours, switching between my seat at the helm station and the stern of the boat, inspecting the waves up-close. It's a terrible night with confused seas, steep waves, and heaps of seawater drenching the cockpit.

Time to reclaim my sea legs!

Griet, Wim, and their son and daughter adjust to the cruising life like pros. The couple has joined us on *Irie* – without their children – one time before. They fit right in. They're the most flexible guests a boat owner can host, and they share in the tasks whenever we allow them. We generally prefer to execute onboard chores ourselves. Doing dishes in a bucket, however, can't go wrong. Griet masters that job. Until the day she forgets to remove the silverware from the bucket before emptying it in the ocean. Like arrows stuck in a target, all our knives and forks pierce the bottom of the bay when she retrieves them the following morning. Thankfully, we're anchored in less than 20 feet. Wim helps Mark with anything boat related, eager to become a sailor himself.

Entertaining four people on our 35-foot boat is fun, but also taxing, not in the least because Mark is busy with the business and we can only stay in bays with reliable internet. Nevertheless, everyone has a good time, and I enjoy playing tour guide and practicing Dutch.

I'm especially happy that we provide an inside look of the boating life to our teenage guests. How cool would it be to raise children while cruising? Such an experience and the perfect environment for hands-on learning opportunities. Being a primary school teacher puts me in an excellent position to home school, as we have seen many families do on the water. The children of these couples appear mature, open-minded, social, articulate, respectful, and smart.

Maybe, one day, Mark and I can raise one or two of our own this way.

꩜ ꩜ ꩜

Everything ends. Even our presence in the Eastern Caribbean.

For three years, our southern terminus has been Grenada and the northern one St. Martin, instead of Puerto Rico. I could've gotten my US citizenship by now if we'd picked a slightly different winter port.

The hindsight hurdles.

But we made these choices ourselves and have no regrets. Mark and I remain a mixed Belgian-American couple for the time being. Not tied to the US anymore by a green, shiny card – or potential citizenship – I am still related to one of its citizens, for good or for bad.

Mark's priorities and moods are shifting away from my passions.

We need the money from the business, but is it worth giving up our freedom to cruise wherever we like? We require a sailboat that's immaculately taken care of, but does he have to yell every time a project causes frustration? Staying in flat, protected anchorages is more comfortable, but am I willing to miss out on attractive destinations and intriguing experiences because a harbor is too choppy? Internet is indispensable to us, but that doesn't mean I happily skip remote islands and tempting bays.

Yes, there are enough places in the world that are easier to reach, but I'm on a boat *now* and I want to see and do the "things to see and do" along the way.

"Do you think I want to work and sit behind my computer eight hours a day instead of exploring the islands?" Mark's question is paired with an accusing look.

I never saw it that way. When anyone does something hours on end, I assume there's a level of enjoyment involved. Is Mark's excitement about the business waning and is he ready for more sailing fun? Maybe he's sick of his wife's curled bottom lip when talking about remaining east and positively affected by her glistening eyes when bringing up the Western Caribbean?

Whatever it may be, the decision is made in Grenada: we're going west! We're heading into the unknown. The one thing we do know is, once you sail west, there's no going back. Unless you take a plane.

"I can't believe you guys are leaving," my friend Rosie chokes. "I'm excited but also sad. Part of me wishes Sim and I could be more adventurous and head west again. Truth be told, we like the Eastern Caribbean. It's easy and convenient here, and there's so much to see and do."

"True. Sailing *is* easy with the trade winds. Three years has been enough for us, though. I'm itching to explore new places. Now that we don't have dogs anymore, we might as well go on longer passages," I say.

"Will you keep going and cross the Pacific?" she asks.

"I don't think so. Mark has always said that *Irie* is too small and ill-suited for an ocean passage. Who knows? We might stop cruising altogether. Boat problems never cease and with the business, life has become stressful and complicated."

"Are you thinking about getting off the boat?"

"Nope, but Mark and I agreed from the beginning that if it isn't fun anymore, we'd quit."

How do you decide what not enough fun is?

It's a question I ponder more and more.

"What will you do then? Sailing surely is more enjoyable than living in a house and working in a cubicle."

"I never sat in an office or a cubicle, so I wouldn't know. And I've never owned a house. Who said anything about going back to work or settling?"

Most cruisers think there are only two options in life: the conventional way of a nine-to-five job while living in a sticks-and-bricks home or sailing on your own boat. They're wrong.

I continue, "There are so many alternatives. Maybe we get a camper again. Maybe we volunteer somewhere. Maybe we travel to Southeast Asia and rent a cheap villa in Bali. But for now, we're off to chase the horizon into the sunset!"

"Have you brushed up on your Spanish?" Rosie asks.

"Not really. I'll have to wing it and speak French with a Spanish flair. I'll use the words I remember and lots of gestures. That should do the trick. As long as nobody provides elaborate responses when all I expect is a 'si' or 'no.'" I snicker, remembering our RV trip in Central America. The long answers I received to my simple questions confused me more than I already was. We'll figure it out. We're not the first *gringos* to sail in South and Central America.

"Be careful! Stay away from the Venezuelan coast. I've heard too many pirate stories, even from people we know," she warns.

We have as well. The danger zone keeps expanding. Isla Margarita has been off-limits for years, and now attractive Los Testigos is also too close to the mainland – within reach of the pirogues' motors – to visit safely. There have even been attacks between Grenada and Trinidad.

"Don't worry," I assure her. "We'll only stop at outer islands away from Chavez's reach. No pirate's outboard engine should be able to make it there."

I embrace her again. I'll miss her. It's wonderful to have found a soulmate, someone to share my thoughts and feelings with, especially since contact with Belgian friends has faded.

"When will we see each other again?" she asks.

"I have no idea, but I'm sure we will at some point, somewhere on this planet."

I refuse to believe this might be it for us. Some connections last a lifetime; this has got to be one of those. Saying goodbye to friends is a familiar practice among cruisers, but often you run into them again. Unless you leave a popular sailing area behind and exchange it for less-visited locales, like the Western Caribbean. At least our need for internet has dual purpose now.

After hugging Rosie and Sim goodbye, we focus on the western horizon and literally sail into the sunset. The prospect of new adventures holds the tears back. It feels as if we're heading to the edge of the world, as if we're leaving everything dear and familiar behind.

Isn't that part of the adventure?

Everything sounds better before it becomes tangible, when it's still far out. In my head, every plan is perfect; the future always looks promising. Mark often refers to it as *in your world*.

Yes, in *my* world there's no room for negativity. Everything is exciting and possible.

Our progress is slow. We're now sailing downwind. It's a novel experience with its own challenges. We only have one small headsail to use and forgo the mainsail. We want to stay on course and settle for a speed of three to four knots. The wind is dead behind us. Imagine a cartoon with Mr. Wind – full, round cheeks filled with air – blowing against the backside of our sail and *Irie* progressing at walking speed. It takes two days and two nights to make our first landfall in South America. There are no Caribbean boat boys trying to sell anything from fruit to fish to handmade souvenirs to island tours, to help with a mooring ball or a rope to shore.

But we do get visitors late afternoon.

"¡Hola! ¿Como estan?" I take the line of the Guardia Costa boat and invite the two officials onboard. Time to find out what the usual procedures are for anchoring in the out islands of Venezuela, while not being checked into the country properly, which isn't required when passing through these islands.

Or so we've heard.

The men smile. They accept a cup of cold coke and make themselves comfortable in our cockpit.

"Where did you arrive from?" "How long are you staying?" "What is your next port?"

The rudimentary questions come in Spanish and are answered in somewhat Spanish. They're friendly and we chit chat. Before our trip west, other cruisers told us to stock up on small bottles of rum "for the Coast Guard when they come by." Here they are and I'm curious about their approach of the booze request. By now they have mentioned a few times that, thanks to them, La Blanquilla is a *muy seguro* place.

Is this the cue?

"Today is my colleague's birthday," one of the men exclaims, looking at his accomplice.

Mark and I exchange glances.

"Really? Congratulations!"

A sheepish smile from the "birthday boy" follows. His buddy continues, "We're having a party tonight. Maybe you have some liquor to contribute?"

I grab a small bottle of rum. The officials appreciate it and ask whether we have more Coca Cola. "El Capitan at the base would love a cold soda as well."

Our only cold coke bottle served its purpose, so we hand them an unrefrigerated one. The visitors get up, satisfied. Checking in is never mentioned. They allow our presence as long as desired, invite us to their base, and hope we enjoy the island, especially Americano Bay.

I thank them and – recalling our explorations of earlier that day – say, "Americano Bay es muy bonito."

I look at the arid shoreline and wince, remembering that little excursion. Mark and I had followed narrow donkey trails from Playa Yaque, where *Irie* is anchored, to gorgeous Americano Bay, named after the American Bob Blankenship who lived on the island before anyone else was around. He built a small house, of which ruins still remain, and landed his plane next to it.

From a cliff, we could see the deep blue ocean through cracks in the rocks. One hole revealed a cave and a whirlpool of seawater. The picturesque bay with its sandy shores had invited us for a refreshing swim and a choppy snorkel. There, our shady spot under a rocky ledge looked out over the peaceful surroundings and a natural bridge.

The unique location made up for the hot and sweaty walk to get there and the cacti attacking me along the path. It had taken Mark half an hour to remove the stubborn needles from my legs, while I let out muffled cries so as to not upset the serene environment. Just like that time in Mexico, when I'd unsuspectingly squatted in a cactus bush to pee and he had to pull needles from my bum. My cries were not so muffled then.

We bid our visitors farewell with another "Feliz Cumpleaños." Smiles are exchanged.

I retreat inside to check our gift/bribe supplies. Still enough rum for Los Roques and Los Aves.

🌀 🌀 🌀

When we departed Grenada, we left civilization behind for two weeks, a personal record. It meant time for the boat, for each other, for sailing, and for exploring. It also meant no internet connection and, in turn, giving the business a break, throwing stress and frustration overboard. Brother-in-law Tim temporarily took over customer support. Mark and I filled the days with the occasional chore ashore, lots of cooking, smaller projects such as sewing, cleaning, fixing boat issues lower on the list, plenty of relaxing, staring at beautiful surroundings from our cockpit, snorkeling reefs, walking powdery beaches and barren land, reading for Mark, writing for me...

We wished it could last forever. But real life awaited and it required groceries, a washing machine, and internet.

In Bonaire, we find all that, plus a national park, excellent dive sites, safe roads, and multiple attractions. Old slave housing, salt flats with flamingos, and the vibrant town of Kralendijk beckon. The water surrounding the island and its little brother, Klein Bonaire, is crystal clear. Colorful fish and healthy coral are abundant. Mark and I don't dive, but snorkeling is rewarding as well. You just jump off your boat and swim to the sea wall, gazing at flashy creatures and vibrant coral.

People even speak Dutch in Bonaire. If it wasn't for Mark thinking this island is too small to live and work, I might consider moving here one day. Temporarily, of course.

After a few weeks of island hopping, Mark and I find ourselves in the C of the ABC-islands: Curaçao.

Our first impression of unfriendly bus drivers and Dutch expats claiming the lagoon of Spanish Waters as their territory has not been favorable. We hope to change that on my birthday. Instead of gifts, I opt for the experience of a *normal* tourist – to have a fun day in the capital of Willemstad, a colorful, clean, and classy haven on the island.

Without a plan, we take the dinghy ashore and mosey over to the bus stop. My only requests: no stress and no rush. In town, we stroll through the shopping streets and cross the pedestrian bridge to Otrobanda on the other side of the river. An impressive pool on the roof of a hotel draws us in like a magnet. After entering the building and taking the elevator, pretending we know what we're doing, we arrive at a man-made beach with clean towels, comfy recliners, and two infinity pools. I peel off a layer of clothing and plunge in. When we want to order one of those colorful drinks and realize we need a room card, it's time to go.

Eating sandwiches on a shady bench in the shopping district follows. Then, we check out the other fancy hotel in the area, the Kura Hulanda. There's a slave museum, but the entrance fee is a bit steep, so we explore the grounds of the hotel instead. We find ourselves in a restored, historical neighborhood, with a maze of alleys leading to a marble garden, decorated rooms, tiny museums, outdoor eating areas, patios, and swimming pools set in tropical gardens; a contrast with our life on *Irie*.

I prefer fresh water over the salty sea any time. Shall we change into swimwear again?

Not needed. After a refreshing torrential downpour, we move to an upscale bar to spend our museum money on elegant cocktails. The view over to Punda, a UNESCO World Heritage Site and the main center of Willemstad, is attractive, even under overcast skies.

Our last stop before the grand finale of dinner is Iguana Café. Yes, you can eat iguana here, but we only order a beer and a glass of wine at our seats near the river; the lights of Otrobanda in the background.

The waterfront restaurant we choose has an array of seafood dishes and reasonable prices. It takes ages before our waitress shows up to write down our order.

After sitting in the outdoor restaurant for another hour without food, Mark finds the manager to tell her what's going on. We receive a different, wide-smiled, and capable waitress. From now on it's bliss! She's attentive, the drinks are on the house, and a discount will be applied to the bill. The food is delicious and filling. Another portion of fries shows up. *On the house.* We feel like kings. We eat and drink until we're stuffed. The bill is the cherry on top.

I thoroughly enjoy the concept of this 36th birthday: letting loose and spending money on enjoyment instead of things required for the boat.

Experiences over material goods.

Similar to what follows after sex, I have but one remark: "We should do this more often."

Chapter 17

Paradise Found... and Lost

When we enter Colombia, it becomes clear that we're exploring the frontier; places not frequently visited by sailing yachts. In the Eastern Caribbean, we mostly encountered retirees who'd cruise for six months on and off, their sailboats safely hauled out during hurricane season.

Now, we meet the hardened and dedicated kind of voyagers: young couples on sabbatical for two years, people who cruise indefinitely and make money along the way, parents following their dreams while the children are still young and manageable. And spunky retirees who sold their belongings and sail full-time with no restraints (except for visits home to see the grandkids).

There's one couple under 45, Mark and Michele, who had worked ten years towards the goal of cruising and are now living the life they'd always imagined. Them, I envy most. They're childless, happy, excited, and committed to being on the water.

As for my Mark and me, we started cruising in 2007 with a timeline of "as long as we can afford it and as long as it's fun." Does our lifestyle still tick those boxes?

Often, we are told we're lucky to make money while traveling.

Don't get me started on the word lucky. People have been calling me that as long as I remember, just because I chose a life less ordinary. What does luck have to do with making decisions or shaking responsibilities to pursue freedom?

Mark and I are fortunate to have been born in a first-world country to understanding parents. Other than that, it's all about choices. People who get stuck in the rat race, have a family, or count on a big income to cover big expenses say they don't have options. They do. Period.

We meet plenty of couples who homeschool and offer their children a worldly education. We know from experience that jobs can be found (or created) and that once you have a sound boat, life aboard costs less than life ashore.

Yes, Mark and I mostly sustain ourselves with The Wirie, but doesn't that have more to do with skills, dedication, and priorities than luck?

What about the fun box?

The last three years, Mark has been working tons for little financial reward. We're still digging into savings and feel restricted about where we can cruise and how we spend our days. We're trapped in a different kind of rat race – I call it the *cat race* – where productivity from the comfort of our catamaran is being hindered by circumstances, remote locations, and unreliable internet.

Mark mostly enjoys the work and the challenge, but it's a frustrating combination, while the inviting settings beckon us to play. Add a never-ending list of boat issues to the mix and it's safe to say that the fun level is diminishing.

Life's still exciting to me, the spouse with few responsibilities. I enjoy being resourceful, living on a budget, and exploring the world by sailboat. Mark struggles with the enjoyment factor but is looking forward to the next set of laid-back tropical isles.

Reaching Panama, we don't want to miss out on the remote and unique San Blas islands, an autonomous archipelago inhabited by Guna Indians, who still live in a primitive, authentic way, somewhat similar to us. They collect rainwater, fish for food, and co-exist with Mother Nature. We're generally welcome to visit the islands and beautiful beaches, but in the more traditional areas a $10 fee is collected by the *congreso*.

The number one rule in Guna land: do not take coconuts. Coconut collection is a major means for the Indians to make money from visitors, Colombian trading boats, and copra factories on the mainland. Another source of income is tourism. The Gunas benefit from visiting yachties, who – in addition to paying for the privilege of being here – buy goods and services from the locals. Jewelry and handmade *molas* (intricately sewn pieces of cloth in different colors) are best-sellers. *Molas* are part of the indigenous women's clothing and tourists use them to hang on the wall or turn into pillowcases.

We want to slow down and savor the land, the water, the sky. We found the perfect spot for that, but how do we keep the business going?

In the Eastern Caribbean, there was wireless internet in most places. The Wirie helped and turned *Irie* into an office with a view. The San Blas Islands are another cup of tea. WiFi is non-existent. Friends told us that 2G service through cell towers works adequately at best, at certain times of the day. Mark and I succumb to taking the internet situation as it comes.

With a dongle bought in Colombia and hauled up the flag halyard and a SIM-card purchased in Guna Yala, we're set. Near cell towers, we s-l-o-w-l-y access the internet. When out of reach, we spend a day or two enjoying the area and move on.

For every four hours Mark spends online, he gets one hour of work done. I give up writing emails and posting blogs after two hours of trying or, on a cloudy day, when my laptop battery is empty.

That's the reality from now on. The trade-off is worth it: we're in paradise.

We sail from one exotic anchorage to another, chasing flat water, peaceful surroundings, and gorgeous views. I indulge in the remote, tropical lifestyle. It's simple and straightforward; we're self-sufficient. We live and survive, using Mother Earth and her bounty. Back to the basics!

We meet friends onshore and buy crabs and lobsters from fishermen rowing up to *Irie* in their *ulus* (dugout canoes). In the more popular areas, Geraldo swings by in his motorboat every week to sell an array of afford-able vegetables and fruit from the mainland. Sometimes he has frozen chickens and beer on offer. His arrival leads to excitement on the VHF radio and causes traffic jams of buzzing dinghies, trying to catch him and his wares before the selection dwindles.

We wake up with the sun, work in the morning, and snorkel, walk, or read in the afternoon. Then, we jump in the clear ocean to take a bath; we get wet, wash up with shampoo, and lower ourselves again to rinse off. We use our sun shower for a final freshwater rinse in the cockpit. Its water is hot enough from the ambient temperature; placing it in the sun would scorch us. We've showered like this for years, saving our tank water for cooking, drinking, and rinsing dishes – and avoiding bathroom clean-up. I still can't believe it took a full year of using Joy dish soap to lather our hair and bodies before we discovered shampoo worked the same magic in salt water. Not smelling like clean dishes anymore was a drastic improvement to our bathing ritual.

We cook healthy, creative dinners with items found in the fridge or the food locker and do the dishes in salt water. Whoever remains inside rinses the cleaned stack with fresh water from a pierced coke bottle. Our 53-gallon water tank lasts three weeks this way. When heavy rain arrives, we clean the roof of our catamaran and collect water. I also have a separate cloth strung above the side deck to guide rainfall into jugs, for laundry. Now that we've reached the boonies, I wash our clothes sufficiently with rainwater aboard or well water ashore.

When civilization is needed to stock up the boat, visit a marine store, deal with internet chores requiring more bandwidth (like sending high resolution photos to go with my articles), or help our friends Axel and Liz cross the Panama Canal, we sail *Irie* to the mainland.

Portobelo becomes our port of call. We take in the fort ruins and reminisce about visiting with Darwin and Kali on our extended RV-trip in 2006. Who would have guessed then, gazing over Portobelo Bay and its dozens of sailboats, we'd be one of them one day?

We have come full circle.

"I guess you two are next," Axel says, after we emerge in the Pacific Ocean on his sailboat *Gudrun*.

The Panama Canal consists of three locks at each end and Lake Gatun in the middle. Each pleasure craft requires a crew of at least five people – the captain and four helpers – to take care of the ropes to shore. These helpers are called line handlers. Mark and I make up half. Cruisers assist each other to gain experience and so their friends don't need to hire crew. Line handling is also a unique way for a backpacker – or for Mark six years ago – to transit the canal. It builds confidence to line up another trip or to take your own boat through one day.

"I don't think so. I'm happy we made it this far with *Irie*. Mark doesn't want to cross an ocean in her, as she's built for coastal cruising. And we're enjoying the San Blas. No need to keep moving now that we found peace and rest."

"I know you guys…" Axel smiles. "You'll get restless again. We'll be waiting for you in French Polynesia or New Zealand."

"Sure," I say, "if you're there long enough, we might visit by plane."

Again, we bid farewell to good friends. They're the ones to venture further afield this time. We wish them smooth sailing to the Galapagos Islands.

It must be amazing to interact with wildlife there.

My thoughts sport a hint of envy. I love animals.

Back in the San Blas, Mark and I catch up with Mark and Michele, who we met in Grenada. Michele introduces me to yoga. I hate yoga. I'm tall and stiff as a plank. Yet, I can't manage a *plank*. I don't like to sweat; I prefer comfort and views towards the sky instead of the sand. As long as I find a shady spot and the ants and mosquitoes leave me alone, these daily sessions under the palm trees become more enjoyable.

In the afternoons, she and I often set out on a snorkel trip. Michele loves underwater photography and I adore snapping aquarium shots with my newish camera as well. Floating in the clear water, observing colorful creatures, dotted rays, and gentle nurse sharks is the highlight of my existence.

꒰꒱ ꒰꒱ ꒰꒱

One day in April 2012, winter becomes summer without warning. Incessant heat, dense humidity, bothersome no-see-ums, and crackling lightning storms dominate. The wind has been switched off and our piece of paradise is erased by rain. Ominous clouds form and head our way. The sky dumps buckets of water, filling our tank and jerrycans, now overflowing. Nothing dries. We gather dirty laundry and rinse water aplenty. But with no sun to dry our clothes that chore has to wait until the color blue returns. The palm trees sway in another squall's strong winds; the choppy anchorages beckon for reprieve.

Thunderstorms vibrate our boat with every roar. Lightning bolts create a painful spectacle for the eyes. With every flash in close proximity, we hold our breaths, hoping it won't hit *Irie* and damage the electronics. Panama is famous for its summer storms and is a prime location for boats being hit by lightning; about 50 percent of cruisers deal with the costly consequences. With a vengeance, bursts of energy brighten the night sky, creating an impressive show. A lightning bolt strikes one of the uninhabited islands. A fireball emerges on the beach. Natural phenomena fascinate us, but after weeks of crackling and flashing, and fear of getting hit, our joy of being in the San Blas Islands evaporates.

The weather influences our internet availability. We move often. The air is heavy. Our foreheads drip over our keyboards. On stagnant days like this, we expect thunder and lightning and a healthy dose of rain by nightfall.

The plants will be happy.

This is how summer in the San Blas looks, feels, and tastes. Every day. The only way to cool off is jumping in the azure blue water. The only way to protect *Irie* from a lightning strike is wishful thinking. Our mast is shorter than on most sailboats. That helps. The only way to avoid the elements is by planning an escape route. If not for *Irie*, then for ourselves.

Mark and I buy plane tickets to fly to the US in July. Together. We need a break. We always have mixed feelings leaving *Irie* and our life behind, but this is the first time we're more than antsy to get out.

After failing to leave our boat at French-owned *Panamarina* on the mainland, because they unexpectedly canceled our reservation, we head to the West Lemmon Cays. It's the only place with affordable and available mooring balls, yet it's not an ideal location to leave a boat long-term without supervision. People anchor sailboats in the deeper areas and abandon them for months, unaware or un-a-care of storms and wind shifts that set their vessels loose. A German man is in charge of keeping an eye on the stored boats. We hire his wife to air the boat out once a week and check the interior and bilges for potential leaks.

The afternoon before our arduous journey to Panama City and onward to the States, we secure *Irie* to her mooring ball. We follow procedures to store loose items and prevent damage from a lightning strike. At least, we attempt this by leading a wire from the mast into the water. Mark's in charge of outside modifications while I tackle *Irie*'s interior. I fill Tupperware containers with laundry powder to absorb the humidity and strategically place them throughout the hulls and cabin. This should reduce mold.

Suddenly, I hear abrupt shuffling on deck.

"Shit! Liesbet, come outside!"

I drop a full container on a bookshelf and run upstairs.

"What's going on?"

Mark doesn't have to answer. I see him grab our boat hook from its snaps on the lifelines, cross the bow to the port side, brace himself, and hold the pole towards an approaching vessel.

Shit indeed.

I join him and lean over the side, pushing both hands flat against the fiberglass of this monohull on the run. It's dragging untethered through the mooring field and misses us by a hair. *Leaving Irie here is the worst idea ever.*

Mark makes an announcement on the VHF to warn other boaters, in the off chance they have their radio on. Then he jumps in our dinghy to inform the caretakers on shore. He helps the German guy and his Guna crew tie off the obtrusive boat. At least there are people around. Hopefully, this will be the only incident in two months.

I distribute the rest of my containers and pack bags for our trip. To avoid forgetting anything important, I go through all the boat nooks and crannies. That's when I remember the mysterious ring.

How could I have forgotten about it?

My hidden treasure is still there. Four years after I discovered the heart-shaped box behind a row of books in one of our aft cabins, I can't contain my curiosity any longer. I had restrained myself because I didn't want to ruin a possible surprise. It doesn't matter anymore. Obviously, this object has nothing to do with me or our relationship. By now, we're married, threw a successful wedding party in St. Martin, and the romance is gone.

Surely, Mark is not saving it for our honeymoon who knows when?

I confront my man, sitting in the cockpit, recovering from the dragging scare.

"It's time you tell me about that ring downstairs." It has been a day full of commotion. I fear Mark can't handle more emotions, especially from me, but it's now or never.

"Which ring?"

My heart sinks. I describe the shape and color of the vintage box. A blank stare. I rush downstairs, fish it from the dusty shelf, and reappear in the cockpit. Blood rises to my cheeks.

How on earth could I have kept this a secret for so long? He doesn't have any recollection of it!

"You don't know what this is?" I present the jewelry box.

Slowly, his memory catches up with him. Almost as an afterthought, he reveals the mystery haunting me for years.

"My mom gave me this ring when I was back in the US for Tim's wedding in 2008."

I remain quiet.

"Remember? You stayed in the Bahamas with the dogs?"

"Of course, I remember. Why did she hand it to you? And why did you keep it a secret?"

"She told me to give it to you one day. The ring was from her mother, carried over for generations. I totally forgot about it. Why are you snooping around?" He smiles, assuming this is a recent find.

I can't help but wonder if he would have eventually remembered the box without my poking. Maybe whenever he'd sell *Irie* and stumble across it, emptying the shelves?

"Why did you hide it in the engine bunk room?"

"It was supposed to be a surprise. I planned on giving it to you sooner," he says.

Quite the surprise this is.

"Well, you can give it to me now." I'm unable to face another wait to finally see, and maybe even wear, this antique ring.

"Sure," he says. I hand him the case. He returns it to me. "Here you go."

After years of anticipation, I open the box and observe a tiny, golden ring. It's cute and simple and only fits the smallest of my fingers.

"Can I have a look?" Mark asks. He scrutinizes it. "Did you read the inscription?"

"No. I would need four sets of glasses to decipher that cursive script. What does it say?"

"Thou art lovely in my light."

"That's so sweet of you to say, baby." I sigh. "I'll thank your mom in person soon."

If she remembers. She is Mark's mother...

The anti-climax leaves me with few words. I never claimed my husband was a romantic. I store the golden item back in its heart-shaped prison and hidden den, to never forget the era of anxiety. Not only do I now know what it is, but I certainly remember where it's located; that's more than I can say about our wedding rings.

Chapter 18

Taking the Plunge?

Mark and I have this cooking app we've used for years. We rave about it to our cruiser friends. It's called *How to Cook Everything* and is written by Mark Bittman. My husband likes to cook. Me, not so much. But I happily eat the wholesome meals he creates. I do the dishes, in my bucket outside. Whoever doesn't cook is responsible for the clean-up in this household. I like it. Doing dishes is much quicker and less hot than cooking, especially on a boat in the tropics.

Usually, I help with the food prep and Mark might do the rinsing inside. We are a team, after all.

While in the US, we made a luxury purchase: a car radio with high quality marine speakers. Normally, we only stock up on necessary items for *Irie*. This time, our bags and finances had room for a treat, a "like to have for enjoyment" instead of a "need to have to prevent sinking."

We had anxiety about the fate of our floating home when visiting our families.

"How is *Irie* doing?" somebody would ask.

"We have no clue," one of us would respond. "We hope she's alright."

We'd learned through the grapevine that our German caretaker and his wife had permanently left the San Blas Islands. The boats on moorings were from then on under supervision of the Guna Indians. Or not.

Worried looks.

"There's nothing we can do from here."

Then, we changed the conversation. Our stay in the taken-for-granted Western world was a spoil, a lavish submersion in comfort. So much so that, back on *Irie*, we forgot on which side of the bed we slept and wondered what the buttons on the electric panel were for.

One of Mark's first projects upon our return to the boat, which – *phew* – floated in the exact position we left her, was to install the new radio. What a joy! For him. After listening to good music through bad speakers, I now listen to bad music through good speakers. Every day. He rediscovers The Grateful Dead. Every day. Loud and clear. He likes them. Me, not so much.

"If we ever cross the Pacific Ocean, I could listen to the Grateful Dead non-stop," Mark says one evening in *Irie*'s cockpit.

"I'd be grateful if you didn't." His Pacific Ocean remark surprises me. With the Panama Canal this close, my thoughts increasingly stall at following our friends Axel and Liz into the next realm. "I don't think you have enough songs to hold you over for three or four weeks. How many minutes are there in 21 days?"

"If we make an announcement about our need for Grateful Dead songs to fill up a Pacific crossing, people will send enough versions to last the entire way to French Polynesia."

The horror!

"I prefer to listen to the whooshing of the boat and the silence of the night."

Isn't that what passage making is about?

"I would listen to my music and cook recipes from Mark Bittman."

Now we're talking!

So, if I desire good food on this fictional journey, I'll have to put up with The Dead.

The thought of sailing in the Pacific elevates my spirits. Is there really a chance we'd keep going? Or is Mark in one of those rare happy moods?

We should have bought that marine radio sooner.

"A Pacific crossing with Mark, Mark, and The Dead," I mutter. Another increasingly annoying, high-pitched electrical guitar medley wafts through the cockpit. I cringe.

Please, let it just be Mark and Mark, or I'll be dead.

🌊🌊🌊

Entering the South Pacific was never an option before, so we never talked, let alone thought about it. With the dogs it was impossible. Plus, Mark believed that *Irie* wasn't built for a "real ocean voyage." He would *never* take this small catamaran into the *Big Ocean*, as we call the Pacific in Belgium.

But after our last conversation, the flame to head further west is ignited. My heart beats faster each time I consider the reality of it. A new ocean, new islands, new cultures! Our discussions keep returning to this topic and I gather stacks of information.

We have to go.

Mark puts things in perspective. Always. The flame wavers.

"*Irie* is an extremely light boat to cross oceans in," he says. "She weighs only 8,000 pounds."

"I know, but hasn't she done awesome so far? And you've been able to fix all the issues that arose." An ego boost might help my cause.

"Cats have strict weight limits. We can't stock up as well as our mono-hull friends and food shopping is expensive in the Pacific. Most of the items are imported."

"We'll eat what the locals eat. We did alright in the Bahamas, never buying pricey goods. Except for that $1 tomato. I can live without tomatoes if I get to live with tikis."

"We have small tanks for water and fuel. We'd need to store extra in jerrycans, which affects that weight limit."

"Our water collecting system will do the job. And we'll be extra careful on the crossings. We'll skip showers or only use salt water. The trade winds should help us sail most of the way."

My optimism is stronger than my realism. Mark is more conservative and prepares for the worst. It's good to have him around, to snatch me out of *my world*.

"The first part to the Galapagos Islands is about ten days, the second one to the Marquesas could be 30. Further west, there are day hops and week hops. *Irie*'s longest trip so far has been two days and two nights," Mark iterates.

None of this fazes me. I can't wait to go.

"That was because of Kali and Darwin. Now, without dogs, it's the perfect time for longer passages."

"I guess you don't remember the vomiting on that dreadful sail to Martinique. You will get seasick again. Following seas make you most nauseous."

Mark almost gets me right there. At least we're genuinely discussing this Pacific affair.

"We were on a deadline for that trip since we were meeting my cousin. We wouldn't have gone out in those strong winds otherwise. No more schedules! I also read that you get used to the motion of the ocean after a few days. It won't be fun at first, but I'll get over it and maybe lose some weight in the process."

It's easy to be positive when sitting in a flat anchorage. If I imagine stormy conditions thousands of miles from land, I admit I'd rather stay in the San Blas Islands. But I only think about the awesomeness that could – no – that must lie ahead.

When will I learn?

Back and forth it goes. Sensible Mark and "happy go lucky" Liesbet. We talk about factors that could hold us back from entering the Pacific. Our instruments – most importantly our autopilot – are 15 years old and bound to break at some point. Spares cost thousands of dollars. The books we read mention treacherous anchorages, dangerous atoll entrances, keel-destroying reef patches, and time-consuming border formalities.

Imagine reaching land after weeks at sea, shaken up and tired, needing hours to set the anchor(s) satisfactorily, then spending half the day to check in, and leaving that same anchorage for another one 100 miles away because the swell is tossing you out of bed.

Why do people go to the South Pacific?

The palm trees wave at me through the porthole. I marvel at our well-set anchor, visible in the clear, shallow water. My cheap rum and coke rests on the table, motionless; I can use both hands to take a photo of the marvelous sunset. The horizon turns yellow, orange, red, and pink. The colors of happiness mix and match to complete the picture of paradise.

On the islands, fresh water and produce might be hard to find; a water maker is out of our budget and not appealing. Who needs another expensive gadget needing electricity, upkeep, and extra spare parts? The distance between us and our home countries will further increase.

As every prospective puddle jumper does, Mark worries that something bad might happen on one of the long passages – you're literally in the middle of nowhere, utterly on your own.

I counter that we're young and healthy compared to the rest of the pack. Entering the Pacific is a commitment, timewise and dedication-wise. It will add years to our cruising journey. Mark is unconvinced that's what he wants. Remaining in the Caribbean or returning to the US is easier. I still have a visa to stay up to six months in the US if Immigration agrees upon my entering. I could try to get citizenship this time.

But I don't want to live in the US. I want to sail to Fiji!

Then there are financial considerations. We need heavier-duty equipment on *Irie* for a trip of this magnitude. Getting the cat up to snuff, transiting the Canal, storing extra diesel, and stopping in the Galapagos Islands will set us back $6,000 more than if we stay in the Caribbean. Almost half of our annual budget. It'll take time and effort to prepare our boat and ourselves.

We are at a stalemate.

Luckily, the conversation remains on the table. I know what I want. Mark is torn. I've felt stuck since we started The Wirie business three and a half years ago. I need to spread my wings. Being this close to the Panama Canal works like a magnet.

"If we stay on this side, we can take advantage of the boating market in Florida whenever we want to call it quits," Mark says.

Calling it quits? We're on the brink of a new cruising sensation.

"Well, I'm not ready for that. *Irie* is in good shape. And thanks to Axel, we have a light sail for downwind destinations." I'm appreciative for the spinnaker gift; it had been too small for *Gudrun*. No reaction.

"We don't have responsibilities preventing us from going. We avoided scooping up a stray puppy. Our parents are healthy. We don't have children yet. And we'll be able to meet friends who took the plunge earlier."

Mark shrugs. "We have friends here."

New adventures or old friends? The choice is easy, like the one between travel or boyfriends in a far past.

I try a different tack. "Think about the wildlife we'll encounter and the incredible underwater world. The Pacific is a peaceful ocean. The weather is benign. We'll have devices to alert people if anything goes wrong. We should take advantage of having our own boat to explore those islands!"

This level of enthusiasm has got to be contagious.

As my list of pros doesn't induce a smile on Mark's face, I inexhaustibly go on. Australia and New Caledonia are good markets to sell a boat, especially a catamaran.

Do I see a twinkle there?

If we don't go this spring, we'll never go. The alternative is less exciting; we've been to Central America overland.

Axel emailed from French Polynesia that the guidebooks are outdated, that anchoring is easy and dealing with officials straightforward. That it's mind-blowingly beautiful there and finding fresh water and produce is possible – you just have to get it whenever you can. First-hand information is indispensable. Heaps of cruisers have done this trip before and enjoyed it; some call the Pacific islands the highlight of their circumnavigation.

We have the time and the energy for a new adventure. Who could possibly pass this up?

Mark?

꩜ ꩜ ꩜

"What's wrong?" Michele asks as we head to the beach for our daily yoga session under the San Blas palms. I concentrate on avoiding coral heads, steering our dinghy to shore. It was my turn to pick her up. We usually chat on the short drive, but I'm choked up. My eyes water.

"Is it Mark's sister?"

I nod, swallowing hard. I give the engine a last *humph,* put the lever in neutral, press the red button to turn it off, and lift the shaft out of the water, locking it in place. The dinghy brushes the sand and we jump out, pulling it well above the water's edge.

"She's not doing well," I say. I'm embarrassed to face my friend. My cheeks shine from the now free-flowing tears. Mark had received a disconcerting email about Dru.

"I can't believe it! She's been fighting so hard, trying anything to beat this damn cancer. She was doing well for almost two years, and now she completely relapsed."

"Ovarian cancer is a tough one. I'm so sorry." Michele hugs me, yoga mat awkwardly pressed under her arm.

It's hard to be away from our families when the going gets tough. This year alone, I had to let go of my aunt Monique, who had colon cancer. She was only 61. And *meter,* my paternal grandmother, died at 92.

"It must be tough to be on the other side of the world right now," my cousin Griet emailed, after I learned the news about our *meter.* We feel helpless in situations like these, but the biggest shock occurs when we return to our home countries and people we used to visit are no longer there. Dru is 52. Too young to die. The thought makes me shiver, despite the 85-degree temperature and the sweat on my temples.

We move to our favorite spot under the palm trees. Michele unrolls her mat, while I open my over-sized beach towel.

Good thoughts...

I sit down on the fabric and try to flatten the ground under my bum. I stare at the horizon and the white sailboats swaying at anchor.

It's not fair.

I'm sitting here in paradise while Dru suffers in cold Connecticut. I feel the sand between my toes, while she is bed-bound. At least she's at home, surrounded by loved ones.

"Which practice do you want to do today?" Michele asks. I shrug. I couldn't care less. At 8:30am, the humidity and heat are already building. Ants join me on my towel. The breeze keeps the mosquitoes at bay. All I want to do is recline in the *corpse* position and look at the palm leaves and blue sky above me. Yoga might be the distraction I need.

Michele starts a session on her iPod Touch, turns the external speakers on, and soon I listen to the soothing voice of Sean Johnson. She picked "Morning Flow," my favorite. I still have to look at her often to understand certain positions, but I'm getting better – more flexible and relaxed. I can finally touch my toes. As a tall, not-so-agile person, that's progress.

Should we fly to the US again? We were just there a few months ago.

I sigh, stretching my arms into triangle pose.

Imagine if she'd pass away when we're mid-Pacific crossing!

I lose my balance. The landing is soft. I ought to focus on the moves and worry later.

Sweat runs down my face as I copy Michele's poses. Downward-facing Dog finally feels like a resting pose, something I never thought possible. We move through the practice, one woman smoother than the other. When the shade has shifted and I'm out of breath, it's time for my favorite, the reward after those intense positions, the closing part of the class: relaxation. My body enjoys the peace, but my mind keeps wandering to Mark's sister. I zoom in on the bright sky, the green leaves fluttering in the breeze. Tropical and peaceful.

It's not fair.

Tears prick behind my eyes. I switch my attention to the soft background music. For three seconds.

What can we do to help Dru? She has been so strong. She can't lose this fight.

🌊🌊🌊

It was bound to happen. Every two years in December, something dreadful occurs in our household. In 2008, we lost Kali in Puerto Rico. In 2010, Darwin passed away during a visit to the US. It's mid-December 2012 now.

Irie is hauled out at the Shelter Bay Marina boatyard near Colon, mainland Panama. We're on a schedule. Christmas is approaching. We have a bunch of projects to attend to and need to be back in the water before the holidays, when yard work comes to a halt.

In a few weeks, my cousin Griet and her husband, Wim, will meet us in Guna Yala for a last hurrah in our favorite island chain. Then, they'll become line handlers on our Canal transit.

Yes!

We bit the bullet. We have a new path, a new destiny. Sailing in the Pacific Ocean. It's the right thing to do. Mark agrees. Grudgingly or not, he agrees. We're now in the boatyard to make the last preparations.

It's happening.

Except, everything has been going wrong.

The harbor of Portobelo, one of our staging points in the past, was a chaotic, dangerous mess due to West winds. It rained constantly. And when it rains, it pours. My camera fell out of my pocket into the murky Chagres river – *bye, bye birthday present.* Twice, we attempted to sail to Bocas del Toro. Twice, we turned around with hanging heads and trembling hands. The first time, the winds were dead ahead, pushing us back to Colombia. The second time, we hit two tree trunks at night, deposited in the ocean by overflowing rivers from the mainland. We returned to assess potential damage. We decided to get hauled, to inspect our underside and to get on with the giant to-do list for our next chapter.

Mark was fed up with the boat life.

Why this bad karma? Are we making the wrong decision?

It's our second day high, but not dry, on blocks. When rain interrupts, we focus on projects underneath the boat. *Sheltering in Shelter Bay.* When the downpour stops, we attempt outdoor activities in the form of maintenance and painting. We rig tarps over our transom steps, which need layers of water-based anti-slip paint. Mark is working on the saildrives and climbs onto the boat for a different tool. It happens on his way down the rickety ladder. It slips. My husband tumbles seven feet before hitting the gravel surface. I hear the events unfold and rush outside.

Besides a few bloody scrapes and cuts, Mark's left wrist hurts at the base of his thumb. In the evening, the pain becomes unbearable. Is his wrist broken?

While trying to figure out how to get a cab at night from remote Shelter Bay to an emergency room in Colon, our neighbor – an orthopedic surgeon – comes over. He saw the accident happen when working on his own boat. He inspects Mark's hand. His diagnosis requires a cast... for at least six weeks. That's the procedure in a Western country.

"There's a little bone in your thumb that might be broken, something that's hard to figure out, even on an X-ray. Better to play it safe," he states.

Our plans, dreams, and hopes shatter. This changes everything: our time in the yard (which is expensive, dirty, and uncomfortable), our final three weeks in the San Blas, our scheduled Panama Canal transit, Mark's upcoming one-week visit to the States late January, our Pacific itinerary. Is it time to abandon the boat life all together? We hit rock bottom. Mark lies in my arms. Our connection strengthens when the going is tough. I console him as well as myself.

We'll be okay. We will figure this out. We always do.

The following morning, we take the marina shuttle into Colon and jump out at the emergency room of Cuatro Altos hospital. In Panamanian fashion, we are "welcomed" at the check-in desk by three women doing each other's nails. They don't bother to look up. One is the secretary, one the nurse, and the third happens to be the doctor on duty. After the nail polish is dry, we register. The air conditioning doesn't work. Everybody fans themselves. The nurse does the rudimentary check-ups and Mark disappears in the "radiation zone." A hospital employee takes four X-rays of his left hand.

Nervous, we wait for the results. We're called into the doctor's office. She speaks broken English, helped by her tablet translator. The X-rays light up. No fractures, only a sprained wrist. Our faces light up. We pay the $95 ER bill and leave.

It's difficult for Mark to do boat jobs with only one hand, but we manage. I offer to be his left hand. Déjà vu to the summer of 2007, when Mark hit the boat out of frustration and wore a cast. With combined hands and determination, we work as a dedicated team to beat the rapidly approaching holidays. Mark wears a robust immobilizing brace. His injury heals over time.

Days before Christmas, *Irie* gets splashed. Griet and Wim join us in the San Blas Islands for a last tour of the splendid beaches and vivid coral gardens. They help fix our emergency hatches for the umpteenth time, while in shallow water. Then, mid-January, we all motor through the Gatun locks, spend a night in raised Gatun Lake, transit its flat body of water, drop back down via the Miraflores locks, and emerge into the Pacific Ocean.

Three months after our big decision, we swap the known for the unknown once more.

🐚🐚🐚

Mark and I have no idea when we'll reach French Polynesia, how long we'll be in the South Pacific, or what year we'll see our families again. Dru's health keeps deteriorating. Mark flies to the States to see his sister, presumably for the last time. We conclude it's better for me to stay behind for emotional, financial, logistical, and practical reasons.

While he supports his family, I take on the mammoth task to provision *Irie*. Panama City is inexpensive and a convenient place to shop if you stay in a marina. We rarely dock, so during my week alone, *Irie* remains in the super-bouncy anchorage of La Playita. I'm glad Mark is gone because this situation would drive him crazy.

Necessity is what keeps me here, thus I deal with the discomfort, sliding pots and pans, and seasickness at anchor. The task at hand is challenging but rewarding. And I'm keen about shopping, organizing, and me time. This situation gives me the satisfaction I desire. I'm productive, work towards the greater good of our imminent voyage, and spend my free time reading and writing.

When Mark asks if he can extend his visit four days, I full-heartedly say "yes." I want him to be there for his family and for himself, but I also cherish being self-secure and independent. I feel stronger without Mark, more positive about our life and our future. *No arguments.*

The draw of our upcoming adventure, the idea of something new – doing what we never thought we would – fuels me. Even after our extended prep work, Mark remains hesitant.

Is he giving in to please me? Is he really getting sick of the boat? Does his frustration have to do with our business? What is the solution to these conflicts – on a relationship level and a personal one?

I sense doom on the horizon but let the topic rest. These are sensitive times.

At the choppy anchorage, I struggle with the elements, space and weight restrictions, and gravity. Hauling groceries, booze, and toiletries – first into a taxi, then into the dinghy – heavy box after heavy box up our steps and into the cockpit, while the boat is pitching, takes all my strength, balance, and focus. I'm proud to report that no item, not even a Liesbet, plummets into the grimy water. I remove cardboard immediately to avoid critters like cockroaches. My *Tetris* abilities yield a place for every item of canned, bagged, and Tetra Bricked food, as well as any liquids, produce, and meat. *I wish my mind was that organized.* We hope to catch fish in the ocean, but you never know.

Irie is stocked to the gills. I'm worried about her weight and Mark's reaction when he notices my burdening of our boat. He'll say I went overboard and might order several items overboard as a result. Hopefully, she still sails fine, despite lying two inches lower in the water.

I'm productive during Mark's absence but feel sad I couldn't be there for Dru. Though, according to my husband, she's not up for seeing crowds and prefers to just have her closest relatives around. Life resembles a collection of emotions, no matter what month of the year or which spot on the globe.

Days after Mark returns, with a suitcase full of boat parts, his sister passes away. Time stands still. The boat does not. Violent wake from container ships, ferries, and pilot boats tosses us around. Tears run as we comfort each other. Dru has always focused on a healthy lifestyle, eating a vegetarian, organic diet, even before it became "in." Her cancer was caused by a bad gene mutation inherited from their father: the BRCA1 gene. This mutation greatly heightens the risk of breast and ovarian cancer. She drew a bad card. There was nothing anybody could have done. Her daughter doesn't carry the gene; a sigh of relief before losing her life.

My affection and care for Mark triples, as seems common in times of distress. Another loved one gone. I embrace my husband and value his presence. I want to be there for him. We are a team. We are strong. We love each other. And we are in the Pacific, ready for new adventures. Together. Dru's spirit will guide us along the way.

Chapter 19

In Darwin's Footsteps

The seawater etches a smile on my face. It's there because of my surroundings and remains because of the icy Humboldt current molding my lips and cheeks in place. My "shorty" wetsuit marginally helps. It doesn't matter. This is one of those once-in-a-lifetime experiences. I don't know where to look first and forget everything else, even this new hole in my mouth from a tooth extraction. Or being in the water without Mark. It's too cold for him, too uncomfortable. A baby sea lion twirls around me, propels to the surface, and plunges back into the depths of the bay, shooting me a mischievous look. I can't follow him too far down but demand his attention – or that of his playmate – by twisting my body in the most crooked contortions, imitating his behavior. Curious about my antics, they return.

Sea lions crack me up, especially these fearless ones. On land, they appear plump and awkward, but here they're in their element, seamlessly gliding through the water, somersaulting around me, unaware of any threats and comfortable with snorkelers like myself. On my swim back to shore, I hover over a couple of spotted eagle rays and follow one of the sea turtles, until I stray too far off track. I'm shivering now. Time to remove the wetsuit and bask in the sun. I join Mark on the beach. Life is good on Isla Isabela, our third stop in the Galapagos Islands.

I'm besotted with the wildlife: prehistoric-looking iguanas that bake on hot rocks, disappear underwater, and spit salty liquid out through their nostrils; giant tortoises crossing our path on a walk; dive-bombing blue-footed boobies breaking the water surface with fresh fish in their beaks (I watch this spectacle for hours sitting on *Irie*'s deck); and cute penguins floating about or hunting underwater, singling out little fish in a school. Imagine visiting this place with children. Such an education!

My heart melts when I think about home schooling and immersing our own kids in a beautiful, exciting world where wild animals are part of daily life. I cherish encounters with sharks, rays, turtles, and their terrestrial equivalents. *Heaven.*

𝔇𝔇𝔇

We covered the 900-mile distance from Las Perlas Islands in Panama to San Cristobal in the Galapagos in a week. *Irie*, with her 35 feet overall length, is small compared to fellow cruising boats. She's a sturdy little cat that hasn't disappointed us yet. We just have to be careful and take her smaller size and lighter design into consideration. This means we reef (shorten sail) conservatively and shouldn't surf down waves at 13 knots. She stands her ground and makes wonderful progress, despite being a tad sluggish.

I did buy too many provisions in Panama. Mark has reminded me of that danger multiple times, but as long as the boat stays upright, all is *irie*.

The first days and nights of the crossing, we constantly slowed the boat down by reducing sails. A steady 30 to 35 knots of wind pushed us along at nine knots. The current helped. I never got sick. From the moment conditions settled, I could see us doing this sailing thing forever. The new autopilot performed splendidly. So did Mark and I. We had no arguments and the atmosphere aboard was one of teamwork, daily chats, shared meals, and enjoying quiet time. Whenever The Grateful Dead shut up.

As we closed our distance to latitude 00.00.00, progress faltered. We celebrated our equator crossing with a rum and coke for Mark and a virgin one (yep, just coke) for me. I'd be on watch. Neptune received a healthy shot as well. Of rum. Belgian chocolate truffles, gifted by my cousin for this occasion, accompanied the drinks.

This notoriously wind-deprived part of ocean had us motor for hours on end. When we grew tired of the noise and fumes and worried about our fuel tank capacity (32 gallons, plus ten extra gallons in jerrycans), we opted to drift.

Thoughts of movie characters acting out sea ventures, sailors caught in the doldrums, and ship-wrecked survivors floating in an endlessly flat ocean crossed my mind. It was dead quiet. Peaceful. Mirror-like seas. Half of my vision filled with water, the other half with air. Both fields separated by a straight line: the infinite horizon.

On day six, I saw ripples in the distance. Within half an hour – joy of joys – a fresh breeze caught up with us. Ready. Set. Action! Spinnaker up, mainsail up, and off we went for the most perfect sail of the century, doing six and a half knots in 12-knot winds.

The night that followed was even more spectacular. The spinnaker charged ahead; the rest of the boat followed. The sky was clear and sparkling with stars. While I watched the illuminated crests of the waves, the Southern Cross watched me. There were no squalls, no ships, and no interruptions.

After five nights of "always something" to break the spell of continuity and bedtime, whether it be a storm cell, turning the engines on, or adjusting the sails, this night Mark and I experienced our dedicated three hours on watch and three hours off and appreciated every minute of it. Our last 24-hour period on the ocean was as enjoyable as a sail trip can be.

That I had to wait six years for this didn't occur to me.

On the open ocean at night, I enjoyed my time alone, writing, reading, and thinking. My mind never rests. Often, my thoughts ventured towards having children. As a long-term couple, the all-important question about kids eventually pops up. Do we want them or not? Because of our lifestyle, we have postponed that question, or better, the answer, for years. Mark doesn't lean one way or the other. I don't know what I prefer. Especially with this husband. During his bursts of frustration, I conclude I don't want to raise a child in that environment. Through the yelling, I cringe and have flashbacks of our dog Darwin cowering in a corner, trying to hide.

Would Mark be a good father? I have his brother, who does anything for his children, to compare. I also recognize Tim's episodes of anger and frustration in Mark. It must be the genes. The clock is ticking... I turn 38 this year. I want children before 40, or not at all. It's the most important and difficult decision of my life. Instead of just answering with *yes* or *no*, like land-based people with a steady income, job, house, family, school system, health care arrangements, and routine, we have to (re)consider our gypsy lifestyle, finances, plans, living quarters, location, amenities, hygiene, and plenty more.

This crossing to the Galapagos did not provide an answer.

≋ ≋ ≋

Our favorite activity on the island of San Cristobal was observing the sea lions when they would come ashore early evening. During the day, fat lazy males lounge in town, on sidewalks, benches, and even reclining chairs. But at night, the ladies return from their hunting missions and find a comfortable spot on the beach to rest. The babies have been waiting. Barking and crying, they do their rounds. They waggle from one growling sea lion to another in an attempt to find their mommy. Chased away by the males and wrong mothers, they eventually find the right nipples to feed them. Or they don't. Females occasionally remain in the ocean for a week at a time, too long for the baby to last without milk. Charles Darwin's "survival of the fittest" and the cycle of life and death are omnipresent in a wildlife Mecca like the Galapagos Islands.

We returned home from town by water taxi for a dollar a person.

The alternative was leaving our dinghy on the municipal beach, above the high-water line, as a trampling ground for sea lions, unwilling to leave.

Approaching *Irie*, we never knew how many innocents we'd find aboard. We rigged up fenders, jugs, and towels to block the entrance to our deck and cockpit. The sea lions managed to overcome every restraining order and left a slimy, hairy layer behind. When chasing them off, we put up with their objections and 600-pound bodies.

They swam past *Irie*'s stern and looked up in disbelief, "Why are these comfy steps blocked by plastic stuff?" To some, the obstacles were a deterrent. To others, a minor nuisance or a pillow. They nudged themselves into a newly created empty spot, heads resting on a fender. When told to leave the transom and bug someone else, the cutest expression on their whiskered faces made me change my mind. Except that time when we found a gigantic daddy stretched out on our cockpit table.

🐬🐬🐬

Before we left Panama City, Mark and I had our teeth checked by a dentist. The weather forecast called for our 30-mile sail to the Perlas Islands the day after. Mark received a clean bill of tooth health. I was less fortunate. One of my teeth had loosened over time and needed a crown. The dentist feared a dangerous infection at sea. It would take a while to get my mouth fixed. I didn't have a while. I researched dentists in Las Perlas. *None.* I discovered an English-speaking *dentista* in Santa Cruz, Galapagos Islands. She could install a crown over two visits. Hurrah for the internet, and a responsive dentist. Not easy to find en route! I'd swing by when we were in town. I favored the left side of my mouth to avoid tooth loss. Neptune did not receive a tooth offering on our first ocean voyage.

My friend Sven from Belgium joined us in San Cristobal for a two-week vacation onboard *Irie*. One of the highlights was a snorkel at La Loberia beach, his first ever snorkeling experience. We spotted rays and turtles in the deeper part of the bay and returned to shore, eyes wide open. On our bellies, in three feet of water, we saw a baby sea lion play with a rock – dropping it, picking it back up – and chase its tail mere feet away. I can't remember the first time I snorkeled, but it sure wasn't anything like this! Years later, he and I still reminisce his visit to the Galapagos Islands on *Irie*.

The three of us ventured further west, mostly under engines. These islands are not known for favorable sailing. There's barely wind. We only planned a couple of days in Santa Cruz, the hub and most touristy destination in the Galapagos. Our first evening in the harbor found me at the dentist. She inspected my mouth and made an *uh-oh* sound: the tooth needed to come out. I didn't see that coming.

"Okay then," I said. "Go ahead. I don't have much time here, so we might as well get it over with."

I didn't realize that pulling a tooth requires surgery and painkillers. I wasn't allowed to be in the sun and needed to rest.

What? I couldn't sightsee in Santa Cruz?

I reconsidered and postponed the tooth removal. I celebrated my renewed freedom of one day with a magnificent beach walk in Tortuga Bay.

After a tour the following morning, visiting two sinkholes created by volcanic eruptions, a lava tunnel, and a tortoise sanctuary, I returned to the dentist. Mark joined me. Sven set out on his own. Local anesthesia, big needles, scary instruments, and 30 minutes later, I went home with a giant gap and stitches in my mouth. After the procedure, the dentist told me she had to remove an abscess as well. My gums were infected close to a main nerve, that if becoming infected itself could have led to excruciating pain, brain damage, and fatal injury. Especially in the middle of the ocean with no help around. I had dodged a bullet.

On the walk back, I was queasy. From this new realization, the drugs, and the assault on my jaw. I held Mark's hand. I felt old. Useless. Like a toothless grandma without even being a mom. The hole wasn't visible when I smiled, but I hated this imperfection. I was incomplete and couldn't eat Mark's wonderful dinner that night. I complained. I'm sure everyone else onboard wished I'd shut up and shape up and appreciate our fascinating surroundings instead.

My first day out of the sun, Mark and I did chores aboard. Sven went sightseeing. The second one was the day we sailed to the last of our Galapagos trio: Isabela. Sven helped Mark with the lines and sails, but, once again, we had to motor the 45 miles. After a few days of discomfort, my smile returned. Right in time to hug Sven goodbye.

※ ※ ※

Before switching oceans, Mark and I decided to quit our Wirie business and enjoy cruising in earnest. Crossing a vast body of water and spending months on end in remote areas without reliable internet would make the job extremely frustrating, if not impossible. We broached the subject with partner Tim in the US. He thought differently. He had come to rely on the extra income. He suggested – for the time being – taking over Mark's customer support tasks. If problems arose, he'd be in touch.

We agreed. Our number of customers was manageable, and no new software development or hardware changes were on the agenda. We could take a break and pick up the workload when circumstances allowed.

The absence of Wirie stress is one of the reasons our time in the Galapagos is wonderful and relaxing. It's also the relief we need to get our relationship back on track, to enjoy each other's presence, and revel, usually together, in the fascinating activities at hand.

If my number one reason to sail is to visit places I can't get to otherwise, my number two is to be surrounded by wildlife. The Galapagos delivers!

On our boat, we blend into the animal kingdom without feeling like intruders. These amazing creatures are as much a part of our life as we are of theirs. We take our struggles with the Spanish language and bouncy anchorages in stride, even Mark, who becomes a new, refreshed person under the tantalizing effects of inquisitive animals and fascinating volcanoes.

It's the best $1,000 we ever spent.

Staying here for two months allows us to taste the variety of flavors these three islands have to offer. But we need to focus on the next part of our journey – the *big ocean*. The stretch from Panama to the Galapagos is said to be the most challenging leg of a Pacific crossing. Since that went better than expected, I look forward to our 3,000-mile journey to French Polynesia.

Unlike most of our cruising peers, we'll sail the tougher stretch to the Gambier Islands, instead of the downwind path to the Marquesas. We want to avoid the increasing group of puddle jumpers heading to those visually striking islands and get there after the masses have left. We're also excited to discover the relatively unknown Gambier archipelago.

Our friends Birgit and Christian on *Pitufa* convinced us this is the best route, off the beaten track. If the trip is too uncomfortable with the waves and wind on our side, we'd veer off towards the Marquesas for an easier ride. We heard on our SSB receiver that every catamaran (all larger than *Irie*) on their way to the Gambier has bailed so far and changed direction towards the Marquesas. *That doesn't bode well.*

In the past, we interpreted weather forecasts and made decisions based on common sense and experience. Once committed to this passage, we have to take whatever comes our way. We top off our tanks, batteries, cabinets, and fridge, and clean the interior and exterior. We test our safety gear and instruments, prepare four meals as easy first dinners, and arrange the paperwork for our departure. Time to take another plunge.

The first Tuesday of May 2013, we lift the anchor and stow it for weeks of inactivity in a big blue ocean. French Polynesia, here we come!

Chapter 20

No Turning Back

*B*ang! The fiberglass creaks and the boat stalls.

Is this the end?

The waves come from three directions on our side, topped with tumultuous chop from the strong winds. They collide underneath *Irie*, creating terrifying sounds and abrupt movements. The boat is constantly swinging, pitching, bucking, and banging into the sea. She sways from left to right, lifts up, goes down. *Luckily not all the way down.* Being jetted up and landing with a smack, *crash*, back onto the water makes napping – makes anything – impossible. The hulls whiz through the water next to our sleepy heads. We're attacked from beneath. Rollers become explosives: *crack, bang, kaboom!* Once in a while there is a ginormous one. It sends a shiver throughout our bodies and our vessel; our entire home vibrates and flexes.

No wonder my husband wants to be done and sell *Irie* upon arrival.

"This too will pass."

Dare I add "It could always be worse? We could sink!"? Better not. Mark hates that statement. It could certainly be worse, though.

Despite being extremely uncomfortable and getting tossed around for days, vomiting, feeling numb, unable to do anything more than hold on and brace ourselves, we don't feel unsafe. We're not scared. We're not hungry. We're not in danger. *Irie* is holding on like a real ocean-going champ and she protects us from the worst of the elements: exposure to sun, wind, and waves. Most of the time, anyway.

An unexpected jerk followed by a thunderous *bang* flashes me back to reality.

"What the hell was that?" I jump up, set my queasiness aside, and check our saloon. Several objects are spread over the floor. This is not allowed on a catamaran! Stuff on the shelves ought to *stay* on the shelves. I crawl over the ground, bracing myself against anything that isn't wobbly, snatching the books, utensils, and souvenirs scattered on the floor.

Hopefully, I won't get slammed against the wall or the cabinets.

By the time I finish cleaning up, my face is pale and I'm in urgent need of fresh air.

I'm so happy we don't have to deal with children yet.

I spew the contents of my stomach in the turbulent ocean.

The 30-knot southeasterly steadily grows to 35 knots, gusting stronger and stronger. The sea grows exponentially. Waves the size of a two-story building are fueled by frequent squalls. They pick *Irie* up and toss her like she's a plastic toy thrown around a bathtub by a frustrated toddler. We both remain in the cockpit at all times, hooked on for safety.

"Look at that wave." My gaze freezes as a foaming mass of water approaches. The all-encompassing tower is about to collapse and spill its contents over us.

"Quick, close the door!"

Too late...

Seawater floods the cockpit and makes its way into the saloon. Back inside I bounce, gathering a dry shammy and a wet sponge. Anything salty on a boat means trouble in the long run. It will always suck moisture from the air, acquiring a permanent state of dampness. Fresh water rinses are of the utmost importance. The cloth gathers most of the intrusive seawater that I keep wringing out in the sink. The tapwater-soaked sponge takes care of the leftover salt crystals. Our living quarters are clean, but I'm sick again and rush outside. Up close, I can tell *Irie* is flying along at seven to eight knots. That's the silver lining; she's performing beautifully speed-wise, covering around 170 miles every 24 hours. It's a hell of a ride, yet she's on top of it.

I miss the early days of this crossing when we progressed at a snail's pace and wondered whether we'd *ever* get there. The water is always bluer on the other side. At least the sea was calm then. We could bake bread and occupy ourselves in a pleasant way. I prefer the pace of a Sunday driver over a reckless sports car any time I cross an ocean.

Our world has been turned upside down with no end in sight. Another attack of water soaks everything and everyone in the cockpit: table, seats, cushions, stack of bananas, plants, geckos, and us. Water leaks into our bathroom through the solar vent. The sealant needs replacing but now is not the time. We duct tape a plastic salad bowl upside down over the vent. Problem solved.

Mark and I improvise a wall with our cockpit cushions, wedging them between the deck and the bimini canvas. We place our lounge seat crookedly against the table to block the incoming waves and protect our plants underneath. We baptize the basil, mint, and spinach with fresh water in an attempt to rescue our nominal crops and hope our stowaway geckos have survived the salty blow. We're all victims of the ocean's mood. It's hard to keep anything alive aboard *Irie* right now. Even our spirits.

Shammies soaked with fresh water make our cockpit livable again, once the seats are dry. The boat moans and groans, shocks and rocks. Flying fish, stranded on deck and on the trampoline, don't need to be removed anymore. The boisterous sea takes care of that by flushing our topsides.

Beep, beep, beep... Now what? One of the water alarms goes off. It's Mark's turn to enter *Irie*'s bowels, while I intently stare at the fractured horizon. Seawater entered the port engine room through the air vent and hose. One of the waves must have hit the miniature opening under the *Fountaine Pajot Tobago* plaque just right. *Or wrong.*

More cleaning up with cloths, sponges, and fresh water cause the customary bruises. Our tired brains are put to the test. How can we avoid this influx of water, and particularly, the clean-up, in the future? I wobble down to join Mark inside. We take the thick, plastic air hose off and stuff the hole in the hull with a towel. Our IQ is fried. Not an hour later, a giant wave pushes the towel out and dumps gallons of seawater into our engine room. *How could we have been so stupid?* We mop and rinse and dab fresh water wherever we can reach. We re-install the hose. I hang over the rails and feed the fish again.

"Are you still having fun?" My husband rubs it in.

No, this sucks. But it's the only way to reach the islands.

Only seven more days of this, or ten, or 15. So it goes. Day after day. Hour after hour. We sit in the cockpit, we check the instruments, we adjust the sails, we try to nap, we deal with unexpected issues and surprises, and we complain, until even that requires too much effort. The month of May 2013 is progressing, slowly and intently. It's okay. I can handle it. As long as Mark, *Irie,* and I eventually get there, without losing our sanity, or more.

꩜ ꩜ ꩜

The violent motion has been going on for eight days.

Why was I so adamant to cross this ocean? Am I insane?

Think positive.

It could be worse. *Really.* As far as the eye can see, up or down or straight ahead, we're engulfed in blue. A blue world is preferred to a grey one or a black one promising storms. We have plenty of food and everything is still intact, boat *and* body parts. Except for my stomach, Mark's scabbed forehead, and our bruises.

"We can do this, sweetie!" I force a smile.

I hate to admit it. Despite the warnings from my other half and my thinking it wouldn't be a big deal – Mark has been known to exaggerate and over-worry – I have gone overboard provisioning for this journey. You could say *Irie* is slightly overweight. As a result, our sailboat moves more sluggishly, which explains her stubborn behavior in the current weather conditions. She's slow to react to the autopilot, lags behind running down waves, and once in a while the bows dip under the sea surface. Every time I see that I beg we won't flip.

Mark was right.

In the past, our nights offered somewhat of a reprieve in settled conditions; a few hours of sleep happily snatched up. Now, our nocturnal watches are extensions of the infinite days of doing nothing, staring into space, and going through the motions of responsibilities. These last eight days have become a real test. Of patience, of endurance, of focus, of caring – or not. Our conversations are kept to a minimum, our sex life is non-existent, our zest for life is extinguished by the movements of the ocean; the same body of water that guides us to our destination.

Cooking meals used to be a welcome distraction from the daily routine. Now, we stuff crackers in our mouths or eat a banana from the never-ending supply. We have 50 left under the cockpit table, all ripe at once. It's too uncomfortable to cook. We eat canned food and don't bother warming it up. Cold baked beans. Juice flies off our spoons with every bite, smudging the table, the cockpit, ourselves. Like the breadcrumbs and lettuce bits last night and the milk at breakfast. The wind is in control. We don't care. About the mess and about the lack of culinary delights. If none of these substances leave my body at the wrong end, I call the meal a success.

We have turned into zombies, following automatic impulses to survive. Every day we get closer to the Gambier Islands, our energy is drained a tad more. We consider changing course to the Marquesas for a smoother trip. Every. Single. Day.

Is that route called the *Milk Run* because the milk actually runs to your stomach instead of down your face when eating cereal? We don't change course. We're stubborn. I'm stubborn. After our determination and suffering so far, I'm not giving up, losing our hard-won headway. Nope. Not. Ever.

We have to visit the Gambier archipelago and join our friends on

Pitufa. It takes my remaining strength to convince Mark. We won't regret it; our situation will improve sooner than later. It has to. I dutifully draw another vertical mark in pencil above our sliding door. Like in prison. I have 13 so far.

How many more will be added?

🌊 🌊 🌊

Everything ends. Even being uncomfortable at sea.

On day 15 of our Pacific crossing, the wind and waves settle down and we return to pre-hell. I don't have to fight seasickness, water intrusion, discomfort, and Mark's foul moods anymore. We eliminate the last veggies stored on a spare bunk. Mark makes a delectable, over-sized pumpkin soup, with three pounds of fresh pumpkin and three carrots thrown in. We prepare favorite dishes, like falafel on homemade spinach flat bread, spaghetti carbonara, shrimp curry, and exquisite salads with eggs, cheese, ham, and beets. Mark Bittman's recipes are put to the test in the middle of the ocean!

One day, Mark produces American-Belgian chocolate chip cookies. The recipe is American, the dark chocolate chips Belgian, thanks to my cousin Griet who delivered them to the San Blas. They're the best cookies in the world: crunchy on the outside, soft with melting fondant chocolate in the middle. Straight from the oven, they're to die for.

Mark and I aren't the kind of people who like routines, but on this trip, with days and nights split 50/50, a schedule is preferable. We settle into a familiar groove. The morning starts at 0600, when we write an entry in the logbook. Military time is implemented on ships, so that's how we start our entries and divide the day. We consult the weather report, (re) consider our course, and (re)adjust the sails. I take a nap after my night shift.

At 0900, the daily Pan Pacific net starts on the SSB radio. We listen to the check-ins from "vessels underway," plot friends' positions, and track their progress towards the Marquesas or the Gambier Islands. If we're lucky, we receive a reliable, current weather forecast of "our area." We can't check in ourselves, since we don't have an SSB transmitter, only a small receiver. We also don't own a water maker, a freezer, or a life raft, which makes us rudimentary members of the puddle jump crowd. The dinghy and two waterproof ditch bags filled with survival gear make up our emergency supplies and are part of our SOS contingency plan.

We sail, stare at the horizon, fish, rest, and figure out routing and weather. Mark does a fantastic job interpreting and incorporating the GRIB files, but the forecasts are never right. The wind directions seem accurate, yet the speeds are over- or underestimated.

On the hour, we put an entry on our navigation computer with the details of the moment: time, longitude and latitude, total miles on the log, speed over ground, course, wind direction and wind speed, and comments. The last column contains one line when Mark enters the information and an entire paragraph when I do it. Did I ever mention I love to write? Even in logbooks.

At 1130, we cook our main meal. While we keep our fingers crossed for protein-rich sea life, today's catch is a vegetarian dish involving spinach. We make sure to spice it up with fish sauce and eat at noon. Our stores are dwindling. Provisioning for a long passage is tricky. The problem is not what to get – you buy whatever is available – but how much. You want enough fresh produce to last the duration of the voyage, but you don't want (too many) items to go bad. After our clean-up, Mark takes a nap, and I write in the shady part of the cockpit.

1700 is the milestone of the day, not with cocktails but with the satellite phone. Mark sends previously written emails out and grabs the meteorological predictions and new mail.

He succumbs to more routing and weather plotting and adds another log on the screen. I scribble the same information in our paper logbook as back-up and mark our course on a gigantic chart of the Pacific Ocean. This is also the moment of truth: how much distance did we cover the last 24 hours? The answer is disappointing or exciting and, either way, resembles a quarter of an inch on the chart. Like our monthly expense tracking, we usually can tell whether it will be a good or a bad day, but the numbers deliver the facts. Only then do we read the incoming emails. It's the most heart-warming part of the day.

We're not forgotten. We're not alone. We're still loved.

We have a dinner of meat and veggie sandwiches and do the dishes. That saltwater pump Mark installed at the sink is safer than a bucket in the cockpit right now and one of the best additions to an always improving *Irie*.

At 1745, the evening procedures begin with reeling in the fishing lines. We trail two handlines off our stern, a short one on starboard and a longer one on the port side. During rough weather, we don't deal with catching fish and the resulting bloody procedures. Now that we're sailing at a decent clip, we anticipate fresh tuna or mahi-mahi any day. But the fish aren't biting. We've tried colorful lures, suicidal squid found on deck, and stranded flying fish. To no avail.

The Pacific fish are either stubborn or smart. Or – more likely – we still don't know what we're doing. Buying a species identification book apparently doesn't help catch them!

We figure out a (new) course and sail trim before the sun sets to avoid the cold, windy, pitch-black, and slippery decks at night. At 1800, daytime officially ends. I rest in our bunk downstairs. The swooshing of the waves lulls me to sleep.

At night, Mark and I take turns at the helm. He starts. In a comfy cockpit lounger, he reads on his tablet and listens to music. *The Grateful Dead* is my guess. He keeps an eye (and hopefully an ear) on all things boat related.

Until we reached the Galapagos, as night passage rookies, we stuck to three-hour shifts, like most cruisers. After talking to experienced British sailor friends, who swear by longer blocks of time, we upped the shifts to six hours. On watch, that seems like a long time to be awake in the dark – it is – but I like it. When the sea behaves. It allows an adequate chunk of me time; six hours doing whatever I please, within the realms of an ever-moving surface, the size of a pickup bed. Even though night and day in the tropics are the same length (12 hours), it feels like the days go by quicker. 6pm is always right around the corner, while 6am appears miles away.

Around midnight, Mark gently wakes me. In a daze, I put my gear on, listen to his observations, and settle into the night scene. First, I'm in the helm seat to get familiar with the movements of the boat and the indications on the instruments. Then, I get comfy on the deluxe cockpit seat.

Our waterproof tablet is my best friend when on solitary duty. I write my diary and blogs, read eBooks, and play sudoku to exercise my mind. I listen. The boat slices through the water and the wind generator buzzes on and off sporadically. The sky explodes with bright stars. Our trail sparkles with phosphorescence. I check the instruments and sails. Every 15 minutes, I stand and scan the horizon in case there's an obstacle on our path. There never is, or I don't spot it. Once in a while, I doze off, to wake up with a start.

Good I'm not driving a car right now.

When something is amiss or appears unusual – an obstacle closing in on the radar, a substantial shift in the wind, an imminent storm, or an alarming sound – I wake Mark. It's our most important night rule, after "do not fall overboard" which is paired with "always wear your life jacket attached to the boat." These rules can mean the difference between life and death. If Mark can't trust that I wake him up when there's a (potential) problem, he won't be able to relax. Our duty to communicate is the key to sleeping; a restful six hours in ideal circumstances. That's the advantage of a long night shift.

At 0600, after a glorious sunrise, I call on Mark. I'm exhausted. He puts our foul weather coat on, combined with his heavy-duty pants and life jacket, and clips himself on the helm seat. It's his turn to be in control of the boat and mine to fill him in about the current weather and sailing conditions. I head downstairs. The cycle starts over. More often than not, we have to adjust the sails together at night. Then, it's back under the covers to listen to the rhythm of the waves; tune into *Irie*'s groove, interrupted only by a mysterious *bang* on the hull or bump in the road.

Every five days, we take a full-fledged shower. Because it's too dangerous to dunk ourselves in the ocean, even with a line attached to the boat, we come up with a different system. Our primary sun shower contains fresh water from the Galapagos and our "spare" sun shower, with its leaking cap and loose hose, is filled with seawater by bucket. There's a lot of resistance from the water when you're gliding or bouncing along at six and a half knots. Caution has to be taken, so neither bucket nor person is lost overboard. After the bags warm up, the saltwater part of the routine consists of wetting, washing with shampoo, and rinsing. The second part is the familiar rinse off with fresh water. Losing our balance umpteen times is part of the experience.

Mark and I have one freshwater tank, holding 53 gallons (200 liters) of water. We also carry four six-gallon jerrycans, of which two are filled for this crossing. This adds 12 gallons (45 liters) of water to our supply, kept for the main sun shower and emergencies. At anchor, these 65 gallons last one month. We use the filtered tank water to wash up, brush our teeth, cook, rinse dishes, and drink. We've become prudent users of fresh water, utilizing seawater wherever possible. This habit comes in handy on a passage that might last longer than one month.

The seas have subsided, and the ride is slow, yet more comfortable. We'll get there after all. And I'm pretty sure there's no yacht broker in the remote Gambier Islands to sell *Irie*.

Of course, I hope Mark changes his mind about that as we discover Polynesia's beauty. The new weather brings inconsistent winds. The anemometer needle bounces around, between SE and NE, and so do we, constantly changing course, adjusting the sails. It's a tiring job. When the wind picks up again, stormy weather is near. We fight it head-on for two days.

🌊 🌊 🌊

Before making landfall in the South Seas, after a multiple-week odyssey (on a not so *pacific* ocean), an advertised image comes to mind: lush mountains, pristine white-sand beaches, turquoise water, a bright blue sky. Local beauties await with baskets full of tropical fruits, and fragrant flowers in their long black hair.

The challenging crossing is finally over. I can smell dirt. We're almost there.

Land ho!

A vague contour line is visible in the distance. Or are those clouds? Twenty pencil marks decorate the fiberglass wall in the cockpit. We're ready to arrive in Rikitea town, on the island of Mangareva in the Gambiers. I can taste the sweet fruit it has in abundance. I wonder who's there. It will be fantastic to catch up with friends, be able to walk on land, and sleep in a stable bed.

My daydreaming doesn't last long. Reality hits with a thunderclap and a gush. As the fantasized land approaches, it speeds up, turns black, and morphs into another full-blown storm. I struggle to write a daily update for my *It's Irie* blog, which keeps family and friends abreast of our progress. "Too rough. Too uncomfortable. Too wet. Too bouncy. Too seasick. Too tired. Too much wind, 25 to 30 knots on the nose! Too frustrating. Too much complaining... to write a full-size blog. Another 68 annoying miles to go. Almost there. Almost!"

After a sleepless night, I put pencil mark 21 above our sliding door. Will this be the last one? Are our prison days over? Where is paradise? Where is this anticipated landfall, this tropical Polynesian island? Where is Mangareva?

Its mountain tops appear and disappear, shrouded by clouds and rain. A few hours of consistent wind and progress are followed by the most dreadful weather. The low-pressure system we'd hoped to avoid – not that we could have planned around it – is coming right at us. We douse the jib, run the engines at full power, and bash into the waves, wind chop, and an opposing current to approach the safety of the lagoon. We creep forward at three knots. Heavy rain drives into our faces and salty waves crash over the bows. *Irie* struggles. The worst is kept for last... We don't feel welcome in this disguised tropical paradise.

De laatste loodjes wegen het zwaarst. The last mile is the longest.

Mark and I navigate an inexhaustible *Irie* through the wide entrance into the Gambier ring of islands. Instead of azure blue, the water is lead grey. Despite being in protected waters, the heavy frontal wind creates short, steep waves. We need to dive into them and bounce our way towards the harbor, following the channel. The raging lagoon swallows us.

The rain stops, but it takes four hours to cover the last ten miles to the main town.

Approaching the Rikitea anchorage, drenched and utterly exhausted, we hear cheering, ringing bells, and fog horns. *Welcome to the Gambier!* Goose bumps erupt on my arms. Tears well up. We made it. *Irie*. Mark. Me. The brave boat, the tested couple, the drooping basil, and the hiding geckos. Everywhere we look, fellow cruisers wave us on and scream compliments across the water. They acknowledge *Irie*'s accomplishment. Our small boat has achieved a big feat. They know what we went through. They can relate.

Once we're settled, Birgit and Christian emerge from *Pitufa*. They swing by to say hello and hand us a basket full of local produce, a fresh baguette, and a bottle of bubbles. She has a *tiare* flower in her long, black hair.

Chapter 21

Cold and Clear

Each day, the anchor snuggles the sandy bottom of a clear lagoon emitting every hue of blue. Mark and I hop around by boat, soaking up the different locales and communities of the Gambier archipelago.

While sailing from one pretty spot to the next is a joy, a careful eye has to be kept on protruding coral heads, patches of reef, and ever-present pearl farm buoys. This lagoon water provides the ideal environment for pearl farming, which keeps local people employed and boosts the economy. These pearls are referred to as black or Tahitian pearls, but the best of the best are harvested here in the Gambiers.

Did my triple-pearl birthday necklace come from here?

It's arguably the most affluent island group in French Polynesia. Being this far removed from civilization due to their location, the Polynesians aren't lagging behind with their gadgets and standard of life. For once, *yachties* appear to be at the bottom of the poverty level. We're not seen as walking wallets, but as curious visitors, welcome everywhere and regularly invited for a cup of coffee or an offering of fruit.

There is a strong sense of culture and tradition, expressed in tattoos, dances, songs, and musical instruments. We indulge in the infatuation with past rituals and the desire to continue these during the annual *Heiva* festival. This native dance and music competition is at the core of every man and woman in the Gambier Islands; the two troupes practice for months.

Finally, for ten days leading up to July 14th (Bastille Day in France and the day indigenous people were allowed to practice their traditions again after years of suppression by missionaries), both groups perform their dances. Together with Birgit and Christian, we watch Mangarevan, Polynesian, and Tahitian dances with elaborate costumes. The bands play hand-crafted instruments. Their glorious voices carry divine songs. Food and games are available in the stands around the sandy stage; alcohol is banned. The prize giving ceremony at the end is extensive, emotional, and festive.

I wonder whether Mark is having a good time.

Despite the colder weather, the pulsing festival pumps warmth through my veins. It's a taste of what awaits in the Marquesas.

A stone's throw away from the "hustle and bustle" of the capital Rikitea, but still protected by the outer reef, is where we find the real charm. Taravai, Aukena, and Akamaru rise from the gin-clear waters with a decent altitude and a proud attitude. Their picturesque scenery invites us to drop anchor and stay indefinitely.

While each island has its own character, the trio has a few things in common. The hilly surroundings provide a beautiful backdrop and an opportunity to hike or explore the interior; each crest reveals a superb view of the lagoon and neighboring islands. To reach their tops, we scramble through brush, get lost in tall reeds, kick stones, and collect scratches and bruises.

The beaches are perfect for swimming and lounging in the shade of palm trees or pine trees. Healthy reefs host a plethora of colorful fish and with immaculate visibility, snorkeling is a pleasure, whenever I brave the chilly water. A wetsuit helps, but after ten minutes of fish gazing, my lips turn blue and my skin resembles that of a plucked chicken.

I enjoy being out and about by myself, but it would be nicer if Mark would accompany me. He hates being cold but still joins me to shore. The air temperature above the water surface appears more pleasant, although it's the same 60°F.

There's a cute church in each settlement, where the grounds are impeccably kept. Ruins add to the atmosphere. The few families that live here take good care of their heritage and are friendly, generous, and welcoming to the occasional tourist. The anchorages remain little visited. A feeling of peace wafts over us. For a little while.

Winter in these islands brings inconsistent weather. The winds whip down the valleys and around the points of land with mighty force. Lightweight *Irie* flies from one side of the bay to the other, wherever we're anchored. Our eyes grow big as we whisk about, barely clearing spectacular reefs or neighboring boats. We count on our scope calculations being correct and our ground tackle doing its job.

When cold fronts are predicted, every cruiser moves back to the protected harbor of Rikitea, which then becomes a can of sardines. Boats of diverse sizes and shapes don't move alike. The dark hours are anything but restful. We keep watch and worry about running into a neighbor. One sleepless night – engines on in order to avoid collisions – our track adds up to three miles of crisscrossing within our anchor radius!

When benign weather returns, most sailors set off in opposite directions again, after buying groceries and baguettes, socializing, and catching up online. The islands offer enough beauty to keep me entertained; to explore, hike, and snorkel. Mark loses interest. The colder it gets, the grumpier his mood becomes.

"You know it's much warmer in the Marquesas, right?" It's his daily statement.

"Yes, but we already plan to spend cyclone season there. That's half a year! Adding more months seems crazy. I'd rather stay here longer. It's more special and less popular."

He sighs, closes the sliding door to keep the cool air out, and pouts behind his computer.

≫ ≫ ≫

I stand on the bow and stare intently at the water ahead. There are no charts for this area south of Taravai. We're smart, waiting for the sun to sit high in the sky in order to see the reefs and skirt them. It's what you're supposed to do: navigate the waters on cloudless days with the sun directly above or behind you. Except, we're wrong. Because we're not smart.

"I can't believe this annoying sun! I can't see a damn thing."

Mark slows *Irie* down to a crawl. The sun emits her strong, gorgeous light directly in our eyes, at 11am.

"Do you see anything in the water? Any dark spots at all?" Mark asks again. I feel frantic. The glare is blinding. Do I say "yes" to instill confidence in my captain? Or do I stick to "no," meaning we can hit a reef any moment? I squint my eyes.

How could we have been so dumb, forgetting the noon sun sits in the north here instead of the south. We need to get used to this Southern Hemisphere thing, and soon. As in, yesterday.

"To the right, to the right!" I scream. Mark instantly tugs at the wheel. I glance back over my port shoulder in awe. Our wake shimmers half a foot away from a black patch of coral.

"We passed an attractive snorkel spot." I smile at Mark. He shakes his head as we inch deeper into the protected, reef-strewn anchorage to settle for the night. Beauty comes at a price. In this instance, the fee is non-material, only frazzled nerves and irregular heartbeats.

≫ ≫ ≫

The north and east sides of the magnificent Gambier lagoon are framed by postcard perfect *motus* (low-lying barrier islands containing white sand and palm trees), one of which is Totegegie, where the airport is located. During settled weather, we venture to these exotic, flat isles. They're similar to the atolls in the Tuamotus, an area we look forward to visiting later. No rocky outcrops or verdant hills here, but long stretches of white sand and plenty of coral. The seawater is transparent, the snorkeling some of the best we've experienced, and coconuts are plentiful. It's a place to stroll the beaches and unwind. The 360-degree view from the cockpit is outstanding, the colors of the lagoon awe-inspiring.

This is what I desire. Live in the here and now; savor glorious moments; have no regrets.

Yet, Mark's discontent increases. Every move with *Irie* seems a hassle and every boat project a burdening chore. That recent Pacific crossing didn't help his declined interest in living on a boat. Add to that constantly being cold and it's a recipe for unhappiness.

Frequently, the wind comes from the south (think South Pole, with no land between here and there) and is icy. On land, the roads and trails are sheltered from the blasts, so during the weekends Mark and I walk in town or hike over hills. When we find a sunny spot, we sit and soak up the warmth, like a lizard in the Galapagos Islands. Whenever the sky is bright blue and the air still, I drop everything and go for a snorkel. Other times, I long for the spectacular coral formations from above. The habitats are inviting; the cold water is not. I feast only with my eyes, while the rest of my body confirms that we're warm weather sailors.

After two months of roaming about the Gambier archipelago, enjoying its treasures and frowning at its quirks, our annoyance with the wind patterns, Arctic air, and funky anchorages has become omni-present. The Pacific is a bitch when it comes to weather systems. We need to move on, so I don't have to listen to my husband's complaints anymore.

Another week-long crossing won't be the solution for his moods, but it's the only way to get to the Marquesas Islands.

Sorry, Mark.

Chapter 22

Majestic Land, Mysterious Culture

I stir under the sheet. *What is that stomping above me?* It's Sunday. I want to sleep in.

That's why I didn't join other cruisers to a Marquesan church service in Vaitahu, two miles away by dinghy. Mark arose earlier and I must have fallen back asleep. I like waking up slowly in the morning when it's not too hot yet to linger in bed. During the week, it's my favorite time, snoozing, dominating the full width of the mattress, while my husband types away upstairs at 6am. This morning, I hear a *creak* and a *bang* instead of the usual *click, click, click* of his keyboard. The anchor locker opens, and slams shut.

What is he doing on deck before breakfast?

Seconds later, his head pops around the corner. He grabs his swimsuit and presses his lips on my forehead.

"There must be something in the water. Michael is snorkeling around his boat and Ursula is about to follow. I'm going in," he says. Our neighbors, friends we made back in St. Martin, also decided to skip church apparently.

"What?" I look at the clock. 7:30am. We never venture into the sea first thing in the morning. I need to sweat before I jump in. Unless there's potential for a wildlife encounter.

I slide down, put my bikini on, and rush outside, stubbing my big toe along the way. Behind *Irie*, three bodies bob in the water, heads down, snorkels up. Around them, small triangles break the water surface. *Sharks?*

I grab my own snorkel gear and get ready to brave the chill. Mark's on his way back already. *Did I miss it?*

"You're not going to believe this. I need your camera to take photos and movies!"

"Of what?"

"Three manta rays are feeding right there, and they don't seem to mind our presence."

Manta rays!?

We heard they occasionally show up in this bay but didn't count on seeing them, let alone up-close. I hand Mark my underwater camera, slip in the water, and swim over. Three gentle giants, with a wingspan wider than my five-foot, ten-inch (178cm) length, mosey about, mouths wide open. Michael and Ursula float with them, GoPro at the ready. Thousands of grey particles restrict our visibility. That's why the mantas are here, to feed on plankton. They circle beneath us, once in a while skimming the surface. We come eye to eye. *Magnificent creatures.* To enjoy this spectacle, we just relax in the water and watch the feeding scene unfold and repeat.

"We're only obstacles in their soup," Ursula murmurs through her snorkel. The three rays stick around, sometimes so close that the tips of their wings brush against our skin. When they approach, we look straight into their webbed mouths, which filter the feed.

I want this precious moment to last forever. I love animals.

After an hour, our bodies are cold and our stomachs rumble. Time for us to eat.

Mark and I are anchored in Hanamoenoa bay on Tahuata, an island teeming with marine life. In a cove to the north, we witnessed spinner dolphins perform tricks for hours from our cockpit. Unlike the Dusky dolphins in New Zealand, they were not fond of my presence in the water and remained out of view. A daily open-air show of these smart and playful animals jumping, flipping, and spinning provided special entertainment.

In our current anchorage, we luck out with more than a manta ray visit. Late afternoon, frigate birds hover over the bay, which turns tumultuous. The sudden rush of water and fins resembles a strong current. Schools of small fish "run" on the water surface with their tails, attacked from above by a frigate bird – successful in scooping one fish up each dive without ever touching water – and from below by a bigger predator. A two-foot tuna surfaces and splashes empty-mouthed on top of the water. Another one leaps out in a perfect arc, dolphin-style, with a fish in its mouth.

I remember the tuna we caught approaching the Marquesas. It shook itself loose, fatally injured, to become food for the sharks. This heart-breaking experience was muted by a visually striking landfall in Fatu Hiva after our six-day sail from the Gambier Islands. Its Bay of Virgins, consisting of phallus-like outcrops, is a magical anchorage. Ashore, we hiked through the jungle to reach the most quintessential waterfall in the most paradisiacal setting. Hospitable people showered us with smiles and tropical fruits, like their signature pamplemousse (a sweet grapefruit the size of my head), mangos, coconuts, and bananas. We traded wares from our boat for a wooden tiki statue, artfully crafted by a local sculptor.

During our time in French Polynesia, we'd exchange toiletries – purposefully bought in Panama – and baked goods for fresh produce, pearls, and fish.

I'm a fan of swapping possessions, talents, or knowledge instead of paying for a service. It fits the minimalistic lifestyle I continue to love. The value of a treasure is more than a price tag.

A couple of hours after our incredible wildlife encounter underwater, I notice the church group has returned home. I decide to pay my friend Lisa a visit. Mark's occupied at his computer. After months of inactivity with The Wirie business, his brain needs a challenge. He feels stupid without the stimulation. I'm fine with a more relaxed and slightly dumber Mark! Whenever we have internet, he deals with customers again and researches possibilities to improve our products. Today is one of these days. His nose is either buried in a boat project or glued to a screen.

I often wonder what my position is on this boat. How do I contribute, other than helping with projects and household chores? I might as well raise a family, like stay-at-home moms, to achieve *something* after our stint on the water. Imagine, after years of sailing, to have only produced blog posts, a few articles, and four translations. The pathetic amount of money made is spent in a week, and all I have left are empty pockets and a frustrated husband. That could hardly be called accomplishment.

Yep, it's a good time to see a friend.

"How was church?" I ask Lisa as I climb aboard her and Fabio's streamlined 48-foot sailboat, *Amandla*. She started this sailing journey as an adventurous, determined, single woman after a successful career in New York City. Her #1 bucket list item is "sail around the world, one ocean at a time." Meeting captain Fabio, an acclaimed writer and photographer, turned her into permanent crew on *Amandla* and brought her closer to achieving this circumnavigation dream.

"It was wonderful in every sense of the word," she says. "The villagers were dressed in their white Sunday bests, the choir sang heavenly songs, and a group of men played local instruments. The entire service was in Marquesan, so we didn't understand a word. Not that I speak French anyway."

It sounds similar to the church service Mark and I attended on Fatu Hiva.

"How was your morning? And how's Mark doing?" she asks. With bells and whistles I recount our snorkel experience and relay that Mark is buried behind his laptop.

"I totally understand he thinks he's brain-dead. Some of us need mental stimulation to feel alive. If you want to explore the island or the water, let me know and I'll join you." Always supportive and positive, Lisa is a friend you can rely on, or have an intimate chat with.

"You know how I've never been able to make up my mind about having children?" I start the conversation I really want to have.

"Uh-huh. I know how that feels as well. Tough decision."

"Yeah, and I'm already the Queen of Indecisiveness. No matter how big or small the topic. Mark hates it. That and my second guessing. Anyway, I told myself that if I ever want to have children, it has to happen before I turn 40. I'm almost 38."

"Better get on with it then. Getting pregnant can take a while, especially at your age."

"I'm not quite ready, but I consider it. Am I getting too old?" These realizations don't please me. But saying them out loud helps with accountability. I need to face reality and can't remain oblivious to life progressing. Fast. And not only for others. "I can't make up my mind and Mark's fine either way."

I sigh.

"Well, you could stop taking your pill and see what happens," she suggests. So simple, yet so effective. The easy way out. Mother Nature will decide.

"That's a great idea!" I'm happy to be a coward. "I love the 'let's see what happens' approach in life, so I might as well apply it for this."

I feel better when I leave Lisa's boat. I have a purpose now; a reason to make this adventure worthwhile. Raising a child on *Irie* while sailing the globe sounds perfect. The boat is roomy and stable, without sharp edges. With my teaching degree and passion for individualized education, I can homeschool until our son is 12 (I hope it's a boy). What better method to provide a kid with a world view than by traveling that world? I'm all for experience-based knowledge. *And Rosie and Axel can be his godmother and godfather.*

We even have a pink bottle of baby sunscreen onboard, which I saved for the occasion. It was given to us by an industrious friend, who thought she would make big bucks selling Dollar Store sunscreen in the Caribbean for a profit. She failed and donated the 100 bottles to fellow sailors. Every time I come across this bottle, stored in a tub under our bed, I think about having a baby and whether this is the moment.

Now *is* the moment. The butterflies in my belly still flutter when I hop on *Irie* and tie off the dinghy.

"I can't believe this stupid internet! I've been trying to load this page for ages. And my computer froze. I lost the notes I was typing," Mark bombards me. My ears tremble and my stomach contracts. The butterflies squeeze out and turn into uncertain words.

"What do you think is going on?" I ask against better judgment.

Why do I always want to engage? Feel sympathy? Continue the conversation if that's what this is? It's not. It's Mark needing to vent.

There's never a solution in these situations. Not for the internet problems and not for his mood. Again, I envision Darwin cowering in a corner and my mind switches to my imaginary son doing the same.

Could I ever have children with a temperamental man like Mark? Is this why I was never determined enough to go for it?

"How the hell do I know?" The expected answer.

I retreat downstairs, not knowing what to do, not knowing what to think. I stare at my half-consumed strip of birth control pills.

Do I even want to have sex with someone like this?

Counting on behavioral improvements of my spouse, I vow to stop after this month's pack. Maybe something miraculous takes place and I can give birth in Fiji next year.

We'll see what happens.

🌊🌊🌊

The drumming makes my heart soar. The colorful attire of the dancers adds to the festive mood and stands in stark contrast with the arid surroundings. The dry vegetation and hilly, brown features give the island of Ua Huka a surreal look, compared to the lush mountains of its Marquesan neighbors. At this three-day festival, Mark and I are engulfed by Polynesian people, their music, their food, their laughs, their positive spirits. The air is full of anticipation and vibrant with authenticity.

The Marquesas mini-festival, containing participants of all six islands – Ua Huka, Nuku Hiva, Ua Pou, Tahuata, Hiva Oa, and Fatu Hiva – is in full swing. It delivers a unique experience of the indigenous culture, its highlights, hospitality, beauty, and traditions. Despite the less than ideal anchorage, I didn't want to miss this body-pulsing event.

It took us from dawn until dark to sail 32 miles upwind from Nuku Hiva, the boaters' hang-out in the Marquesas. Acting like the purists we usually aren't, we decided to sail the entire way to Ua Huka, zigzagging for 13 hours, covering 70 miles in total – more than twice the actual distance. Consistent swells roll into Hane Bay, where we squeezed into a tight spot. The bay was packed with other cruisers. Waves rock us to sleep at night and wet landings on the rocky beach are inevitable. We row ashore and leave the dinghy engine on *Irie*'s railing, so it doesn't get ruined if we capsize. We hitch a ride and pile into a pick-up truck to reach the festival grounds. The drive has a desolate beauty, with magnificent seascapes.

With heartfelt, intense performances of the troupes, this native festival consumes us. We're one with the sounds, smells, and emotions. Our feet tap to the rhythms of the drums. *How I adore those drums!* Our ears embrace the singing voices, and our eyes feast on the elaborate movements of the dancers, their bronze bodies scantily clad in loincloths, skirts, and bras made of natural materials. Intricate tattoos, flower headdresses, and necklaces of boar teeth embellish their appearance. The Tahitian dances are slow and sensual, the Marquesan versions tribal and exhilarating. Performers as well as spectators are caught in a jarring, blissful trance.

I love it one hundred percent and I'm glad Mark is with me. Only after untangling a couple of boats – the wind had shifted – and moving *Irie* to a safer spot in the outer bay, was he okay to join the festivities. We prevented our floating home from crashing into a neighbor, fortunate to have still been around.

I know he was right to wait out the weather and make sure our boat, and the others, didn't get into more trouble. But the time-consuming ordeal tested my patience. I envied everyone else already at the event, ignorant to the chaos in the anchorage. They had fun, while we argued about my need to get ashore as soon as possible and his need to rescue boats. Our priorities clash.

On the last day of the festival, dedicated artists finish sculpting stone and wooden *tikis*. The *va'a* (canoe) races are canceled due to yacht congestion in the bay. The six troupes showcase a dance interpretation of the theme *the challenge*. When the dancing, singing, and drumming conclude, traditionally prepared dishes appear. A communal, free *kai kai* lunch is offered.

As we eat the exotic food on plates of banana leaves, hollowed bamboo, or coconut shells, we have no clue we'd face our own *challenge* the following day. Instead of being bent over the lines to sail to a comfortable anchorage, we're bent over the toilet bowl, pulsing stomachs replacing pulsing beats.

🌊🌊🌊

"Did you miss me?" Mark asks. I embrace him after three weeks apart.

"Not really. You know how it goes over there. A million doctors' visits to get everything checked and running around between friends, my *oma*, and other family, securing enough time for my parents. They were happy to see me after a year and a half. I'm glad I went."

My hope was for them to visit us in the Marquesas, an island chain they would enjoy. The mountains, the lushness, the hikes, the waterfalls, the food, the language. But French Polynesia is far away – literally halfway across the globe from Western Europe, with a 12-hour time difference. Plus, my mom gets sick in planes as well as boats, cars, and buses.

"Why don't you both come to Belgium instead," she suggested. "We'll pay for your trip." It sounded like a good alternative, since I enjoy the company of friends, family, and a real shower. Plus, we always need boat parts and chocolate. Mark wasn't comfortable accepting a $2,000 plane ticket.

"Tell your parents to do something fun with my share," he had said. I accepted the flight and appreciated my time apart.

"I thought about you once in a while." I kiss him on the lips and show my implant, a metal stud with a cap.

"Ouch. Did you feel anything?"

"Nope. But I heard *everything,* and my jaw was shaking from the drilling." I shiver at the thought, grateful it all happened quickly. Two days later I was on a plane with a metal piece in my jaw, some stitches, and pain killers. "I'm set up for a replacement tooth now and there's no rush anymore. I have to figure out where that's affordable. We might have to sail to India," I half-jokingly suggest. "How are you doing?"

"I fell on a winch the other day when I slipped on the cockpit cushion. My chest hurt a lot and now I have this raised scar tissue here," he says, feeling around his right nipple. "Luckily, the bump doesn't hurt anymore."

"How about your elbow?"

"The same." Mark has visited French doctors aplenty since we arrived in the Marquesas. First, it was for a painful elbow. "Oh, I see," the man in the white coat said. "It's tendonitis. Nothing to worry about. It'll disappear in a year or two." *Huh?*

Then, it was a cracked filling, which a French dentist fixed for free. On a different island, we visited the hospital to request a cortisone shot. The pain in Mark's elbow had become unbearable. Fixing *Irie,* let alone sailing her, was nearly impossible. Despite a bit of practice after his two right-handed misfortunes of the past, doing everything with his left hand created more bruises, cuts, and frustration than usual. Three months later, he requested a second shot. It remains a mystery how he suffered from tennis elbow without playing tennis.

"What did your family think about your tattoo?" Mark asks.

Seeing every person in the Marquesas sport these detailed skin decorations had made me consider one. My interest grew with the months. What better place to get a tattoo than where the art was invented? I decided on the imprint of a gecko. The day after Christmas, I told the tattoo artist in Nuku Hiva to use his imagination with the design and details of the lizard on the side of my right foot, tail curling around my ankle. My other request was a depiction of "adventure" inside the animal's body. The result was satisfying – a black gecko representing a cryptic journey from the waves of the oceans to the tops of the mountains. The wound was still fresh when I jumped on a plane the beginning of January 2014.

"As expected, my dad lifted his nose and my mom said 'ah, not bad.' When I took my socks off at my *oma's* house, she asked 'Is it real?' but I think she liked it. Wearing socks and shoes prevented more looks but felt nice for a change."

I don't think Mark can relate. If it were up to him, he'd never wear anything but flip flops ever again.

"How did you manage by yourself in Taiohae?"

We should have called more often.

"Fair. After that giant French boat dragged and almost hit *Irie* the day you left, I moved. It's a longer dinghy ride to shore but I feel safer, not surrounded by French cruisers."

I smile. Despite the majority acting arrogant and inconsiderate, we have made wonderful French sailing friends, like Marie. She and I are both trying to get pregnant (well, she's trying, I'm open to it) and joke we'll share a hospital room in Fiji to give birth on the sail west. Fiji is our tentative destination, where we'll decide what to do and where to go next. With or without a baby. But that's too far in the future to talk about. What we do talk about is Mark being in French Polynesia, where he can't speak or understand the language, which is getting old.

"Where is the router you brought?" Mark gets to the important stuff.

"Just a minute." I love unpacking and displaying the bounty I traveled 10,000 miles with.

I unload the *fondant* chocolate and new boat parts. Then, I fish out a small black box made in Lithuania. Mark has been thinking about integrating cell data connection in our Wirie products, so customers can choose between WiFi and cell service to connect to the internet. It's an idea he's been playing with for years, but the technology wasn't available. With this router, he'll experiment and figure out what can work. His new project. *Yay.*

"Have fun challenging your brain!"

I unpack my bag and find a place to store the goodies, edible and non-edible. That night, we finally have sex again. I'm not sure whether it's ovulation time, but I hope so.

To make this baby thing work, I ought to plan a bit better.

🌊🌊🌊

As cyclone season nears the end in the South Pacific, Mark and I talk about leaving the Marquesas for the Tuamotus. It has been a bouncy seven months and Mark needs a change. Even I am ready for a different location and not only because of my husband's complaints. We contemplate heading south before the storm season's over. The mountainous islands of the Marquesas are a safer environment than low-lying *motus,* which don't offer protection from heavy wind and waves, but white-sand beaches, picturesque atolls, and azure water beckon; our patience is wearing thin.

The need to work on *Irie* in Apataki's boatyard is the main reason we plot our route to that atoll. If a cyclone threatens, we'll get out of the water sooner. *A sound plan.*

After our conclusion to sail south, Mark joins his other lifetime partner: my rival, the machine.

How could he prefer sitting behind the computer all day when surrounded by beauty?

I want to see the sights. Mark is losing interest in our lifestyle. His focus keeps shifting.

Is this temporary?

He hasn't been happy since the Galapagos Islands. It makes me unhappy as well. *I miss his roaring laugh.* I hate how his moods influence me. But when you live together 24/7, that's what happens. When he's miserable, I'm miserable. *Why this ripple effect? Why don't I "just" ignore his behavior?* Because I care about him. I love him. If his feelings, his soul, his core self wouldn't affect me, I have no business being in this relationship anymore. Fact is, each time he yells or boils over with frustration, I can't focus on things I enjoy, like writing. All I do is cower.

Everything was easier in the Caribbean.

We often reminisce about our time in the West Indies; the happy hours, good friends, the relative ease of getting things (done). We fantasize and romanticize. Mark regrets leaving the Caribbean. At least, that's what he says when he's grumpy. I look at him from the corner of my eye, unable to do much else. Pathetic.

Me? Or him?

Women starve themselves and spend hours at the mirror and the gym to feel pretty. Entrepreneurs lock themselves up until their next invention. Business owners don't know the difference between weekdays and weekends. And software engineers are attached to their computer 14 hours a day to create the perfect Wirie product. Each of them is determined and dedicated.

These thoughts pop in my head when I watch Mark. His computer is an extension of his body. He's guilty as charged for being single focused on The Wirie. When we go to bed, he's tired. I hate to enforce scheduled sex sessions, so I don't.

Maybe we can make a baby in the Tuamotus.

Chapter 23

Perilous Postcard

The spires of Ua Pou become smaller and smaller. So does our distance to the atoll of Apataki. Goodbye mountains, rocks, and murky bays. It's time for lagoons, clear water, and sand. Clouds swallow the Marquesas. We're alone in the big, wide ocean. We check the instruments, adjust them. We check the sails, adjust them. We eat fruit, gifted by the locals upon our departure. As usual at sea, we need to consume the stack of bananas as quickly as possible. It must be the salty air; they all turn yellow at once. We want to share them with the people of the Tuamotus – where the *motu* soil isn't very fertile – if they're not rotten by then.

The sun induces a nap. Our peace is short-lived. Inconsistent wind causes us to bob about with limp sails one moment and charge ahead under full canvas the next.

Sailing is about wind. People say sailors are free. Free-spirited maybe, but the weather is your boss and the wind your manager. It decides where you go, when, and how fast. Or slow. Forget about the rain in squalls. Sure, it's wet and inconvenient, but it's the wind that messes things up.

The same goes for waves and swell. The sea would be calm if not for the wind. The harder it blows, the more discomfort the ocean creates and the choppier the anchorages become. The wind orchestrates your pace. And your well-being.

In the Caribbean – where the breeze is relatively consistent and pre-dictable – we plotted our course based on a conservative five knots of aver-age speed. We often arrived ahead of schedule. In the Pacific, that's too fast for reality. We are frequently becalmed, obstructed by a countercurrent, or sail in the wrong direction. This adds distance. And time.

The first two days of a long voyage are always the toughest. You have to get used to the constant motion, having to hold on, banging toes and heads, and staying up half the night. All you want to do is sleep. On day three, some routine has been established and you feel more inclined to be productive – take a shower, make banana bread, or fish – if the conditions allow such activities.

Enjoying turns annoying when the wind suddenly shifts or stops. For hours I wish for breeze. Not only are we becalmed, but no matter how flat the sea is, the incessantly flapping sails and erratically banging rigging would drive the sanest person crazy. There's no sleep for the off-watch crew with that racket.

Since the forecast calls for ever lighter winds, this situation is not a good sign. We reluctantly accept not arriving within four days. We drift for hours. We hope for more wind. We ask for more wind. We scream for more wind. We turn the engines on. It's loud, hot, and smelly. Despair takes over. Motoring for 25 hours would empty the fuel tank, wear the engines – and us – down, and deliver *Irie* to Apataki lagoon too soon for slack tide. Off they go. Quiet returns.

A wisp of air! A smile on our faces. The spinnaker shows her colors and at three knots, we move forward again. We might get there before Mark's birthday.

Apataki, like all atolls (islands consisting of a lagoon surrounded by *motus*) with passes (entrances), should only be entered at particular times. It would be foolish to attempt this at night, what with the reefs, wrecks, narrow gaps, and lack of navigation aids. Even during the day, timing is important. The tides aren't the problem in the passes; the currents are. The best time for a boat to enter or leave a lagoon is around slack tide, which happens every six hours.

Of course, the South Pacific being the South Pacific, there's no reliable tide schedule. Cruisers use what's called the "current guestimator."

With that information, we successfully slip into Apataki's channel and tie up at the village dock for our atoll introduction: a tranquil setting of pearl farms, palm trees, and the clearest of waters. From the moment we're settled, colorful fish nibble on the algae attached to our hulls. We stare into an aquarium. The locals greet us and hand out food, fresh produce, and fish. Our overripe bananas are eagerly accepted in return.

In pursuit of peace and beauty on Mark's birthday, we untie *Irie* and move to an uninhabited *motu* on the south side of the lagoon for two days of snorkeling and relaxation. From there, we want to sail to the boatyard, pick up a mooring ball, and get hauled out to start our list of boat projects. It's a foolproof plan. Except, when we enter the expansive lagoon, ominous clouds surround us.

We drop anchor in 16 feet of turquoise water accentuated by the last rays of sun. *Irie*'s butt faces the beach. Mark's ready for some rest; I can't wait to snorkel on the reefs behind us, an activity we haven't done in months.

Out of nowhere, the wind shifts 180°, swinging *Irie* into 52 feet of water towards the abyss of the lagoon. We sit tight when the first of many squalls needs an hour to pass. We watch the instruments, hoping for reprieve. Slowly, we turn around and our depth decreases. We lie in our initial spot again. The predicted north wind returns. And picks up. The waves build. *Irie* pitches. We barely manage the discomfort and want to press the stop button on the anemometer. There are no such buttons. The situation deteriorates. The wind shifts more and the gap between our bow and land is now 20 miles.

The anchorage – if you can call it that – becomes a nightmare as the waves build. One squall after another passes. *Irie* jumps up and down like a bucking bull. Three-foot waves smash against the hulls and hit the bridge deck. Everything is tossed around. We scrutinize the depth meter. *Are we dragging to the reefs? Shore?* We don't even see the island behind us anymore to gauge our distance. Rain pelts on the bimini. We're stuck and have to sit it out.

The night engulfs us. We don't sleep. It was calmer on the ocean; the current movements of the boat compare to sailing upwind in choppy seas. It's the most dangerous, uncomfortable, and dreadful 12 hours in our seven years of boat life and Mark's most awful birthday in 43 years.

This doesn't help my cause to keep cruising.

We realize then and there that it would be impossible to haul *Irie* in these conditions. A call on the VHF radio confirms our worries.

We have no choice but wait out this weather system at the village quay. After a miserable ride, we safely tie up. It rains hard and the strong wind pins us against the dock. We couldn't go elsewhere even if we wanted to. Every three hours, day and night, we adjust our fenders (bumpers), because the tides move *Irie* up and down and the currents propel us forward and backward.

"It could be worse. At least we're safe here and the water is flat. *Irie* hasn't been this stable in ages. We're alive and comfortable. What more do we need?" I smile at Mark.

He shoots me an exhausted stare. "What *I* need is to be settled on shore somewhere and not worry about the weather or this boat anymore."

It was a rhetorical question.

It *could* be worse. While I tell myself that to feel better and think positive, I don't count on it actually getting worse. But, it does. We are in the wrong atoll at the wrong time.

At night, a giant squall hits. Heavy, 30-knot north winds smash our boat against the dock and churn up the channel. The combination of high winds and funky currents creates chaos. *Irie* pitches violently, tightened by four lines to a cement dock, jerking her down with force. The ropes moan and screech. We worry our cleats will rip out, setting us loose in this mess. There is no getting away. We're literally pinned down. The storm only lasts half an hour, but we learn another lesson.

When I jump ashore, straight out of bed and buck-naked to fix the fenders at 4:30am, there's already a fisherman on the dock. *Oops!*

We retrieve the latest weather forecast: 20 to 30 knots of northwest winds. Imagine 48 hours of what we just experienced...

There's one option left: an anchorage at the north end of the atoll, 15 miles away. We hope to find protection there in three hours. We need to leave *immediately*. We can't wait for less wind or slack tide. Four bulky guys push us off the dock and away we scramble. An opposing current of four knots thrusts *Irie* left and right. Mark does a fantastic job steering through the eddies and preventing the boat from turning sideways, which would be disastrous. With the small engines on full throttle, we try to get out of the tricky pass and into the lagoon.

Mark and I drive against the wind, waves, and rain with 100 percent concentration. He hand-steers since the autopilot can't manage the rough conditions. Argus-eyed, I stand at the bow, watching for imminent danger. It lurks everywhere. Left, right, ahead, underneath. We have no time to eat, drink, or get a raincoat. Before long, the feared weather system is upon us.

This is when a boat should be holed up someplace safe and comfortable. We're too late...

It's blowing 30 to 40 knots; the waves are six feet high and close together. With constant squalls and even grander wind bursts, the rain drives down horizontally and whips our faces and bodies. Waves crash over the bow and into the cockpit, swamping us. I'm on deck, fully exposed to the elements – the wind claimed my bandana early on – with poor visibility. Mark focuses on the instruments, which show accurate charts of the Tuamotus. I point at every obstacle I see and scream to Mark which side and how far away I estimate them to be. Dark spots, pearl farm buoys, floats, lines.

We are the perfect team. Especially under pressure. We trudge on, skirt reefs, maneuver around floats, shiver from the cold, and swallow salt water. We curse. For six hours. That's how long it takes to bridge those 15 miles to safety, flat water, and underwater beauty.

After a few days of relaxation and snorkeling, a glorious 17-mile sail brings us to the Carenage. The lagoon is choppy as ever, while we wait until the yard workers are ready for *Irie*.

"Do you see that?" I alert Mark as we approach the haulout facility.

"Yep. Looks sketchy to me. I assume those black spots are coral heads and not weeds?" He nods at the dark areas scattered ahead. From the bow I have a better idea about their depth.

"They are. If you take it slow, we can weave through. There must be a safe path since boats get hauled here all the time."

Mark maneuvers *Irie* around the shallow reefs and crawls towards the beach. When the bows are a foot from touching sand, he keeps our floating home in position. I throw lines ashore. First the two from the front cleats. They're tied to palm trees ashore. Then, the two from the stern. Two workers hold them, while standing belly deep in the water. Our cat is temporarily immobile, so the trailer – pushed by a tractor – can get underneath the bridge deck. A diver attaches the straps. By the time we leave the water, it's 5pm. The workday is over. Our first night out is spent on the trailer.

The following morning, Alfred, the owner, positions us in a "nice spot," next to a group of trees which provides shade early afternoon, so we "can keep working without being too hot." We deal with the inconveniences of that location: no breeze to cool off, no batteries being charged (no sun), no rain collection due to tree debris on the roof, heaps of mosquitoes, and multiplying ants. They thrive on bugs falling from the sky, and so does *Irie*'s gecko population. *Everything is a trade-off*. This is to be our *motu* paradise for a week.

Our home doesn't move; we're finally safe, anchored on terra firma. Well-prepared with parts carried from the Marquesas and ordered from Tahiti, we focus on the job. We have our portable Honda generator to run power tools. There is no electricity on the island. No running water either. Every day, a metal barrel on our site is filled with well water. When we need to rinse something, we use a bucket and a cup. It's a tedious process but it works. Lit coconut husks create smoke when the sun sets behind the horizon, a decent attempt to repel mosquitoes. Back to the basics in exchange for a location that can't be beaten. After work, we rinse off our sweat, grime, and exhaustion in the glistening lagoon. A tropical breeze towels us dry; palm trees frame another spectacular sunset, as we sip a cocktail on the dock.

From 7am to 5pm, Mark and I labor as a well-oiled pair. I prep *Irie's* bottom and at last – high and dry and ready to apply – I put two layers of new paint on. Done are the days of scraping barnacles once a week. With a feeling of accomplishment, a clean boat, and a shorter project list, we leave this *enterprise in paradise* to enjoy the other Tuamotus.

꣠꣠꣠

Imagine a postcard depicting a quintessential white beach, heavily laden palm trees, turquoise water lapping the sand, and blue skies above. That's the image welcoming us to the southwest corner of the Fakarava atoll.

"What shall we do first?" My smile is as bright as the sunlight. Mark's appreciation of the tropical scene fails to hide his concerns. We're in a con-flicted situation. This scenario is what we've looked forward to for a year: agreeable weather, a pristine setting, and exciting activities in and out of the water. But a few days earlier, we saw a nurse in Fakarava's main town, Rotoava, to inquire about that stubborn bump in Mark's chest. It had been there for two months.

"Probably scar tissue," the orderly said. "From the moment you arrive in Tahiti, you should get it checked out at the hospital." Sound advice, but we're not sailing there any time soon. Cyclone season officially ended, we survived another exhausting boatyard stay, and we're finally ready to explore the gorgeous Tuamotus. The island chain is called the "dangerous archipelago" because of its tricky entrances, hard-to-see reefs, and hard-to-reach location.

We're here for months.

"We can dinghy to one of the *motus* or snorkel with the sharks in the pass and check out the resort there. Or we can find a sandbank and just hang out," I go on. Mark is open to any of it.

"Although, swimming with sharks is probably not the best idea right now, since my period started." *And I'm not pregnant again.*

Mark shrugs. "Okay. To the beach it is."

My husband pulls the dinghy closer, so I can jump in. He joins me, starts the moody engine, and I untie the line. We putter to the edge of an islet, wade in the water, and relax on the sand. Baby reef sharks cruise the shallow waters. I observe them in awe and can't wait to join their relatives. I watch the bright sky, swaying palm trees, and turquoise water. The reflection of the lagoon is so vivid that it turns the underside of the white-winged birds above us azure blue. My camera works in overdrive.

I grab Mark's hand as we stroll the shoreline. I wonder whether he's appreciating the beauty as much as I am. We sit down again, and I sigh. If only these moments could last forever.

I think about our RV trip through Mexico and Central America, a lifetime ago. I was excited then as well, sharing my delights every minute of the day. It was met with grumpiness. I acted too overbearing. It ended in a devastating breakup. I push the thought away. Often when I allow myself to be happy, those bad memories creep up. The here and now is what's important.

I know.

There's validity to enjoying these experiences internally and not express each sentiment that enters my head. I refrain from ooh's and aah's. I cherish the moment, his head on my lap.

The following day, Mark and I set out for our underwater discoveries in the pass. People from around the world come here to dive with sharks. Apparently, snorkeling with them is mind-blowing as well. We mosey over to the Tetamanu Village Resort and park our dinghy on the beach. Already, we see black-tipped dorsal fins circling in the shallow bay. We test the waters, walking among these intriguing creatures. I'm antsy for our shark encounter. When I researched "period" and "sharks" in the same sentence,

Google didn't come back with anything frightening. I'm determined to debunk the myths about these so-called blood-thirsty animals.

We motor our dinghy against the current. We don our snorkel gear, Mark attaches the tie-up line to his wrist, and we slide in the cool water. The current guides our bodies through the channel. We float belly down, tender within reach. Reef sharks rest on the bottom, fins spread wide. They appear small, 70 feet below. When we swim to the coral walls near the resort, a black-tip reef shark slithers by at eye level. Back in shallower water, the fish are colorful and abundant, the reefs vibrant, and the increased shark population moves with us, then against us. Mark stays at a respectable distance. I join the schools and snorkel alongside these mellow, vicious looking creatures. It thrills me to swim in their midst. And I can safely report that reef sharks don't seem to have more interest in bloody me than in anyone else.

That night, still in a trance of the day's experiences, I lie on our trampoline, gazing at the bright stars. Watching the sky outside is an inconvenience for Mark, so he's downstairs in his comfy bed. Often, I suggest spending the night under these majestic stars. And we have. But it always turns into a quick escape inside. Because of fabric imprints on our limbs or rain. I love being up here with a pillow and comforter, deep in thought, but it has become a rare occurrence.

Staring at the twinkling dots above brings me joy and sadness at the same time. Always, I'm amazed and apprehensive about the scale of the universe, our world, and our lives in general. And always, I think about our loved ones who left us. Ever more. Kali, Darwin, Mark's sister Dru, my aunt Monique, and my *meter*. As I reminisce about these important people and pets, tears fill my eyes. Happiness and sadness, they seem to go hand in hand. Once we experience loss, can we ever truly feel joy again? I'm grateful for my current life, but I can't help thinking that everything made more sense when we were in our twenties.

I don't want to be unhappy. I'm in paradise.

I switch my thoughts to the present, to the blackness and sparkles above. For no apparent reason, a daunting feeling envelops me. I shiver. It's not from being cold. Something indescribable, like a sixth sense, whispers into my mind. When the undefined message is transferred into my brain and deciphered, I sit there; transfixed, shocked, and in disbelief. Instantly, I feel utterly alone and immensely sad. This abrupt sensation convinced me that I will never be pregnant. That I will never have a child. I believe it's real and truthful, but where did this come from? I don't cry. I don't share this new information with anyone. I take it in, not quite understanding what it means, not quite ready to accept it.

Southern Fakarava is amazing and everything we hoped to find in the Tuamotus, but other islands call, particularly uninhabited Tahanea. I'm eager about the destination, not the journey, which promises opposing winds, waves, and current. Mark couldn't care less. After visiting three atolls (we stopped at Toau as well), he adopts the "if you've seen one, you've seen them all" attitude. Sailing east is a hassle and Mark is tired of difficult sailing trips. I'm worried about pushing his buttons too much. Maybe we can sail to Kauehi instead?

I'm sick of fighting with Mark about the places and islands I want to see. In the grand scheme of things, our conflicts about which Tuamotus to visit – or whether to remain on *Irie* and sail to Fiji or abandon this lifestyle – are not important. Something else nags us: Mark's bump.

Heading to the more attractive *motus* in the island chain means moving farther away from Tahiti, from civilization, from the only Western hospital within thousands of miles.

"Everyone says it's nothing." As I voice the words, my heart pounds. This could be serious.

I shouldn't brush this off in order to explore the Tuamotus. What's wrong with me?

"It should be nothing," Mark agrees. "But what if it isn't?"

The thought retracts my stomach. I swallow hard. *What if it isn't?* I cannot fathom this kind of "if." Our strategy has always been "better safe than sorry."

We'll have to come back after the check-up.

The decision is made.

We are heading to Tahiti. Immediately. No further discussion. We have to confirm Mark is healthy. Health is everything, as we have experienced increasingly. Despite the weather predictions (I should call them "weather contradictions"), we leave *now*. The 260-mile journey will take two days and two nights. We can't waste another minute.

Chapter 24

Reality Happens Everywhere

We're invited over for drinks by our retired American friends Lili and Steve. *Liward*, their beautiful, well-maintained 48-foot Hans Christian, is comfortably docked at Marina Taina in Tahiti. *Irie* is attached to a mooring in a not so comfortable fashion, pitching back and forth.

The mooring field provides the same choppiness and annoyances as the crowded anchorage, with the added "bonuses" of a hefty user fee and a chance of losing your boat due to the poor quality of the buoys. However, the perceived feeling of safety and convenience slightly makes up for that. The bus to the capital Pape'ete stops here, and marine stores, laundry and shower facilities, and two bars dot the shore.

We are made at ease on *Liward*. As always, we're impressed with her immaculate shape and the positive, relaxed attitude of her owners. They truly appear free, content, and well-off. As we sip on cocktails, I'm in one of my complaining moods. I can't help but be envious.

"I wish we didn't have to worry about money and could go out for dinner more often," I moan, in response to one of their stories. Mark and

I, since the start, only buy the necessities. We don't shop for what we want, but for what we need. We eat to live; not live to eat.

"We've worked hard our entire lives, Liesbet," Steve counters. "You and Mark might not be rich in funds, but you're rich in time. You're still young and healthy. That's worth a lot!"

I let that sink in. Yes, we have the advantage of our age, compared to the average cruiser. Yet, I'm in awe about what these 60- and 70-somethings achieve, while I huff and puff, hoisting sails and hauling our dinghy onboard or on a beach. Back ache, knee pain, and headaches are my foes, and I'm practically half their age.

Immediately upon arrival in Tahiti, part of the Society Islands, Mark and I dinghied ashore to figure out where the hospital was. Despite being tired from the 48-hour trip, there was an inexplicable urgency to our movements. It took inquiries, patience, and determination to find the location of the French-run hospital, and two walks and bus rides to reach it. A physical exam of Mark's chest did not bring answers; neither did a return visit and two scans.

Eventually, a female doctor did a biopsy of the lump. Taking a chunk out of the mass with a thick needle aided by the ultrasound machine took a few pokes. This tissue was sent to a lab in France for identification. Mark and I await the results of this biopsy, a formality more than anything else.

As Steve says, at 38 and 43, we are relatively young. A bright future awaits. I smile and clink my glass to everyone's health and sailing adventures.

🐬🐬🐬

It's Easter, 2014. Mark and I are stuck on our bouncy sailboat near Marina Taina, waiting for Mark's test results. I feel lazier than on other Sundays. Through the porthole of our bedroom, I notice Yvan Bourgnon's beach cat *Ma Louloute* pitching near shore. His posh support boat looks gigantic compared to the tiny multihull he's sailing around the world to set a few records. He aims to be the first to circumnavigate in a 6.4-meter

(21-foot) cat without a cabin and GPS, using only a sextant and paper charts for navigation. I'd never attempt what he's trying to achieve! But then again, he's a Frenchman. The French accomplish the most amazing feats, without thinking much of it. That arrogance makes them heroes, but also villains. *Life is less stressful with that attitude.*

I remember the conversation we had with a French couple in the Gambier Islands, days after finishing our Pacific crossings.

"We never worried when doing the trip and had no issues. We weren't even tired when we made landfall," the skipper confessed, contrary to everyone else we talked to.

"How is that possible with two children aboard?" I had asked.

"Aaagh, easy. After dinner, we all watched a movie and went to bed." The four of them. Going to bed. For the entire night. For three weeks. Without night watches.

Irie and *Ma Louloute* have shared the mooring field for two weeks. Part of me wanted to go over earlier and say "hi," another part of me – the lazy part – reasoned *who cares?*

I lie in my bunk. *Easter*. It doesn't feel like a holiday. I should be writing. I haven't accomplished anything this month. Mark, on the other hand, has been working non-stop – days and evenings, weekdays and weekends, pursuing the idea of a new Wirie product.

I only *imagine* what I *could* be doing. I'm good at that. I stare into the forepeak, see the mold on the walls, and come up with ways to clean it quickly and effectively. I have grand ideas, lounging about. About articles, blogs, *and* cleaning projects. Unfortunately, results don't materialize that way.

I could go over, meet Yvan in person, and ask him a few questions. Would I dare? I used to be braver. What if he's not home? Get your act together! Complaining you don't accomplish anything, and then ignoring the chance for a story? Who knows how much longer he'll be here?

I gather a piece of paper, a pen, my camera. And my courage.

"I'm going to say 'hi' to Yvan Bourgnon," I tell Mark, as I walk out the door. His body is bent over his laptop.

"Okay," he says. "Good luck!"

I dinghy over to *Ma Louloute*'s support boat to conduct my first ever interview. It's informal and unplanned, and I'm ill-prepared, but I return home with a decent story, glad to have sprung to action. The following day, I keep an eye out for *Ma Louloute*. It would be nice to photograph him sailing out of Tahiti. When Mark and I come home after sundowners with friends, Yvan and his beach cat are gone.

"I still can't believe he's doing this," I say.

"Let's hope he makes it alive," Mark replies.

🌊🌊🌊

Mark enjoys our stationary time in Tahiti. The internet works adequately, so he makes progress with Wirie projects. I take care of errands on shore and onboard. At least, there are no excursions to hassle Mark with. Having our business means sacrifices in terms of enjoying the cruising life. It's always the forefront, whatever we do and wherever we go, like having a responsible job on land. Except that owning a business means no break from it. Ever. Plus, full-time cruising has its own challenges, even without a company to run. The combination can hardly be called ideal. But the view from our office can't be beat! Being in Tahiti, we take advantage of the facilities to tick more boat chores off that never-ending to-do list.

Our months are (s)expensive again. Mark agrees to a copulation schedule around my ovulation time. Spontaneous as we are, doing something planned is not our thing. And not romantic. Plus, none of our attempts lead to success. With a twinge of jealousy, I learn Marie is pregnant, but it looks like she'll return to France to give birth. Fiji won't "expect" her.

"What would *you* want to do if I became pregnant?" I ask Mark. "Sell *Irie* and move back ashore?" This isn't to be an enjoyable conversation, based on his shifted priorities.

"I'd get off this boat right now, regardless of you being pregnant. We've been sailing for almost seven years. Don't you think that's enough? Aren't you uncomfortable? And annoyed with the weather, the lack of internet, choppy anchorages, the hassle to get groceries?"

I sigh as I hold on to the table to avoid sliding off my seat. It's one of those bouncy, swell-over-the-reef type of days. I can't argue this is getting old.

"No," I say. "The annoyed one is you. I'm still interested in seeing more islands and countries and cultures and wildlife. I really want to sail to Fiji. Why don't we see what happens when we get there? We can take a break from sailing and fly to New Zealand. That shouldn't be too expensive. We'll store the boat and do maintenance when we return. Or sell *Irie* there."

Did I ever ask Mark if he even wants to sail to Fiji?

He's fed up with this lifestyle, but I'm not.

He used to be the sailor. What happened to his dream?

I know we don't have to settle ashore when this adventure finishes – I'm an advocate of alternative lifestyles – but I prefer a satisfying conclusion for this journey. Tahiti is not the place; Down Under too far away. Fiji makes a good compromise. And, it buys me an extra year aboard.

🌊🌊🌊

The phone rings as I soap up on the bottom step. Mark answers and leans over the stern.

"It's the doctor from the hospital. Can you talk to her?"

I shake my hand free of suds. I strain to hear what she says. My French is far from perfect and the breeze is not making it easier.

"Can you come to the hospital? We need to talk about Mark's biopsy results," she repeats.

I look at the sun and estimate it's around 3pm. Getting to the hospital is a hassle. I don't even know if we'd make it before closing time.

"Can we come tomorrow?" I ask.

Why can't she say that everything is fine over the phone?

"Tomorrow is a holiday," she says. "And then it's weekend and I won't be here either."

Those damn French holidays. We have the same ones in Belgium, but for Mark and me, traveling around and working every day, they never come in handy.

"Okay. Will you wait for us?"

"I normally leave at five, but I can wait if I know you're on your way."

I return the phone to Mark, jump in the ocean, rinse off, and towel dry. I put clothes on, grab a bag, lock the door. We get in the dinghy, yell at the engine (it starts after the seventh pull), navigate the continuous wake from boat traffic, and hurry to shore. Do we hitchhike to the city or do we wait for the bus? A bus approaches. Decision made. At the bus station in Pape'ete, we walk to our connection, wait, and find a seat on the vehicle marked "Pira'e." Near the hospital, we jump out and cover the last bit on foot.

"I have bad news." The doctor starts the conversation in English from the moment we sit down in her office. *What did she just say? "I don't have bad news," right?* She must possess enough knowledge of the language to realize the significance of one word.

I look at her as my heart stops.

"Sorry, what did you say?"

"I have bad news," she reiterates. "We received the biopsy results. Mark has cancer."

The room turns black. The world spins. I drop from the planet. Everything stops. Dizzy, I glance at Mark. His face is white. He doesn't say anything. Time stands still, yet seconds pass.

"What kind of cancer?" My voice trembles. The big C-word. This is it. The end of so many things.

"Breast cancer." Her explanation is lost on both of us. I remember leaving her office at some point, with a paper in my husband's hands: the pathology report of the biopsy, in French.

We stumble through the long, modern hallway in an attempt to find the exit of this giant hospital. *This can't be true.* My legs shake as we approach what looks like a door to the street.

"This doesn't make sense," I say. "Something isn't right. You are a guy.

You can't have breast cancer. Someone made a mistake." I can't see straight but I'm not crying either. Mark remains quiet. I cannot imagine what goes through his head right now.

"Hey, Liesbet and Mark! Do you guys want a ride back to the marina?" A chirpy voice overpowers the traffic noise as we walk back to the bus stop on automatic pilot.

"Yes, please!"

Lili and Steve pull up to the side of the road and we quickly get in.

"What are you doing here?" Lili asks.

Mark doesn't answer. He must be in shock. How do I share my overwhelming emotions?

"We picked up Mark's test results. He has cancer. Breast cancer." Tears prick behind my eye lids now. This is dramatic news of the first degree. How does one react to that?

"It's okay," Lili, in the passenger seat, says. "It will be okay. Believe me. They will take care of you in the US. It'll be tough for a few months, but it'll end well. You'll be back on *Irie* and sailing again in no time." She speaks from experience.

Lili is positive, but it doesn't help. Not yet. We can't digest this devastating turn of events. We appreciate her support and the ride. I have no idea how else we could've made it back.

From the moment we're home, we try to translate the biopsy report. We call our friend JP of the motor vessel *Domino,* who's a retired French/American doctor. We read the sheet to him.

"Don't worry," JP says. "This is probably nothing. At your age, Mark, and as skinny as you are, there's no way you have breast cancer. It's an extremely rare disease for men." The following days, he consults with former colleagues and confirms his thoughts. "It's likely a benign tumor. Get it taken out here and you'll be able to move on with your life." Our friend puts us at ease. His conclusion coincides with what we read online.

As JP suggested, the next step is to remove the entire tumor – which is called a lumpectomy – and have that tested. Mark and I face a dilemma that takes days to sort out.

We talk to a surgeon in Pape'ete, collect information, and need to make a decision. Do we have the surgery in French Polynesia for about $3,000, which Mark's insurance won't cover? Or do we spend $2,000 on a plane ticket for Mark to fly to the States, where he has health insurance? We want to finish this nightmare as soon as possible. We trust the French doctors and their Western education. Staying seems to be the easiest and quickest solution. But what if it is, indeed, a cancerous tumor? Then, Mark has to go to the US anyway. That's one thing we know for sure: if this is serious, Mark needs to be in the States for treatment.

We spend our money on one roundtrip plane ticket from Pape'ete to Boston. Mark leaves immediately. He expects to be gone for two to three weeks, enough time to have the surgery, get the tumor removed and tested, and recover a bit. I await his return on *Irie*.

"Are you still there?" Mark asks, after sharing his news with me. It's quiet on my end of the line, thousands of miles away. That could mean the connection dropped, the internet is flaky, or I don't know what to say. Or all of the above. Currently, I'm shocked. I wish the only thing I had to worry about was a bad internet connection.

I clear my throat. "Yes. I'm here. I'll buy a plane ticket and get out of here as quickly as possible."

It's mid-May. The result of our French biopsy report has been confirmed. Within a week of being back on the US East Coast, Mark saw his general practitioner, met with the surgeon, underwent surgery, and received the diagnosis of the removed tumor. The good news is that the mass was taken out with "clear margins," which means the tissue around the tumor is healthy. We're in the dark about whatever else needs to happen. After our Skype call, I book my plane ticket with a stopover in Los Angeles, prep the boat, and pack my bag.

"Why are you in the United States again?" The Immigration officer's voice is stern. I was in LA on my layover from the Marquesas to Belgium not that long ago.

Here we go again. Interrogations until I drop.

I'm exhausted, willing to do anything to get through the border and in transit to the other side of the country. The past weeks have been taxing, mentally and physically. This guy doesn't care about that. He wouldn't understand what it's like to have your other half diagnosed with cancer in the middle of the Pacific. To be separated from him until further notice and to wrap up your floating home within 24 hours.

In record time, I organized *Irie* for cyclone season in November, in case we won't be back by then. I removed or secured everything that could blow off, finally scrubbed that forepeak with bleach, distributed laundry powder to deter moldy conditions, lifted the dinghy, and placed the outboard inside. All while the boat rocked madly, inducing nausea. Every ten minutes I had to rush outside and gag, losing precious moments to catch my breath and let my stomach settle, before continuing the insane preparations; preparations that typically take Mark and me days *together*. In manageable conditions. What kept me going was determination. And helpful friends.

"I'm here to be with my husband, sir." I remain polite.

"Where is he?"

"Newburyport, Massachusetts."

"Why is he there?"

"He's sick and needs treatment."

"Why does he need treatment?"

"Because..." I hesitate. I still have a hard time with this new reality. *And why is he asking this?* I want to say, "None of your business," but I know what can happen at an American border.

"Because he has cancer." I choke and can't take much more.

"What kind of cancer?" *Really?*

"Breast cancer." He looks up from his screen. No matter what I answer at Immigration, it always sounds ridiculous, false, too far-fetched. I can't win.

"How long will you be here?"

"I have no idea." My voice diminishes. Tears flood my cheeks.

They hate this answer. You're supposed to know when you'll leave the country, especially with a B1/B2 visa. *Especially* when you've gotten in trouble before. But I honestly don't know. I don't even know whether Mark will survive or whether I'll ever see *Irie* again.

The man takes pity on me. *Bang.* The stamp lands on my passport. *Six months.*

"I hope your husband gets better soon," he says and hands my documents back.

"Thank you," I mumble, before making my way through the blurry hallways of LAX.

Chapter 25

A Surreal Fight

In 2008, cancer became part of our lives. Our two precious dogs passed away on the animal front, and then I lost my aunt Monique to colon cancer. Her recovery actually went really well after the surgery and chemo. When the doctors recommended preventive radiation "to make sure the cancer is truly gone" it ruined my aunt's vitals, leading to her demise. Needless to say, radiation treatment in my Belgian family is heavily frowned upon since then. More recently, Mark's sister passed away following a brave battle against ovarian cancer.

Now, my husband has cancer. This terrible disease will define the rest of our lives. I can't imagine how my mother-in-law must feel, as losing your child is one of the worst experiences for a human being. Barely a year later, her youngest son, the second child out of three, is diagnosed with cancer as well. The outcome is unknown. But I shouldn't forget that Mark's dad survived colon cancer and my *oma* dealt with colon *and* uterine cancer, all before the innovation of modern medicines and treatments. Those examples give me hope.

What will happen to Mark? What kind of breast cancer does he have?

If we have learned one thing these last weeks, it's that there are almost as many different breast cancers as there are victims. Between the types and the individuals, treatment differs greatly and results as well.

How will Mark be treated? Will he need chemo? Will he survive?

We read and read – articles on the internet, books, statistics, personal stories – and reach one conclusion: none of it matters. Mark doesn't belong anywhere. When have we ever fit in a box or social convention? *Not even in a cancer category!* He's male. He's only 43. He's as skinny as a straw. He has breast cancer. We lack results, proof, statistics, and accurate prognoses about his disease. There's no information available about cases like his. He *is* the case.

Mark's type of breast cancer will determine the options and possible treatments.

Fear dominates our lives those first two weeks I'm back in the US. We pity ourselves, hug, and cry. Our family and friends are supportive, but what is there to say?

The final diagnosis will be upon us shortly. Then, it's time to take action. Or be patient. Or both. Waiting isn't one of my strengths, and I'm hopeful to be back on the boat soon. My cousin Griet and her husband Wim have booked plane tickets to exotic French Polynesia for another visit on *Irie* the end of June, a month from now.

It takes three weeks and a plethora of appointments and opinions before we learn what Mark's cancer is about. The initial diagnosis in the local hospital of Newburyport was worse than the final verdict by the specialists. We're relieved and appreciative that he's referred to Boston, where a dedicated and experienced cancer team will take care of Mark in the renowned Dana Farber Cancer Institute. The array of "solutions" (each creating its own set of emotions) ranges from a suggested double mastectomy to a less drastic lumpectomy in combination with radiation, possible chemo, and a predicted treatment period of three to seven months. It's hard to believe that only recently we anticipated a sail trip within the Society Islands and a family visit, to then slowly head west to Fiji for cyclone season. Planning anything at this point is useless.

The diagnosis of Mark's cancer is Invasive Papillary Carcinoma, an extremely rare type of breast cancer but – apparently – a "good" one; one that is less likely to spread and one that is responsive to treatment. One out of a thousand breast cancers are detected in men; less than one percent of invasive breast cancers is Papillary Carcinoma. Ten percent of breast cancers in males is caused by the BRCA2 gene mutation, not the BRCA1 my sister-in-law Dru contracted, and which might be the cause for Mark's trouble. It's suspected – and later determined – that he has the BRCA1 mutation as well, putting him in a unique class as cancer patient. *I always knew my husband was special.* It explains why nobody believed the result from the Tahitian biopsy, which was pretty much on target.

A positive about Mark's situation, other than the type of cancer, is that he presents a fascinating case study. Therefore, the head of the radiology department and the top (women's) breast surgeon are involved in his treatment and recovery. While it wasn't an easy decision, Mark and I chose the combination lumpectomy (which happened already with clear margins) and radiation treatment. This way he keeps his breast tissue and nipple and doesn't undergo invasive surgery, which would immobilize him and potentially cause permanent damage to his muscles.

Once the procedures are finished, he has to take the hormone drug Tamoxifen for five years. First, he needs another operation to remove the sentinel lymph node(s), to make sure the cancer hasn't spread. Four to six weeks of radiation will follow, after the results of the pathology report are known and radiation mapping has taken place.

Let the road to recovery begin.

꩜ ꩜ ꩜

I have no one to talk to. My in-laws have their own grief to deal with. Mark has his family and his friends. I'm in sparse email contact with a couple of Belgian friends. They have their own lives and I've been away for over a decade; they have no idea what I go through. Few people our age have dealt with cancer up-close.

My parents taught me, indirectly, to be strong and keep things to myself. That last bit isn't my style. Yet, it's hard to communicate about Mark's cancer with them. My mom lost her sister. She wouldn't agree with Mark's radiation treatment. My best friend, Rosie, who sails full-time and is unreachable by phone, takes the brunt of my feelings. We've stayed in touch, despite the distance. Our friendship – typed words on a screen – has grown stronger over the years. Composing daily emails to her and documenting what I go through for myself keeps me sane.

My current grief is an egotistic one and has little to do with the diagnosis. I am angry with Mark. I'm mad he has cancer. The thought of leaving him enters my mind again.

How awful, abandoning your husband in the middle of a crisis.

Do other people have morbid thoughts like this? You know you won't do it, yet the idea crosses your mind. Like imagining what it would be like to jump off a roof while peeking over the edge. "Through sickness and through health. Until death do us part." I've memorized and understand the saying now. I can deal with his sickness. *Really.*

My personal devastation has nothing to do with his frustrated moods this time. As a matter of fact, he handles his situation and the consequences better than I ever thought. I'm proud of him, surprised he takes everything in stride.

I am the weak one. The disappointed one, the impatient one, the rude one. *Why?*

There is one implication I hadn't realized until now. Because Mark needs to take this hormone drug for five years, we can't get pregnant anymore. Too risky; the chance of a birth defect is too high. This stupid cancer means I'll never have a baby. We've waited too long. I'm almost 39. When Mark's done with the Tamoxifen drug, I'll be 44. *Too old.*

That weird sensation I had on *Irie*'s trampoline in beautiful Fakarava makes sense now. I cry myself to sleep. I hate this predicament. I hate Mark. I can't share this sentiment with anyone but Rosie. I'm the most selfish bitch on the planet.

I join Mark at the Nuclear Medicine Department. A doctor injects him with radioactive material, which is supposed to flow into the sentinel lymph node(s). This enables the surgeon to find the correct node(s) with a Geiger counter before removal for another biopsy. It's the only way to determine if the cancer has metastasized; the fluid follows the same path as the cancer cells. *What an experience. What an adventure.* Is Mark glowing? It's not dark enough to tell.

We wait. Mark disappears into the pre-surgical area to be hooked on an IV. I join him later. Two more hours pass. Our surgeon runs late. We don't mind. We're happy the procedure takes place today, a week earlier than scheduled.

Anything to return to *Irie* as soon as possible...

Mid-afternoon, I leave my husband in the capable hands of nurses, anesthesiologists, and his doctor. She finds me an hour later to report that the operation was a success. Only one lymph node (as opposed to two) had to be removed for further investigation. Dopey Mark takes a while to wake up before we get into the car.

It's a slow, traffic-laden ride back to Newburyport. When being part of a string of vehicles, I'm always glad this is not my daily life. Our identities seem to be lost when running on automatic; we resemble sheep in the herd. Like ants in an ant colony.

I give Mark one night to recover from the surgery. We need to get pregnant, *pronto!* My ovulation period is only this long. Or short. If my calculation is correct.

"You're kidding, right?" My naked body snuggles against Mark's for one purpose only.

"No, I'm not. You don't have to do anything. Just be comfortable."

Am I that desperate? Or is it impulsiveness popping its head up again? Maybe it's an act of cowardice – if Mother Nature decides I'm pregnant, it's a done deal.

"But my side hurts!" The stitches under his right armpit are covered with a bandage. And he's taking strong pain medication. He'll be fine.

"Stay on your left side," I suggest.

I try to get him excited. It works. Marginally. He groans. I can't tell whether it's from pleasure or discomfort. I can't care right now. I have to focus. I make sure his sperm lands – and stays – where it's supposed to be. I'm gentle, but determined. I can't waste another month. He'll start the hormone drug after his treatment and during radiation it's unsafe to get pregnant.

This is our last chance. He can recuperate after my ovulation period. It's not that we have anywhere to go. *Irie* is stuck on a mooring ball in choppy Marina Taina. Whenever cruising friends pass through, they check her lines. Griet and Wim have postponed their flights to Tahiti.

My priority is getting pregnant. Surgery or not. It's now or never. *I'm selfish. I'm rude. I want a baby.*

Out of breath, Mark fires a look of pain, disgust, and disbelief. I have to think about myself. This part of myself, anyway. We have lost enough.

I bought one pregnancy test and own limitless determination. Mark gives in. Every other day during ovulation, I collect his sperm and let it settle, my legs straight up in the air. I read this increases your chances.

In addition to the cancer procedures, this sex schedule isn't fun either.

"Don't you want a baby?" I'm disappointed at my husband's lack of cooperation.

"I have other things to worry about. Don't you think it's important that I heal first?"

"Of course, but this is our only chance to get pregnant," I say. "We were going to try for a year, remember? With this stupid cancer, our chances are gone."

"We can always freeze my sperm." Mark echoes what a consultant and his oncologist mentioned. As well as our sister-in-law Kris. Having recently given birth to the most adorable twins, she believes it's a terrific idea for us to have a child and wishes to help.

"How on earth can we afford that? Freezing the sperm, storing it for who knows how long, and then dealing with in vitro fertilization?" I sigh in exasperation. "Even if we go that route, we'd have to live in the US during this long, difficult, emotionally and physically draining procedure. That doesn't suit our lifestyle."

When I talk to Kris again, she suggests we at least have a conversation with a fertility specialist. Not only does she recommend the right person, she and Tim pay the consultation fee, our postponed wedding gift. We ask questions and consider options. It's all incredibly expensive and massively time-consuming. My decade-long indecisiveness about having children confronts me with a hard reality. Usually, if I really want something, I attempt it immediately. Like taking that perfect photo or embarking on a particular adventure. Circumstances constantly change.

I've followed most of my desires and interests. But I failed to *really* want – and have – a child. My mom confirms that "mistake" – or choice – in a phone call.

"I don't know what to do, *ma*. I wanted to get pregnant naturally. Now, it's too late!"

I sound like a sulking child. I am one. Hers.

"Well, you've had enough chances to get pregnant in the past." She's down to earth as always. "If you really wanted children, you'd have them by now."

She's right. Not only did I keep delaying a potential pregnancy, I never even committed to desiring one. Until last month. Fate decided for me. Yet, I'm still not willing to give up. Mark agrees to postpone his Tamoxifen treatment for six months to buy us more time to get pregnant. We have to wait until his radiation sessions are finished and the poison has left his body.

This isn't the right way to get pregnant.

Where is the love? The passion? The mutual desire to have and raise a child?

I'm at a loss. My ambivalent thoughts towards pregnancy, our relationship, Mark's feelings, the scheduled sex sessions, and his mood and fatigue don't encourage "planting the seed." We try. The emotional roller coaster continues.

According to Mark, that part is worse than the physical part. He never feels ill, but his mind and destiny are messed up. Our present is what it is; we deal with it. Our future, however, changes forever. As a couple. As a family.

$$\text{🐢🐢🐢}$$

Radiation technicians "map" Mark's body for the four weeks of therapy to follow. He receives five permanent tattoos – blue dots – to help line up the laser beams. After a dry run, his 19 treatments start. Five days a week, he lies in a fancy, white contraption and gets zapped. The actual radioactive ray only hits him for one minute. Once these sessions are finished, and we meet with our wonderful, skillful, and experienced medical team (all three doctors are professors at Harvard Medical School), the next step is Mark's five-year hormonal treatment. This, with a personal choice of natural remedies and a healthy diet, should minimize bad cancer cells from lingering, multiplying, or recurring.

We appreciate living in the room above the garage of Mark's parent's condo, our home away from home. It provides two desks, a bathroom, privacy, and an address to order boat parts. We are Carol and Stan's "live-in help" as she says ever so fondly.

We've been here a couple of months now. It's unusual for parents to have their adult children move into their close quarters or for those middle-aged kids to live with them, but everyone adjusts. Yet, I can't wait to return to our *Irie*. I hope this cancer wake-up call convinces Mark to enjoy life again on the water and as an adventurer. So far, he seems happier in the Western world with all its conveniences.

Mark focuses on the business and implements his ideas for the new Wirie product. He makes lots of progress, thanks to available resources. He also develops a website for *Irie*, to sell her, initially at a high asking price. We plan to launch that site later, in Tahiti. I'm busy writing. I'm thrilled *Cruising World* accepted one of my stories about the French sailor, Yvan

Bourgnon.

After multiple revisions, my article for them is finalized. I'm ready to submit the last version. Right before hitting "send," I learn devastating news.

Yvan has crashed into the rocks off Sri Lanka, destroying *Ma Louloute*. He only had 5,000 miles left to the finish line. He survives and is determined to continue. I get in touch with Yvan and rewrite my *Cruising World* article to include the current events and his ideas for a continued voyage. The story becomes more exciting and dramatic because of the crash.

Thanks to my "crazy French sailor," I land my first article not only in *Cruising World,* but also in the UK's prestigious *Yachting World,* and the most popular sailing magazine of The Netherlands, *Zeilen.* I submit feature stories to *Multihull Sailor* – the sister magazine of *Sail* – and *Sailing Today.* Every one of them gets published; at last, I'm a *real* writer!

Mark's side effects from the radiation treatment are benign. He gets tired every afternoon and has a tingly sensation in his mouth. Once in a while his chest hurts and his throat feels coughy, as if his asthma is acting up. His chest area is red; it looks sunburned. The surgical wound is painful due to a skin infection.

🌊 🌊 🌊

I'm thrilled to find out that my best friend, Rosie, and her husband, Sim, have made it to the States to haul out their new-to-them sailboat, *Wandering Star.* After not seeing Rosie for two and a half years, ever since we left the Eastern Caribbean, she's in the same country! I'm even more excited when Mark feels well enough to take the multiple-day trip down to Beaufort, North Carolina, in a rental car. Happy times! It feels so good to finally laugh again, catch up on each other's adventures and stories in person, and enjoy girl-time for a couple of days. This visit with our friends is the perfect finale to our four-month stay in the US.

Back in our sofa bed in Newburyport, I'm restless. I can't sleep. It's early August 2014. Soon, we hop on a plane out of here. I'm more than ready to return to the tropics, to French Polynesia, to my real home. We've been surrounded by people, traffic, and sickness long enough. Mark is recovering nicely. We stuck it out as a team. We fought this disease – together – and my husband should be cancer-free. We survived strong emotions, meltdowns, disbelief, fear, anger, and treatments.

Unfortunately, Mark isn't fond of picking up the boating life again. He enjoys our unchallenging life on a day-to-day work, eat, and rest level.

When I eventually fall asleep, wondering what's next, I have my reoccurring dream about *Irie*. The weather is benign, but something happens to her anchor. We detach from safety. Mark and I are both aboard as our home drags and runs aground, destroying the keels and hulls. Water enters through the cracks, rising steadily. We collect our most valuable belongings within minutes. Next, we face an immense restoration process. Our catamaran never sinks in these nightmares. Sometimes, we drive her on land or weave through congested boat traffic, missing objects by a hair.

But, no matter what, we never sink.

Chapter 26

Is This What We Want?

*H*ealth is the most important thing.

Ever since I was young, grownups around me have been sharing this wisdom.

"You are rich in age and health. That's important," Steve on the good ship *Liward* told us in Tahiti, before we knew any better. It's the first question my mom asks when we talk on the phone: "How is the health situation?"

My dear *oma* is always relieved when she hears Mark and I haven't been ill. She's unaware Mark had cancer. I avoided the topic during calls from the US. Once she lost her daughter, my aunt Monique, her health and mind declined rapidly. My fear of losing her increases equally as fast. Part of me believes she's gone already, her soul wandering in strange places. At 94, she finally moved into a retirement home. I'll never visit her again in the kitchen where she coddled my brother and me each afternoon of our kindergarten years.

I rarely thought about health in my 20s. I backpacked through Southeast Asia for two years without travel insurance. When Mark and I took our truck camper to Central America in 2006, we'd see a local doctor if needed; healthcare was cheap. On this indefinite journey with *Irie*, Mark has health insurance provided by Massachusetts and I have my Belgian policy. We're covered in our own countries, but uninsured abroad. If something small happens, we'd take care of it locally; if there's an emergency, we'd fly to our home countries and deal with it there. That's exactly what happened.

These days, I no longer take our health lightly. We're still uninsured outside of our countries, but the implications are known first-hand. Mark's cancer episode, including its consequences, will loom forever. It's a dark cloud, always present, even on the sunniest, most tropical day. He will require check-ups every six months for at least five years, needs to stay out of the sun, has a heightened chance of developing skin and prostate cancer, and worries from the moment anything feels unusual in his body.

After those four months in the US, Mark and I finally return to French Polynesia and *Irie*. It's where we belong. Loaded with a year's supply of health supplements for Mark – wheat grass, vitamins, green tea pills, fish oil, and flax seeds, the same pregnancy test for me (*we keep trying*), and a ton of boat parts, we jump on the plane. Fiji is no longer a feasible destination. It's too late in the season and Mark needs to ease back into boat life. The procedures, surgeries, radiation, and emotional stress wore him out. We'll get there next year.

After his cancer scare, Mark should be ecstatic to live on a boat in the tropics, a dream of many people. To most, cancer is a wake-up call, when they change their priorities from the mundane to the extraordinary. The opposite happens for Mark, who'd be happy with a settled life right now. The timing of his disease was just right. He needed a break from *Irie*, an extended stay in a Western country. He successfully focused on the business and the newest Wirie product (which aims to combine long-range WiFi *and* cell data connections). How will he keep up progress in the islands?

We load four bulging travel bags of gear and three carry-ons onto a bus to Boston airport, into a couple of planes to Los Angeles and Pape'ete, on a piled-high cart through French Polynesian Customs, and in a taxi to Marina Taina in Puna'auia, Tahiti. We arrive home with everything and everyone intact.

It's August 15th, 2014, the day after my nephew Lenn was born as a sibling to my five-year-old niece, Lena. My brother shared the happy news while Mark and I waited for our connection in LA.

Irie is still connected to mooring A19. Her waterline is filthy, a foot up, due to the constant swell and scum passing through. The city's polluted air turned her decks grimy. The bimini is ripped from heavy winds. It's to be expected. We'll take care of it, in a comfortable location. After an absence of four months, I step inside to unpack our heavy bags and Mark inspects the bow of the boat.

"What are these piles of dirty lines doing on our trampoline?" Mark asks.

"Which lines? What do you mean?" I walk outside. Like Mark, I stare at the mysterious mess of tangled ropes.

"Look at that!" He points down. "There's only one line attached from *Irie* to the mooring ball, and it's slack. We're riding on top of it! Our Apataki bottom paint is being scraped off."

Before Mark left, we made sure that the boat was safely prepared for his – and later my – departure. *Irie* was securely fastened with three lines leading forward. This set-up had three goals: it kept the ball in the front and middle of our boat, so nothing was touching the hulls, chafing of the lines was less likely, and there were always two ropes to hold *Irie* steady in case the third one developed a problem. Now, the leftover line is poorly tied around the outside of the hulls, wiping our expensive paint off and leaving blue marks on the fiberglass.

"I wonder what happened. Imagine this line or the loop of the ball chafed through because of this awful set-up. *Irie* could've dragged through the mooring field and crashed on the reefs!" I shudder.

"This is insane," Mark says. "If our friends saw this, they would have fixed it."

"None of them mentioned anything out of the ordinary. It must have happened recently. Do you think this hat is related to the mystery?" I show Mark the beige headgear I found in the cockpit. "It looks familiar."

I double-check with sailing friends who passed through about this perilous set-up. *Nothing.* Asking the neighbors doesn't reveal anything either.

Why would a stranger get aboard and replace a well-prepared situation with one that can cause damage or the loss of our boat?

Mark and I are annoyed, but don't dwell on it too long. *Irie* is safe. This is a new start. We need to think positive and enjoy the cruising life again. We unpack, store the spare parts, put our clothes away, and fill the cupboard with American goodies.

It's good to be home.

Tired from the journey, we take a nap. The mooring field is as uncomfortable as we remember. We'll do what's strictly necessary here and head over to the anchorage in Arue as soon as possible.

In the afternoon, we lower the dinghy, carefully attach the outboard – tricky in the constant chop – and struggle to get it running. The sun beats down. Mark sweats and curses. The tenth pull evaporates his good mood.

"I should have flushed it with fresh water," I yell. This is my fault. Before I left, I took the outboard engine off the dinghy with a Swiss friend and put it in the saloon, on its side. Our friend suggested rinsing it before storage, but Mark had told me earlier over Skype not to worry about it. We had other things on our minds. The salt water inside must have caused corrosion.

"That's not the problem," Mark calls over the wind. "You put it on the wrong side when laying it down."

How was I supposed to know that?

Mark rinses, cleans, and lubricates engine parts. I fret and hand him tools when needed. I wished for our return to be smooth and enjoyable. I should have known better. He works on the outboard for a few hours, before I hear the familiar rumble of our aged, well-used motor. *Phew.* The

8HP engine – our lifeline to shore – runs again!

I look at my husband. We haven't even been back for 24 hours and his annoyance with the boat life has returned. His chest – half of it hairless from the radiation – is soaking wet from sweat. His right nipple shows a white scar. I feel bad for him. I wish I knew more about boat maintenance. He should take it easy, but I'm pretty much useless.

We anticipated issues after "neglecting" *Irie* for months. Mark replaces our old toilet seat and a broken burner. The sun goes down; it cools off. The island of Moorea beckons in an orange glow, like it did before we left. When it's time to warm up cans for dinner, another problem arises. The solenoid for our propane stove fails. A new one is easily found – hurrah for spare parts – and an hour later, food is served. We survive the first day back aboard without fights.

We can do this!

Two days later, we've cleaned *Irie*'s scruffy bottom, stocked up on groceries, and paid our hefty mooring fees to the manager. The bill was higher than expected, because the marina raised the weekly rate while we were gone and didn't honor their quote. We feel taken advantage of, but complaints don't achieve anything here. We buy more odds and ends in marine stores, make sure both diesel engines run smoothly, and move anchorages.

In Arue, the chores on *Irie* continue in a more comfortable fashion.

One day, the catamaran *Paradocs* enters the anchorage. Passing our boat, a crew member yells: "Hey *Irie*, I saved your boat two weeks ago in Marina Taina! It was floating about."

What?

We have no chance to ask questions. Once the new arrival is settled, Mark and I take our dinghy over to request more information.

A couple of weeks prior, the sailor came home from playing ukulele. It was around midnight when he saw *Irie* drag through the mooring field. The mooring ball and all three lines were still attached. He banged on the hull, but nobody was home. Our boat was about to crash into another catamaran, so he woke those owners up. Together they fended *Irie* off. Our savior contacted the marina staff, who – begrudgingly – towed our boat to an empty ball. When A19 was fixed, the manager put *Irie* back with only one line. A man in charge who is unable to responsibly tie the boat of a customer to an unsafe mooring, for which he demands lots of money... It's hard to believe. Or is it? And he never told us about it.

I hitchhike to Marina Taina to confront the manager. I walk upstairs and into the office. The Frenchman sits behind his desk, an arrogant smirk on his face. We found what we assumed was his hat on our boat. I planned to wear it to see his reaction, but I chicken out. Instead, I tell him who I am and the name of our boat.

When he doesn't show any signs of recognition, I explain what happened to *Irie* two weeks ago and that her mooring broke during our absence.

"I don't remember. Moorings break *all the time*. Many boats drag here." My blood boils.

"It happens *all the time*? Why don't you do anything about it?"

"The moorings are checked regularly by the dive shop and repaired when necessary. They're old and not of good quality." He shrugs.

"Wow. So, we risk leaving our homes on them? And you are okay with that?"

"Everyone knows the danger. That's why you have insurance." He leans back and smiles.

I'm speechless.

"I have my boat here as well, and I make sure my insurance is up-to-date," the man adds.

Mark and I have boat insurance, but that's not the point!

I have no idea what to say next. If I'd be playing myself in a movie, this is where I spit in my enemy's face, crumple his brimmed hat, and throw it on his desk. I'd erase the boat names on his white-board, pivot on the heels of my flip flops, and slam the door behind me.

In real life, I shoot him a furious look, leave the building, jump on his hat until it's flat, throw it in the dumpster, and hitch a ride home.

Paradise is in the surroundings, not in the circumstances. People experience the same location differently, based on their state of mind. A picture doesn't say more than a thousand words. It screams observations trapped in a small frame: beauty, happiness, freedom.

At least the tropical photos I share with my loved ones do.

I don't experience these blissful scenes during our uncountable moments of frustration, agony, annoyance, and full-out dread. Despite my surroundings claiming otherwise, my situation sucks. I'm sick of Mark. Sick of how I feel. Sick of not seeing a way out. I consider leaving my husband. Again. He's to blame for my unhappiness. I think about our wedding vows. Nowhere did it say: "Through frustration and despair." They ought to rewrite that nonsense or instruct a wife how to change her partner into a desirable, caring, grateful one. Even if it's a temporary fix. I'd take an hour. Or a minute.

I sit in the cockpit, wearing shorts and a bikini top. It's hot and humid. Sweat runs down my face. The Austral summer has been brutal. But I don't care about my discomfort. My mind is blocked and my body in shock. The shock of reality hitting; a reality I don't want to know, don't want to believe, and managed to ignore brilliantly.

Until now.

I need to get out and clear my head, but I'm stuck on this boat. Even worse, I'm stuck on this boat with my husband. I look around me. The water is turquoise blue, clear, attractive. Coral reefs await within swimming distance. An appealing white beach stares back at me from shore. The palm trees wave and encourage me to embrace their shade. Sheltered water full of life beckons. The sky is a perfect deep blue, a favorite view I never tire of.

Except today.

Day after day, week after week, month after month of fights, struggles, stress, frustration, complaints, yelling, and marital confrontations caused a massive knot in my stomach and took their toll. I cannot live in my bubble any longer. I have to face it: Mark is finished with this life, our life, on *Irie*; the only life we've known for almost eight years. Trying to cheer him up and point out the bright side has become useless. Mark doesn't see it anymore, can't do it anymore.

No, I won't dwell on everything that has gone wrong. Yes, I realize we've been unhappy for a long time. But I didn't want to admit defeat. Until today. Today, I *have* to give up our life. All of it: the hospitable Polynesians, the snorkeling, the colorful sea creatures, cocktail hour with old friends, making new ones, going to the beach, watching the glorious sun set behind the watery horizon.

I partly blame our business.

It's one of the reasons why Mark is annoyed. The demands of running The Wirie have increased and our remote environment doesn't allow convenient work conditions. Since returning to *Irie* in August, Mark's main focus has been the company. We brought a prototype router with us, chose anchorages based on internet availability, and stayed as long as needed for the different stages of its development. He found a manufacturer in China who could build our custom-designed router and sourced companies for the other parts. He took care of existing customers – *if only he could be as cordial with me as with them* – and kept working on the new products. We updated the website, decided on names for the new Wiries, wrote manuals and quick start guides, and launched the first of our new inventions, The Wirie^{AP+}, at the end of the year from our boat in the Society Islands. This device offers WiFi only and is a significant upgrade from the previous version.

When the cellular router – the heart of our mixed product – was finally finished after a year of negotiations and arduous communications, we received a unit here. But the problems aren't over. The Chinese company always wants more money and new issues arise weekly. That our contact in the Far East barely speaks English and can't admit mistakes doesn't help. Because of Tim's hyper-busy life in the US, conversations between the two brothers are close to non-existent. I'm of little help either; the technical aspects are over my head.

Mark has to make every decision himself and can't consult anyone. Still, the software and hardware testing continued. He improved and adjusted; we wrote press releases, revised materials, and did odds and ends needed to launch the other products. In the meantime, Tim continued our operations in the US and helped with planning and designing the new manufacturing aspects.

Life on board was hectic, exciting, frustrating, nerve-wracking, and stressful at the same time. But with our new prototype, we grabbed emails and weather forecasts in the most remote and protected bays of the Society Islands, allowing us to safely sit out storms during cyclone season and stay connected.

In the beginning of 2015, we officially launched The Wirie^{xG} (2G/3G/4G service only) and our revolutionary all-in-one Wirie^{pro} from this island, Huahine, French Polynesia. We received positive feedback and sold and shipped units throughout the world. Magazines, including *Cruising World*, requested a Wirie to test and review. Favorable articles online and in print appeared as a result. Later, *Practical Sailor* crowned our Wirie^{pro} as a "Gear of the Year."

When it comes to starting and running a business from the middle of nowhere, The Wirie and its inventor, Mark Kilty, are a success story. When it comes to our personal lives, not so much.

My husband is bent over his computer, oblivious to the beauty around us. He wears shorts and a T-shirt with holes and smudges. When he's not sitting at our galley table, he's fixing a boat problem, cursing out loud, struggling physically as much as psychologically. It's hot and humid inside, too.

Instead of lying into the wind, *Irie* faces the current. The free mooring ball bounces against the hull and smears bottom paint where it doesn't belong. *Bang. Bang. Bang.* No breeze, not even the slightest wisp, enters through the gaping windows and portholes. We're glad the flies and mosquitoes haven't found us. *Yet.* The mosquitoes carry Chikungunya now, like Zika last year. Lathering up with mosquito repellent and/or monoi oil is routine. So far, we've been fortunate. Most cruisers we know have succumbed to the Dengue-related disease. It's only a matter of time, we fear.

It's quiet, apart from Mark's grumbles. I'm waiting for an outburst. It's not an if but a when.

I should escape. Go ashore, sightsee, jump in the water to snorkel. Maybe I'd see a shark, a ray, a turtle. They guaranteed a smile in the past. I have no energy anymore. My head replays the last six months. Every time something breaks on the boat, it's a disaster, and I hold my breath. After Mark diagnoses the problem, a litany of curse words flows over me. They're not directed at me but hurt, nevertheless. There's screaming and complaining. Every day. I shrivel and want to hide, but on a 35-foot sail-boat there's nowhere to go.

I could take the dinghy to shore for a husband-break, but I need Mark's help to get the dodgy engine started. Thing is, when Mark's in a mood like this, I'm paralyzed. I can't do anything. I'm frozen in place, despite the heat. I feel what he feels. I am him. We are one. An escape to shore means abandoning him to suffer alone. *Treason.* I can't call friends or family. Even if Skype would work, they won't understand.

I'm living the dream in paradise.

"Shit, the signal dropped again!" *There we go.* "Aaargh, I lost every-thing!"

I cringe. *Please, let the issue be resolved quickly. Please, let him get back online without losing his work. Please, let this be an easy fix. Please.*

"I'm so sick of this stupid internet and this stupid business!"

I understand his annoyance, especially when he's on the phone with a customer who complains about his inability to stream Netflix and our connection drops. It's ironic. It's infuriating, unprofessional, yet only one of the situations Mark deals with on a daily basis. His accumulated frus-trations – worse every new day – puts me over the edge. I worry about the last drop in the bucket, the last straw, when all hell breaks loose from breaking loose.

"I need to get off this fucking boat!"

"I need to get out of this French-speaking country!"

"This place is killing me!"

"I'm so sick of this damn boat!"

He's desperate. Done with this challenging lifestyle.

We need to get off this boat. I don't want to get off this boat. How do we get off this boat?

I offer a suggestion, an alternative, a break. My head is snapped off. I patiently sit out another word storm. I, too, am exhausted. Any joy I had left – the rewards for the trials and tribulations, the beautiful snippets that made me smile – is gone. Crumbled.

The picture-perfect paradise surrounding me doesn't help anymore.

Chapter 27

A Break from the Boat

At what point do we break mentally and collapse physically? Am I willing to risk everything by being stubborn and refusing to admit that, *really*, it's time to get off the boat?

You can't have it all. You always want it all. My mom's words repeat in my head. I have always wanted *it all.* And I've been quite successful at it. Why would I choose if I don't have to?

This is different. It's my relationship. My future. Our future.

"Don't forget that there are two in a marriage." Yes, mom.

Have I been sacrificing by living with a verbally explosive husband? Or has he been sacrificing by staying on the boat with his disappointed, spoiled-with-adventure wife?

I face reality. Reality hurts.

We need a solution. Abandon our home again? It feels like we just returned from the US. In actuality, we've been back half a year. *Irie* has been for sale as long, without serious interest. She's represented by three brokers in French Polynesia, Australia, and Hawaii. We advertised wherever we could. After dropping her list price multiple times, it's currently less than we paid, before spending tens of thousands of dollars on improvements and upkeep.

"*Irie*'s value is more than we're asking," I stated in disappointment.

"Her value is whatever someone is willing to pay," Mark responded.

I wipe my forehead. My bandana is soaked. It truly is something, every damn day. Wait until another boat system acts up or the outboard refuses to start again.

What are we to do?

We can't afford staying at one of the high-end resorts on shore for a rest, nor do we want to, having a fine and free home on the water with exactly the same view. We don't have money to go on a vacation. I looked into a week-long holiday on Easter Island last April, but then the cancer happened and this delightful plan disappeared forever. I can't believe that was almost a year ago. Mark's frustration has grown to immeasurable quantities since then.

And I struggle with my own demons.

Mark and I "tried" to have children for six months. Our haphazard attempts took our aversion towards a sex schedule, our tiredness, and our bad moods into account. The result was predictable: no pregnancy. Mark started taking Tamoxifen for at least five years. That and the flax seeds should help prevent a recurrence of his cancer. No baby for me. Ever. I don't know what I would do without Rosie. Our email exchanges could fill a tome.

I also have trouble giving up on Fiji as an end destination. Getting there would bring closure. I want to reach a stopping point by choice, not by necessity.

On an immediate level, I prefer to explore, snorkel, socialize, immerse myself into cultural events. Mark likes to sit behind his computer and get intellectual satisfaction. This causes more frustration. It's a vicious cycle we need to break. *Now.*

I might as well abandon "destination Fiji," if I can't give birth there.

Mark did agree to visiting the major Society Islands these past months. We set foot on Tahiti, Moorea, Huahine, Taha'a, Raiatea, Bora Bora, and

Maupiti. We welcomed Griet and Wim for another wonderful visit and retreated to Huahine in March 2015.

So, here I sit, losing the respect and love of my husband. I need to get my priorities straight. Compromise. No, give in. Be the smartest for a change. We would cruise until "we ran out of money" or "it wasn't fun anymore."

The time has come to switch gears. To stop the complaining. To enjoy life. To smile again.

But how?

We can't fly back to the States for a break. Plane tickets to Boston are $2,000 a pop.

"If I go back to the States, I'm never coming back," Mark says.

I believe him. We have arrived at a critical stage. We need to figure out how to save our marriage, our business, and our happiness. And, ideally, get our sanity back.

When a behavior that crushes you inside and out is repeated for months, you've had it. The patience is gone.

Enough is enough.

Love turns to hate. Compassion to annoyance. This must be what leads couples to a divorce. Instead of trying to help, you want this madness to stop. You lose your wits, your composure, your positive attitude. You don't have to take this. You have to let it out. It's your turn to explode.

"You complain all the time without trying to find a solution. I'm so sick of it!"

"Well, that makes two of us," roars the reply.

Now there are two people yelling. Who cares about the neighbors?

Enough is enough.

You think about leaving the boat. You don't want to be with this depression-prone creature anymore. *Remember his visits to that shrink in Oakland?* He was bound to make you miserable. It happened slowly and effectively. You blame your despair on him. It's time to end this suffering and have a life – a much happier life – without him.

I need to get off this boat.

Yes, it's what he's been screaming for months. You finally agree.

"I wish I had cancer again, so I *had* to go back to the States!" Mark's words pierce my mind and body. I snap out of my own depressed state.

This is bad. The point of no return.

🌊🌊🌊

Ashore on Huahine, squished together in a small pocket of shade, Mark and I sit in silence. We stare at a propane tank, hanging upside-down in a tree to gravity fill ours, a process that takes an hour if all goes well. Using a pencil to hold a washer and tiny nut perfectly aligned to push the pin of our tank valve in order to hook the hose up correctly took only a few minutes. I expected the worst – several attempts to securely connect the hose, loads of sweating, cursing, and butane escaping during the trial and error period. Which, in turn, could cause passers-by to watch in disbelief and request we move our butane bomb elsewhere. None of that today.

Sporadically, Mark releases air to create room for the liquid. When positive events occur, I make my husband aware. He hates it almost as much as my "It could always be worse" speech.

"That went extremely well. Now we can relax and listen to the sound of traveling butane." I crack half a smile.

He doesn't care. It's a job related to the boat life; a job he doesn't like, a life he's sick of.

"I have an idea," I say, wallowing in the goodness of the day. I'm not even sweating; a bonus. And the sky is blue. *I love blue skies.*

"What?" Mark sighs.

"Why don't we fly to New Zealand for a couple of months? The plane tickets should be much cheaper than to the US and it's a shorter, direct flight. It's a Western country, offering a break from the tropics and the boat. We can focus on the business, reconnect and regroup, and rest our exhausted bodies and minds."

Mark looks at me in thought, so I continue: "We have friends there, people speak English, and I have always wanted to revisit it with you." I become genuinely excited about the prospect. Of the countries I explored before meeting Mark, New Zealand had the only "potential" for me to settle. That was in 2001.

To my surprise, the suggestion isn't dismissed immediately.

"It will still be expensive," Mark says.

"You think so? When I was backpacking there, it wasn't too bad. Hopefully, we can stay with Axel and Liz in their apartment until we figure out what to do and where to go. And we have friends on boats, too. *Amandla* and *Iona* are moored a couple of hours north of Auckland, in Whangarei." The more I think about this plan, the more feasible it sounds.

There we go, again.

"What would we do with *Irie*? We can't leave her here in unprotected Huahine."

"Remember, Moorea has an affordable marina. Maybe they have a spot available."

"A marina slip costs a lot of money as well, which we don't spend at anchor."

"Our happiness and health are more important than a few hundred, or even thousand dollars at this point. Don't you agree? Plus, it will be much easier for you to work."

Back on *Irie*, I set the plan in motion. I contact Axel, who now lives in Auckland with his Kiwi wife, Liz, and their baby son, Arno. How times have changed since we joined them as line handlers on *Gudrun* through the Panama Canal in 2012. I write the harbor master of Vaiare Marina in Moorea and look up prices of plane tickets.

We're taking a break from this nightmare!

"I wish I didn't have to return to Tahiti," Mark says, as we depart towards New Zealand. The multi-hued lagoon and the impressive topography of Moorea are so beautiful. All I see is paradise. We'll be back. Or at least, I'll be back. Maybe I'll leave my husband down under.

It's interesting how a plane ride transports you into another world. In a matter of hours, we swap cultures. Life in New Zealand for two months would be the answer to our problems. *Not.* You can't escape your struggles. You can only carry them elsewhere. The idea of going to *Aotearoa* a was followed by that exciting feeling of anticipation.

Unfortunately, I never plan ahead and always assume things will work out.

When we arrive in Auckland, we're homeless.

Did I forget we are the most frugal people on this planet?

New Zealand is expensive. Nothing like 2001.

How will Mark and I survive here? Where will we live?

Our generous friend Axel comes to the rescue. With a newborn, hosting visitors in his apartment is inconvenient, so he puts us up at a hotel to get our act together. I research and book a campervan for three weeks in the South Island, while Mark is busy with the business. Until that adventure starts, we borrow Axel's car and meet other cruising friends further north.

"So, you leave *Irie* to be off the boat and now you're staying on other people's sailboats," my mom states the ironic truth in one of her emails. While it's wonderful to visit our favorite sailing family on *Iona* and catch up with our dear friends Lisa and Fabio on *Amandla*, I fail to tell my mom that our lives have become even harder than before. Mark currently directs the business and customer calls from a car seat instead of a comfortable cushion at our saloon table.

Axel signed us up for a housesitting site, but no opportunities materialize during our time in New Zealand. A better alternative pops up.

When we return to Auckland, our friend has rented another apartment on his floor to use as an office. It has a kitchen, bathroom, and lots of space. Mark and I borrow Axel's camping gear, move into the flat, and become neighbors for a week.

In the South Island, we experience van life and the underestimation of fall in this country: short days, colder weather than expected, and an all-encompassing time difference with the US.

Mark gets up at 6am, when it's still dark, and works a few hours at his computer, dressed in foul weather gear, hat, and gloves. The heater is insufficient, due to the lack of insulation. We live in a metal box in freezing temperatures.

After a late breakfast, we pack up and drive to our next destination, where we have a couple of hours to explore until the sun sets around 5pm. Even this time of the year, it's busy everywhere. The locals don't appear as welcoming as I remember. The explosion of tourism might have something to do with that. We enjoy wonderful sights and activities but combining our travels with the business is extremely difficult.

While testing the reality of Mercedes Sprinter van living, Mark and I conclude it's too soon to do this full-time. A van is certainly in our future – as long as it's well-insulated – but right now, we're ready for a more settled and comfortable life.

"What if we don't sell *Irie* by the summer, or worse, November, when another cyclone season arrives?" Mark had asked back in January. I made him a promise that wasn't mine to make: "In April, we'll be off the boat, you'll see."

Well, April came around and we *are* off the boat. Only, it's temporary and in New Zealand, instead of permanently and in the States. We hope *Irie* sells within these two months.

Imagine we could go back to Moorea, appointment with a buyer in hand?

When such interest is actually generated and – after lots of commotion, communication, emotion, and expectation – falls through, we're even more desperate about the sale.

If she would have crashed on the reefs when dragging at Marina Taina last year, we'd be done. And, we'd have collected insurance money; more than Irie's asking price.

In Auckland, after sampling van life, Mark and I have three weeks left to taste flat life in the center of this most vibrant city. Axel inaugurated his office. We're welcome to move in again. He has added a fridge, super-fast Fiber Optic internet, and multiple desks; two of which occupied by us, the rest by Axel and his assistant.

There's true enjoyment about living in comfort, being surrounded by friends, and communicating in English; quite opposite to our last two years in French Polynesia.

꧁꧂꧁

I walk home after meeting Lisa, who came to town and showed me her favorite street art. A weird sensation overwhelms me. I jiggle the house keys in my pocket. My heart sings along.

I have my own keys! I'll soon see my husband. We'll pick up fresh produce in the store downstairs, have a healthy dinner, and watch a movie in bed. It's all so simple; utter bliss.

"Hi sweetie! How was your day with Lisa?" Mark looks up from his computer. I go over to collect a kiss. He stands up and hugs me.

"Great! The graffiti in this city is amazing. Did you get a lot of work done today?" I glance at his desk. Both iPad and computer are in job-mode.

"Yep. Other than the time difference, the business is much easier to deal with. Want to move to New Zealand?" He smiles. Since we settled in Axel's apartment, he has been caring, sweet, focused, and productive. *Happy.* But as our time here is dwindling, I sense a change in his mood. The dreaded reality of returning to *Irie* casts a shadow. I'm not sure his question is serious, but I am convinced that Mark can only function in a Western environment right now. He needs to be in the States.

The last seven weeks, we lived in an apartment, on boats, and in a camper. At last, I know what's next.

"No, I don't want to move here. Too remote and too expensive. But I've been thinking..."

"You think way too much. What?" he asks.

"I think you should fly to the US from here." There it is, that butterfly feeling of doing something right. Or is it that clenched stomach feeling, where you're nervous about the consequences of what you just proposed?

"I can't do that," he says. "We have return tickets to Tahiti already and

I'm not leaving you alone on *Irie*."

"I don't want to hear any excuses." I made up my mind. When that happens, I become stubborn and determined. Mark is going to the United States. *Pronto.* "You'll be happier there, with your family, friends, reliable internet, other amenities... and the correct time zone."

As I support my decision, we hear a *ping* on Mark's iPad.

"What is it?" I ask. His face changes color.

"It's an email from my mom. My dad had a stroke."

Chapter 28

That's It

A sigh of relief escapes through my nose.

Let it all out!

My entire body relaxes. I'm on *Irie*. Alone. It's quiet. The saloon is empty. The table is mine. I sit on our settee and look around. Most decorations have been taken down. The shelves are empty. Some personal belongings flew to the US with Mark. Whatever else I wish to keep has to fit in two checked bags and two carry-ons. Worries for later. I savor being home. This is the closure I require. Two full weeks alone on my boat – to say goodbye to her, the island, the culture, the friends I made ashore and afloat.

Our two-month trip to New Zealand confirmed what I suspected: Mark needed to get back to the East Coast of the United States. He made more progress with The Wirie; it's where his passion lies. We also enjoyed having unlimited water, electricity, and other basic comforts we'd been missing. After discussing our options – which abruptly ended when we found out Mark's dad suffered a stroke – we canceled our return flights to Tahiti and replaced them with one-way tickets from Auckland to Boston via French Polynesia. I picked a different date than Mark for the last leg. This solution proved cheaper than a new airfare from Tahiti to Boston.

Mark stayed on *Irie* for ten days, enough to help me get settled and prepare the boat for an indefinite absence. He left, hoping to never return.

My last two weeks on Moorea are extremely busy. Unsatisfied with our lowered asking price for *Irie*, I try to sell a pile of gear instead of leaving everything for the potential buyers. I pick a spot along the main road around the island – across from the Champion grocery store in Vaiare – and set up shop Saturday and Sunday mornings.

Another day, I take the ferry to Tahiti and the bus to Marina Taina, loaded like a donkey. At the flea market there, I earn more francs. The size of my backpack reduces, and my wallet gathers the equivalent of $100, enough to hold me over until I leave.

The docks in the capital are bulging as I return to the Moorea ferry. Another set of Puddle Jumpers arrived in Pape'ete after completing the Pacific crossing from North America. They start their adventure in French Polynesia, bright-eyed and excited. The skippers and crew are energetic, eager to sail west. I can't blame them. There was a time Mark and I felt the same, heading east. That was ages ago. *Eight years.* I've never lived anywhere that long as an adult.

I scan the well-equipped yachts at the marina. I stall. That boat in the back row looks mighty familiar. I squint and put my glasses on to read the name.

You're kidding! Four Choices!

Our old monohull looks exactly the same as in 2005, when we sold her in Monterey, California, to head to Mexico in a truck camper. Ten years later, she still has the same name. Images of nasty boat projects, living aboard with a view of the Golden Gate Bridge, and our dogs Darwin and Kali spring to life.

Has it really been a decade?

I hang around the locked gate until a boat owner leaves, slip inside, and walk over to *Four Choices*. I introduce myself to the captain.

"No way!" he exclaims as we shake hands.

"She's looking good. How was the ocean passage?" I ask.

"The boat did great. We love how seaworthy she is. Do you want to go inside?"

"Yes!" I can't hide my excitement. While we only owned her for nine months, she was our home for five of those; a roomy and comfortable one at that. Not much has changed.

"My wife and I always wondered what the name *Four Choices* stands for, speculating about your four choices to go cruising," he says. "But why the unusual spelling?"

"Actually, there is a triple meaning to the name," I explain. "The *Four* stands for the four of us taking off, Mark, our dogs Kali and Darwin, and I and the different directions to sail: north, south, east, and west. The world is your oyster. It was also important for me to state that cruising is a choice – *our choice* – and not luck, hence the middle part of the name and the spelling: *F/Our Choice/s.* "

"That's a mouthful."

"I know. I have a soft spot for phrases with multiple meanings. My husband... not so much. Our current boat is called *Irie*. Short and sweet." As I pronounce her name, sadness washes over me. Soon, she won't be in my life anymore. *Bitter and sweet.*

"Is it true that you sold *Four Choices* because of your dogs? I read that in an issue of Latitude 38, years ago."

"Yep. Our dogs were more important than going cruising. Not everyone agreed and a heated discussion ensued in the magazine." It had been an easy decision. We never envisioned seeing our dogs miserable on a tilted vessel. I was often seasick when the boat hobby-horsed over the waves. *Irie* was a much better fit for us; all four of us. *How I miss Kali and Darwin.*

I wish the captain a fabulous journey across the rest of the Pacific Ocean. Smooth sailing, uneventful passages, following seas, and the like. *And MacGyver capabilities when (not if) needed.* Then, I head back to my beloved *Irie.*

From my first sailboat to my last one.

I gaze at the azure waters, sparkling reef, dramatic silhouette of Tahiti, and Moorea's green peaks. It's hard to give it up. I'm untethered right now, doing what I want during the day and cherishing the space in bed at night. I embrace my cold showers ashore and balancing on the rickety plank to get there. I hike the interior of the island with Birgit and Christian. Their *Pitufa* is anchored in the shallows. While I know how tricky that anchorage is in heavy winds and funky currents, I envy them. I wish I could jump off *my* boat for a snorkel. Never again.

A mother and baby whale cruise through the channel. Out of reach. One day I will be able to swim with them. *One day.*

🐋🐋🐋

The islands, the mountains, the splendid lagoons and dangerous reefs, the tropical surroundings, the 50 shades of blue, the white caps, everything becomes smaller and smaller as the plane takes me higher and higher, away from the familiar, towards another unknown.

I feel empty yet glad to have been able to say farewell to my home of eight years, my friends, the hot and humid climate, the wildlife, and French Polynesia as a whole. I have no idea what Mark and I face next. That, at least, is a familiar sensation. We're officially homeless. But I have good prospects for the summer: an extended stay in Belgium. I need more me time. To let everything sink in. To consider what the future might hold.

Our future. Once we sell the boat.

We don't allow ourselves to think about that, as long as *Irie* is ours. We've learned from our "planticipation" attempts. Plans and anticipation lead to disappointment. We'll take life as it comes, one step after the other. *I can live with that.*

The horizon turns puffy as we turn towards Los Angeles. I'm weightless. My body and my mind. It's time for something else; a new adventure ashore, whatever it may be.

I choose Mark over traveling. It's exactly what I did when I left Karl. Eleven years later, I abandon the sailing life instead of the camping life. For the same guy: Mark, my mate. I want our relationship to succeed. And

I could use a break from all the traveling and commotion this last decade. We'll figure this out, as a couple, as a team, as we always have. I want the business to flourish. We'll be happy and relaxed. I welcome this change to a convenient lifestyle.

For now.

My sense for adventure will eventually prevail. I'll miss our life on the water.

That's why I have photos, blogs, and memories. And cruising friends to stay in touch with. Plenty of boats to visit, all over the globe.

We'll pause this quest for new horizons and embark on another one in the near future, maybe in a campervan. *I can live with that.* I contemplate the pursuit of happiness. Do we search for it or do we let it find us by going with the flow?

Happiness comes from within. It's presented in fleeting moments; it's found when you feel at peace with the decision you've made.

I have a mental plan. I can't wait to reach Boston and run into the arms of my dear husband. I turn from the window and smile at my neighbor. We exchange pleasantries.

"Where do *you* live?" he asks, after we chat for a couple of minutes.

"Nowhere and everywhere."

Epilogue

The Interlude

I lie in bed, spooned with my husband and smile. While not mine, the mattress is comfortable and stable. I listen to the breathing of my love and of Lola, the dog we're taking care of in Northern California. Her people are in Mexico for two months. There is nothing to worry about tonight. *So nice.*

I'm glad we left *Irie* when we did. It was a conscious decision – the "wait and see what happens" attitude didn't cut it anymore. Action was needed to restore our relationship, work ethics, and general happiness.

Shortly after leaving our floating home, I stared at the wall-sized map of the world in my childhood bedroom in Belgium. As usual, I marveled at how the pieces must have fit together millennia ago, like a jigsaw puzzle. I imagined cutting around the edges of the continents and attaching them with glue into one big, connected blob. It always intrigued me.

Unlike other times, when I looked at this map in anticipation, the spark was gone. Not a trickle of excitement about the countries and the land masses – a not-so-usual sensation. The world map annoyed me. So many places.

Who has the energy to explore such a vast empire?

I wanted to rest and sleep forever. I wanted to be comfortable. To take a hot, pressurized shower every day, to step out the door without sweating, to sit on a comfy couch. I wanted to do nothing, connect with friends, and eat whatever.

No more adventures.

I was exhausted and suffered from travel burn-out. The thought of jumping on a plane or crossing a sea churned my stomach.

Irie sold to an Australian couple in August 2015, a month after I left Moorea. Mark's return to French Polynesia to meet the broker and potential buyer materialized into his worst nightmare. His week consisted of missed planes, messed up schedules, midnight phone calls to me, sleepless nights, impossible conditions to run the business, heaps of stress and frustration, lots of prep work, multi-colored bruises, bleeding body parts, and having to shit in a bag because the boatyard toilets were locked. You'll have to ask him whether the sale was worth the hassle.

Once the Polynesian chapter finished, the future was ours. Once the money arrived, a weight lifted from our shoulders. *Irie* ceased being our anchor to a previous life.

When I joined Mark in the States, settling was not on the agenda. Again, we faced the question: *now what?*

Without the funds or the desire to be in one place, and eager to spend time with dogs without adopting one, we chose a new lifestyle. One that offers us the best of all worlds: we became house and pet sitters. Finally, our responsible, meticulous personalities are put to good use. The free exchange – caretaking in return for a place to live – benefits every party involved.

Since we work from home and don't want to move every few weeks, we prefer long-term sits. This way, we immerse ourselves in our new surroundings and focus on what matters most: our Wirie business, my writing, and the variety of dogs we love, walk, and cuddle. We appreciate the small things that bring us comfort and incorporate what we learned on the boat – a small carbon footprint, care about the environment, and respect for the creatures that share our planet.

"Do you miss the boat life?"

Without a second thought I reply "No!" to this question from cruising friends. Sure, I'm envious when I see their photos of turquoise water, tanned bodies, flip-flopped feet, colorful reefs, wildlife encounters, or exquisite beaches. But, I know reality is more than what's captured on SD cards and shared on Facebook.

As many times as I see gorgeous scenes, I read about weather delays and boat issues. It's satisfying to enjoy the conveniences taken for granted by so many people and to contemplate our next step. Excitement lures around every corner; the options of what to do in life are immense. Mother Earth always delivers beauty, adventure, diversity, and knowledge, no matter which continent you explore. It's up to us to decide how, where, and why we live.

Right now, that's in the US with my new green card.

I have no regrets about my choices, but adventure is waiting. There's an entire world to be discovered once our batteries are recharged.

I'm excited about the future and cherish what I have: a caring, like-minded husband, falling asleep in my arms every night. I love Mark and he loves me. We are a team. Still. A well-oiled machine with two gears, sometimes spinning apart, but most of the time in unison. He tells me about news in the real world, I share my social media tidbits with him. We grocery shop together, walk the dogs, work during the day, and talk over lunch and dinner. *Ups and downs.* Like a normal couple. The Tamoxifen drug affects his sex drive, but *quality is better than quantity* I always say. The baby dream is a part of the past.

Yvan Bourgnon eventually finished his around-the-world tour in *Ma Louloute*, his 21-foot beach cat, on June 23rd, 2015 in Ouistreham, France. He didn't have time to celebrate. The next day, his brother Laurent went missing while diving in the Tuamotus and was never found.

A year and a half later, my own precious *oma* leaves my life. She passed away at the ripe age of 97. I hold her close to my heart. Like other deceased loved ones, I miss her dearly.

Life goes on with highs and lows, like the tides come and go and the ocean flows forever. Mark and I have yet to go on a honeymoon. We like this housesitting lifestyle, but the travel itch is growing stronger.

Will we get our own dogs again?

My thoughts finally dissipate into slumber, then sleep.

First thing the following morning, Mark is immersed in his iPad as usual. A sudden call from the bathroom startles me.

"I've found our next camper! Wanna take it to South America?"

Your Opinion Matters

Dear reader,

Thank you so much for reading *Plunge* and coming along for the ride. If you enjoyed my book, I would really appreciate it if you could leave a short review on the site where you purchased it, on Goodreads, and/or on Amazon. A couple of sentences will suffice. Your opinion is invaluable. Plus, reviews help other readers find my book and encourage me to keep writing. Word of mouth – verbally or expressed by a keyboard – is the finest way to spread news and show support.

With gratitude,
Liesbet

Acknowledgements

Before I plunged into this book, I wondered, *why do authors always have such a long acknowledgement section*? I surely would be the only one writing the story! A couple of years into the creation of what was to become *Plunge*, I still could only thank myself. Oh, and Janna Cawrse Esarey and Jennifer Marine, fellow authors who I bounced ideas off and who generously shared their time and expertise.

Then, seven beta readers got involved. My team was growing. As the end of this major project neared, stress and anxiety took hold of me. I needed assistance with the steps required to self-publish my travel memoir. Fortunately, help arrived. Now, I am one hundred percent aware of the support an author requires *and* receives, and I am one grateful being!

I want to thank my beta readers Rosie Burr, Ellen Jacobson, Alexandra Palcic, Volkan Akkurt, Ryan Carty, Karen Hume, and Kathy Gottberg for their valuable feedback. Maria D'Marco proved to be a great substantive editor, who nudged me in the right direction and substantially improved my manuscript.

Thank you to my two proofreaders: friend and language aficionado Holly Horgan and the best magazine editor in the world, Sally Erdle. They were inadvertently promoted to copy-editors and did an amazing job polishing this book. Of course, my talented cover designer, Kelly A. Martin, should not be forgotten. Also helpful were the tons of articles I read from industry experts like Jane Friedman, Sean P. Carlin, David Gaughran, and the KindlePreneur.

My favorite Facebook groups offered a tremendous amount of insights and support: kudos go to the knowledgeable members of the Insecure Writer's Support Group (especially Victoria Marie Lees, Beth Camp, Jamie Richardson, and Jennifer Busick), to the invaluable and friendly We Love Memoirs author group (specifically Marian Beaman, Robert Fear, Simon Michael Prior, Neil Loewe, Cynthia Reimer, Mike Cavanagh, Alexs Thompson, and Lisa Wright), and to my adventurous writing peers of the

Women Who Sail Who Write crew.

I am thankful for Meggi Macoun, Amy Bovaird, and Janet Howle's help with my query letter and for the witty, experienced, and honest input from author and writing coach Dawn Bates regarding my blurb. Special thanks also to publisher Edward Renehan, publicist Erin Carey, and author/circumnavigator Lin Pardey for sharing their tips. I welcomed Kate Johnston and Amy Alton's suggestions as well.

Heartfelt gratitude goes to the faithful readers of my *Roaming About* blog. Their continued kindness, encouragement, and positive comments kept me on track. As did my supportive friend Rosie Burr, with her unfaltering patience and listening ear. And, there's Ryan Constable, who would not buy my book unless he'd be mentioned.

Last but not least (sorry for the cliché), I am indebted to my lovely furbabies of the past and present (namely Kali, Darwin, and Maya) for keeping me sane and smiling. I wouldn't be where I am today without my versatile husband, Mark Kilty, who has always been there for me through the *ups and downs*, provided sound advice, and played a major role turning *Plunge* from a concept of words into a published book. Thank you, sweetie, and cheers to many more adventures together!

Photo Gallery

Liesbet, Kali, and Darwin hanging out inside *F/Our Choice/s*

Mark, Liesbet, Kali, Darwin, and
F/Our Choice/s in California

Elephant seals along Highway 1 in
Southern California

Heading to Mexico – overland

Camping spot on the shores of Lake Atitlan in Panajachel, Guatemala

Mark and Liesbet's wedding ceremony in Annapolis, Maryland, USA

Irie's interior – the galley

What do you want us to do on this Astroturf? Nap?

Doing the dishes in *Irie*'s cockpit

Approaching the iconic Pitons in St. Lucia

Liesbet on watch for coral patches from *Irie*'s boom

Mount Pelée looms over the town of St. Pierre in Martinique

Irie bashes into sea and wind in the Caribbean

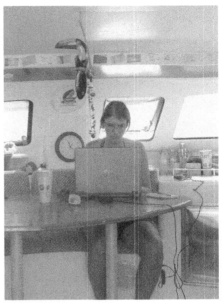

Coiling the lines after dropping the mainsail

Liesbet writing an article or a blog at her computer inside *Irie*

The Wirie products – built aboard and ready to sell

Solo weekend away from *Irie* to hike on Saba

Cleaning *Irie*'s waterline and bottom – a frequent event

Mark proposes last-minute to
Liesbet in St. Martin

Liesbet and Mark on *Irie*'s bow in
the San Blas Islands

It's easy to see why the San Blas Islands are called "paradise"

Liesbet line handling on *Irie* in the Panama Canal

Provisioning in Panama City before crossing the Pacific Ocean

Sea lion visitor on *Irie*'s back steps, Galapagos Islands

Reclined in the Galapagos Islands!

Surfing down big, following seas towards French Polynesia

Baguette delivery to friends in Rikitea, Gambier Islands

Anchored off Taravai in the Gambier Islands

Dinghying over crystal clear water near Totegegie in the Gambier Islands

Quintessential Pacific waterfall on Fatu Hiva, Marquesas Islands

Unexpected wildlife interaction: snorkeling with manta rays in Tahuata

Cultural immersion at the Marquesas Mini Festival

Tiki in Tahiti with Mark and Liesbet

Swimming with sharks and rays in Moorea, Society Islands

Irie anchored in Cook's Bay, Moorea

To view this photo gallery in color, go to
www.roamingabout.com/plunge-photogallery

For bonus photos, go to
www.roamingabout.com/plunge-bonusphotos

About the Author

Liesbet Collaert is a bilingual freelance writer, translator, editor, and photographer from Belgium who has been writing and traveling her entire life. Her work is published internationally in anthologies and magazines, including Cruising World, Blue Water Sailing, Ocean Navigator, Eldridge Tide and Pilot Book, Islands, Yachting World, Sailing Today, All At Sea, Caribbean Compass, and Zeilen. She also created walking tours for Marigot and Philipsburg in St. Martin.

The author has been interviewed about her alternative lifestyle by Multihull Sailor, Modern Day Nomads, Ocean Navigator, The Wayward Home, The Professional Hobo, and Grey Globetrotters among others. She contributed to extensive cruising surveys for All At Sea and Caribbean Compass and became an editorial assistant for Caribbean Compass in January 2019.

Liesbet loves animals, nature, and the promise of adventure. A nomad since 2003, she calls herself a world citizen and currently lives "on the road" in North America with her husband and rescue dog. Find her stories and photos at www.itsirie.com and www.roamingabout.com. *Plunge* is her first book.